MUSTANG

Stewart Wilson

INTRODUCTION

Welcome to the second in our Sovereign Series of books, this one covering one of the great fighters of any era, the North American P-51 Mustang. As with the first book (Spitfire) I have tried to approach a well known subject from a different angle.

The book's several major sections comprise a potted narrative history of the aircraft; a detailed review of the various Mustang marks and models with specification and performance data (including the P-82 Twin Mustang, Cavalier Mustangs and Piper Enforcer); serial number listings; summary of operators; and the major chronological section which tells the Mustang story in 'diary' form.

The idea of this approach is to provide a different perspective, one which compliments the rest of the information in this book and that which has been presented in other publications.

I make no claim to the chronology section being definitive but hope it does provide technical and operational information which may otherwise be missed. Included in the chronological section are breakout boxes covering various topics associated with the Mustang, its powerplants and operators, these designed to present some additional aspects of the story.

I hope readers find something of interest within these pages.

This book has special significance to me as it is my 50th, which I suppose is something of a milestone. Of those 50, no fewer than 27 have been published by Australia's Aerospace Publications under the stewardship of Jim Thorn. Jim is not only my major publisher but also a good friend whose ongoing support cannot be understated.

My thanks also to others at Aerospace Publications, especially production manager Gayla Wilson and Gerard Frawley, who along with Jim looked after the proofreading. Thanks also to Juanita Franzi for her profile drawings and to Neil Mackenzie for supplying some of the photographs.

Stewart Wilson
Buckingham 2001

Published by Aerospace Publications Pty Ltd (ACN: 001 570 458) PO Box 1777, Fyshwick, ACT 2609, Australia. Phone (02) 6280 0111, fax (02) 6280 0007, e-mail mail@ausaviation.com.au and website www.ausaviation.com.au – publishers of monthly *Australian Aviation* magazine.
Production Manager: Gayla Wilson

ISBN 1 875671 51 X

All rights reserved. No part of this book may be reproduced or transmitted in any form or by any means, electronic or mechanical including photocopying, recording or by any information storage and retrieval system, without permission from the publisher in writing.

Copyright © 2001 Stewart Wilson and Aerospace Publications Pty Ltd
Proudly Printed in Australia by Pirie Printers Pty Ltd, 140 Gladstone St, Fyshwick, ACT 2609.
Distributed throughout Australia by Network Distribution Company, 54 Park St, Sydney, 2000. Fax (02) 9264 3278
Distributed in North America by Motorbooks International, 729 Prospect Ave, Osceola, Wisconsin, 54020, USA. Fax (715) 294 4448. Distributed throughout Europe and the UK by Airlife Publishing Ltd, 101 Longden Rd, Shrewsbury SY3 9EB, Shropshire, UK. Fax (743) 232944.

FRONT COVER (top to bottom): P-51 41-37322 *Mah Sweet Eva Lee* of the 154th Observation Group USAAF; Mustang I AM148/RM-G of 26 Squadron RAF; P-51B 42-106703 *Snoot's Sniper* of the 352nd FG/328th FS USAAF; P-51D 44-13464/MX-A of the 31st FG/307th FS USAAF; and CAC Mustang Mk.22 A68-82 of 3 Squadron RAAF. (artwork by Juanita Franzi)

CONTENTS

Mustang Magnificent 9
Mustang Described 23
Marks and Models 36
Mustang Chronology
    1938-40 56
    1941-42 64
    1943 80
    1944 91
    1945 111
    1946-84 121
Mustang Operators 132
Mustang Serial Numbers 140

Impressive lineup. P-51D and K Mustangs of the Royal Australian Air Force's No 84 Squadron at Townsville in North Queensland during 1945. The RAAF operated both US and locally manufactured Mustangs. (via Neil Mackenzie)

MUSTANG MAGNIFICENT

MUSTANG MAGNIFICENT

Factory fresh P-51Bs await delivery at North American Aviation's Mines Field (Inglewood) facility in Los Angeles, in company with a barrage balloon.

There is no doubt that the North American P-51 Mustang was one of the most important aircraft to emerge from World War II, a single engined fighter with the range of a bomber, an interceptor equally comfortable as a ground attack aircraft and in its later, post war years, an aircraft which remained in front line service with one smaller air arm until the 1980s. The Mustang also had a career as a sporting, racing and even executive aircraft in civilian life.

Conceived and built in an astoundingly short period of time, for many the Mustang became the classic American fighter of the war and the subject of adoration which persists and even grows today. Total production of the P-51 by North American Aviation reached 15,484 of all models plus another 200 built under licence in Australia by the Commonwealth Aircraft Corporation.

Whether or not the 1944 Truman Senate War Investigating Committee's description of the Mustang as "the most aerodynamically perfect pursuit plane in existence" is entirely accurate or not (its maximum Mach number was less than the Spitfire's, for example) the fact remains that the aircraft was remarkable, and one which resulted from an equally remarkable set of circumstances. Lacking in altitude performance in its early models, the Mustang was transformed by the mating of its advanced airframe with the Rolls-Royce Merlin engine in 1942, the combination resulting in a long range high altitude escort fighter of the highest calibre capable of ranging from Britain to Berlin and beyond while simultaneously 'mixing it' with the best fighters the *Luftwaffe* could offer.

The Merlin engined Mustang's dominant feature was its range. An absolute tactical radius of 1,000 statute miles (1,610km) was just about possible with full usable internal fuel and external drop tanks, meaning that bomber escort missions from England to the far reaches of the Third Reich were a reality without sacrificing any ability to indulge in combat.

A round trip from England to Berlin was about 1,100 miles (1,770km) and therefore an easy journey for the Mustang but almost a physical impossibility for other fighters, especially if there was combat on the way.

Before the Mustang, the fighters available for these escort missions were less than adequate. The Spitfire, although generally recognised as being the better pure fighter had poor range, the Lockheed P-38 Lightning and Republic P-47 Thunderbolt had better range than the Spitfire on internal fuel and much better when external tanks were fitted. Their flaw was that when the external tanks were jettisoned for combat, little internal fuel was left for fighting, escorting the bombers into Germany and then returning home.

Of course the Mustang also had to jettison its external tanks for combat, but its large internal fuel capacity gave it a useful endurance far greater than anything else. In addition, it was compact, manoeuvrable and single engined.

The Mustang transformed the ability of the USAAF's daylight bombers to do their job more effectively.

The NA-73X prototype shortly after rollout in September 1940 and before the experimental civil registration number NX19998 had been applied. The short period between the aircraft's go ahead and its completion was a major achievement for North American.

Without fighter cover the B-17s and B-24s were highly vulnerable to *Luftwaffe* fighters and as a result tended to restrict their targets to those within the radius of action of the fighters. With the Mustang came a great increase in that radius and therefore the number of targets which could be attacked within the relative safety of the fighter screen.

The Mustang's range was also put to good use in the Pacific and the American's 'island hopping' campaign towards Japan. Whether escorting B-29s to the Japanese mainland or operating alone on interdiction/ground attack missions from island bases hundreds of miles away, the Mustang was able to perform missions beyond the capabilities of any other single engined fighter.

A good example of the Mustang's extraordinary endurance is provided by a flight performed in January 1945 by USAAF aircraft. The pilots were legendary aces Captain Charles 'Chuck' Yeager and Major Clarence 'Bud' Anderson, both in P-51Ds. This was to be their last mission before being sent home and it resulted in the pair 'Doing Europe', as American tourists tend to say.

From England, the two Mustangs departed over the English Channel where they split from the rest of their squadron, then, with Yeager leading the way – and with a delightful contempt for the rules and regulations – flew over the Alps (buzzing Mont Blanc on the way through), to Switzerland (where he led the pair at treetop height and full throttle over a Geneva restaurant he's once dined at and a hotel he'd stayed at), France (including Paris) and various other parts of Western Europe until finally returning to base seven hours later.

A Fighter for Britain

Despite British Prime Minister Neville Chamberlain's "peace in our time" utterings in 1938, there were those within the British Government who considered a war with Germany to be inevitable.

As a result, the British Direct Purchasing Commission led by Sir Henry Self visited the USA in 1938 with the intention of obtaining US built aircraft for the Royal Air Force. The United States was observing a policy of neutrality at the time, although provided a country intending the purchase of US equipment was not actually at war, the government had no objection to some foreign sales.

Self and his Commission visited several US aircraft manufacturers during the trip and placed orders for 200 Lockheed Hudson reconnaissance bombers and a similar number of BC-1 (AT-6A) advanced trainers from North American Aviation of Inglewood, California. Called Harvard in British and Commonwealth service, the first of these was delivered just four months after the contract was signed, the predecessors of more than 4,700 members of the AT-6 Texan/Harvard family supplied to the RAF.

The worst fears of the British were realised on 3 September 1939 when war was declared on Germany following the invasion of Poland two days earlier. Suddenly, the Royal Air Force found itself in desperate need of more combat aircraft and once again turned to the USA as a source of supply.

The NA-73X in flight. It first took to the air on 26 October 1940 and quickly displayed substantial performance superiority over the aircraft it was designed to replace, the Curtiss P-40.

Britain ordered a total of 620 aircraft as the Mustang I, the first contract placed in May 1940. AG345 was the first of the production models, flying in April 1941 but retained in the USA by North American for trials. (NAA)

Ostensibly continuing its policy of neutrality, the US Government placed an embargo on the export of military equipment in 1939 but left a loophole for the benefit of the British and French, a demonstration of goodwill. The loophole provided for the export of equipment provided it left American shores in the holds of ships owned by the purchasing country.

With this in mind, the RAF and French *Armée de l'Air* in late 1939 ordered a total of 1,740 Curtiss P-40 Hawks to be shared between the two services. Although suffering by being powered by the low blown Allison V-1710 vee-12 liquid cooled engine, the Hawk – then just entering service with the United States Army Air Corps – was adjudged the best aircraft available, although deliveries to Europe could not be made until late 1940 at the earliest due to Curtiss' United States Army Air Corps (USAAC) commitments.

The British therefore decided to attempt to establish a P-40 production line with another, less committed manufacturer. Remembering their favourable experiences with North American Aviation and the Harvard purchase, they put the idea of P-40 licence manufacture to NAA's president, James H ('Dutch') Kindelberger, an idea which did not overly impress him or his company's board of directors, who responded with a proposal that a new and more capable fighter utilising the P-40's Allison powerplant be developed, a project on which some preliminary design work had already been done.

This was January 1940, and following discussions with the British Direct Purchasing Commission's Colonel William Cave and Air Commodore G B A Baker, North American set about completing the design under the direction of Kindelberger, vice-president Leland Atwood and a design team headed by Raymond Rice and comprising Edgar Schmued (chief designer), Larry Waite and E H Horkey.

Although North American had not previously designed a high speed fighter, the British DPC was sufficiently impressed by the company's work to sign a letter-of-intent for 320 NA-73 aircraft on 10 April, following this with approval of the preliminary design on 4 May and the signing of a formal contract on 29 May worth over $US15 million.

Some of the conditions of the contract were restrictive, the prototype having to meet all specification goals and be flying within eight months, the cost per aircraft should not exceed $50,000 and North American was required to obtain all current data on P-40 development from Curtiss as a hedge against NAA's lack of experience with high speed fighter aircraft. Included was a considerable amount of wind tunnel data.

If the required timescale wasn't already tight enough, it has often been reported that the company took the decision to tighten it even further, setting itself a limit of 120 days from contract signing to rollout, the same time required if the P-40 had been built under licence. Some dispute this, but regardless, what was achieved by NAA's design team in a very short space of time was remarkable.

By working 16 hours a day, seven days a week, North American was able to roll out the prototype NA-73X airframe (the manufacturer's designation as the US military was not yet involved in the project) just 102 days

The first RAF Mustang I for the RAF arrived in Britain in late October 1941, No 26 Squadron at Gatwick receiving its first aircraft in January 1942. (NAA)

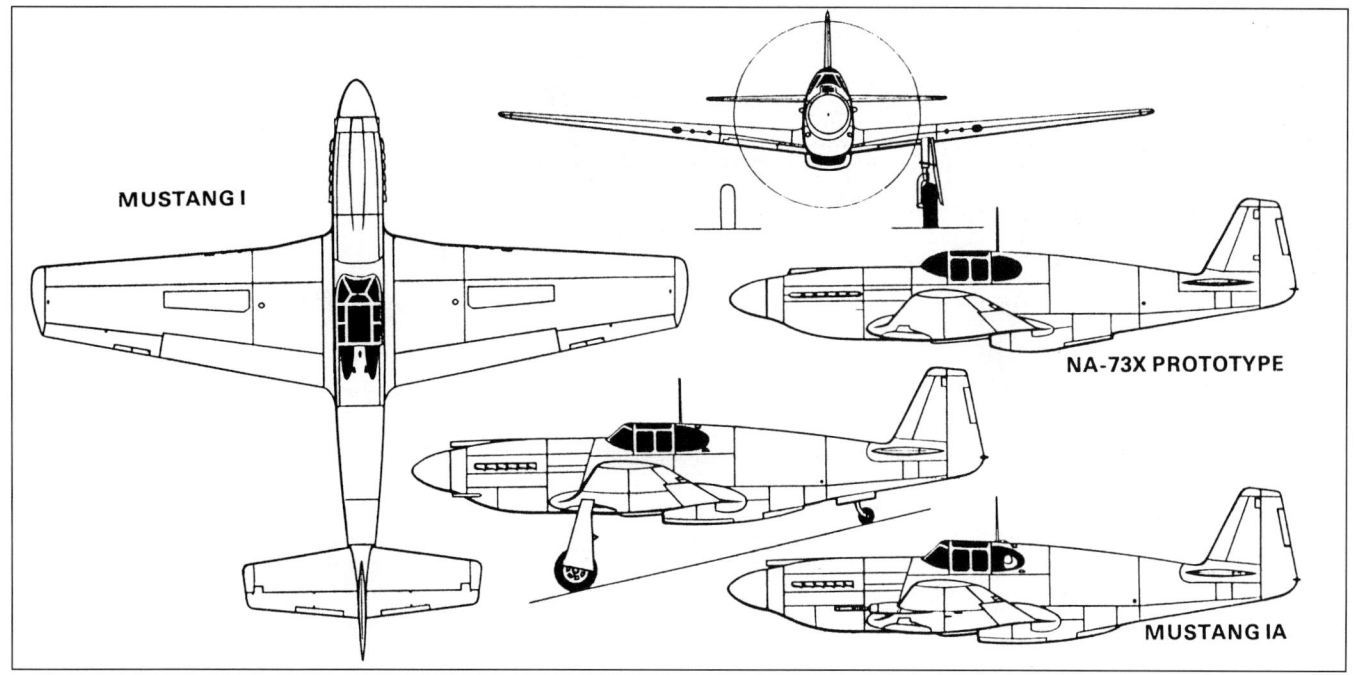

after the contract was signed. A delay in delivery of the 1,150hp (857kW) Allison V-1710 engine due to the engine manufacturer's commitments to Lockheed P-38, Bell P-39 and Curtiss P-40 production caused a further 20 days to pass before the complete aircraft emerged from the factory. A small concession to the short time involved was that the prototype was rolled out on wheels and tyres borrowed from the Texan production line!

Nevertheless, 122 days from contract signing to roll out was a remarkable performance and well within the contract's stipulations.

Underneath the shiny aluminium skin of the new fighter – which carried the civil registration NX19998 – was a design which featured several innovations. The outstanding feature was the aircraft's wing which was of basically laminar flow section, a concept developed by the National Advisory Committee for Aeronautics (NACA) and involving moving the thickest section of the aerofoil aft to a point near centre chord. This provided a long sloping incline on the upper wing surface which gave an increase in the area of even airflow before breaking up at the thickened point. The theory was that this made for reduced drag and resultant better overall performance and longer range.

Many of the aircraft's other design features were also intended to reduce drag and increase performance: the tightly cowled engine, the low set canopy, the minimal fuselage cross section, the ventral radiator air scoop and the use of secondary curves in the design of the aeroplane instead of the more usual straight angles (which were easier to manufacture) and single curvatures. 'Conic geometry' was the term used for this kind of design, the compound and non uniform curvatures providing smooth airflow over the NA-73's surfaces.

Construction was all metal with a semi-monocoque fuselage and two spar stressed skin wing. All control surfaces were metal covered. The prototype had provision for two 0.50 calibre Browning MG53-2 machine guns in the lower engine cowling with 400 rounds per gun, a single example of this weapon in each wing close to the propeller disc and a further pair of 0.30 Browning MG40s in each wing with 500rpg. Internal fuel capacity was 180 US gallons (681 litres) – nearly twice that of the early model Spitfires – divided between a self sealing tank in each wing. The Allison engine drove a three-bladed Curtiss constant-speed propeller of 10ft 6in (3.20m) diameter.

Potential Demonstrated

The NA-73X made its first flight from Inglewood on 26 October 1940 in the hands of freelance test pilot Vance Breese. Breese flew the aircraft three more times during the following month before handing it over to NAA's own Paul Balfour.

Balfour's first flight in the aircraft, on 20 November, ended in disaster. The NA-73X's engine died while engaged in airspeed calibration tests and while Balfour was attempting a dead stick landing in a ploughed field short of the runway the aircraft flipped over onto its back. Fuel starvation was the cause of the engine stopping, the result of Balfour failing to select the correct fuel tank.

Interestingly, years later Breese said he'd made a bet with some of the North American Aviation hierarchy that Balfour would crash the NA-73X on its first flight....unfortunately he was right! The NA-73 was eventually repaired to fly again, Bob Chilton taking over the testing duties from the hapless Balfour.

Despite the accident, the NA-73's potential had been demonstrated....it handled superbly and was 25mph (40km/h) faster than the similarly powered Curtiss P-40 it had been designed to replace. On the strength of this, a further 300 were ordered for the Royal Air Force (under the manufacturer's designation NA-83) and the name 'Mustang' bestowed upon the aircraft by the British.

By now the belated interest of the USAAC had also been aroused and they requested a pair of production Mustang Is be allocated from the initial production batch for evaluation. Given the designation XP-51 and initially called Apache by the manufacturer, these aircraft were the first of many thousands of examples of North American Aviation's latest product to reach the United States Army Air Force, as the service was

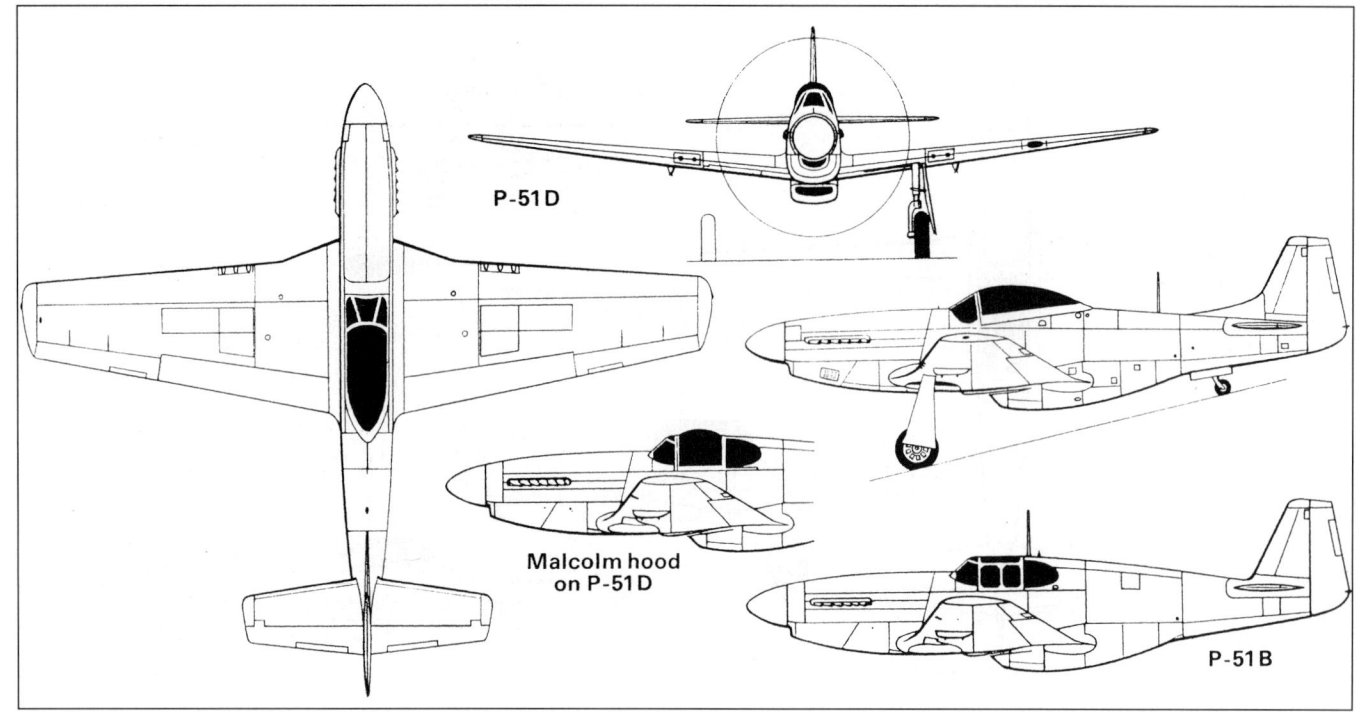
Malcolm hood on P-51D
P-51D
P-51B

renamed in June 1941. The 'Apache' appellation didn't last long, the USAAF quickly adopting the British 'Mustang' name for the fighter.

Early RAF Service

The first production Mustang I (AG345) was flown in April 1941 and handed over to the British a few weeks later, although the first example to reach the RAF (AG346) didn't arrive in Britain until late October. Following trials which confirmed the flying qualities and low-medium altitude performance of the aircraft (top speed 384mph/618km/h at 13,000 feet) – and the fact that performance deteriorated badly above that height – No 26 Squadron RAF based at Gatwick began to receive the first service Mustangs from January 1942.

The lack of altitude performance restricted the single-speed supercharged Allison powered Mustang to low-level army co-operation, strafing and armed photo-reconnaissance duties in RAF service, roles at which it excelled due to its high speed at low altitudes, heavy eight gun armament and outstanding flying qualities. In air combat at low to medium altitudes the aircraft proved to be a match for just about anything, including the Focke-Wulf Fw 190.

The Mustang's first operational sortie occurred on 10 May 1942, when a camera equipped 26 Squadron aircraft (AG418 flown by F/O G Dawson) undertook a reconnaissance mission over the French coast, the pilot strafing some targets of opportunity while he was at it.

This was to be the Mustang's forte in its early Allison powered versions, and soon some 14 RAF Army Cooperation squadrons were flying 'Rhubarb' strafing and 'Ranger' reconnaissance sorties over France. A Mustang also became the first single engined RAF aircraft to fly over Germany when in October 1942 a reconnaissance was made over the Dortmund-Ems canal.

The first production Mustangs to carry the official United States P-51 designation were the batch of 148 Mustang IAs ordered by the RAF for delivery from 1942. These differed from the initial 620 aircraft only in their armament installation, four wing mounted 20mm cannon replacing the eight wing and engine cowling machine guns which had been fitted before.

The reason for the adoption of the P-51 designation came about due to the introduction of the USA's Lend-Lease Act of March 1941. In an effort to continue the illusion of its neutrality, the USA had ceased selling military equipment to foreign powers but instead drew up an agreement which allowed the equipment to be leased out. It was in effect a thinly disguised way of helping Britain, but required the equipment – in this case aircraft – to be first ordered by an American Agency of Military Service and therefore given a US serial number and designation before being transferred to the customer.

Into US Service

At this still pre Pearl Harbour stage the American military could find little use for the Mustang as it was already committed to the Lockheed P-38, Republic P-47, Curtiss P-40 and Bell P-39. But the events of 7 December 1941 saw the USA embroiled in a global conflict whether it liked it or not, and the USAAF immediately decided to take a further look at the two evaluation XP-51s it had on strength.

The result was the diversion of 57 of the RAF's Mustang IA order to the USAAF, which fitted them with two F.24 oblique cameras in the rear fuselage and assigned them to photo-reconnaissance units in the USA under the designation F-6A, although as the aircraft retained their cannon armament, they were still often officially referred to as P-51s.

Following the perceived success of the Junkers Ju 87 Stuka in Europe and noting the stability and performance of the P-51 in the dive, NAA proposed a dive bomber variant of the Mustang to the USAAF early in 1942 and received an order for 500 such aircraft under the designation A-36A and unofficially named Invader.

Utilising the basic P-51 airframe and the 1,325hp (988kW) Allison V-1710-87 engine, the A-36A featured a structure strengthened to cope with the stresses of dive bombing, racks

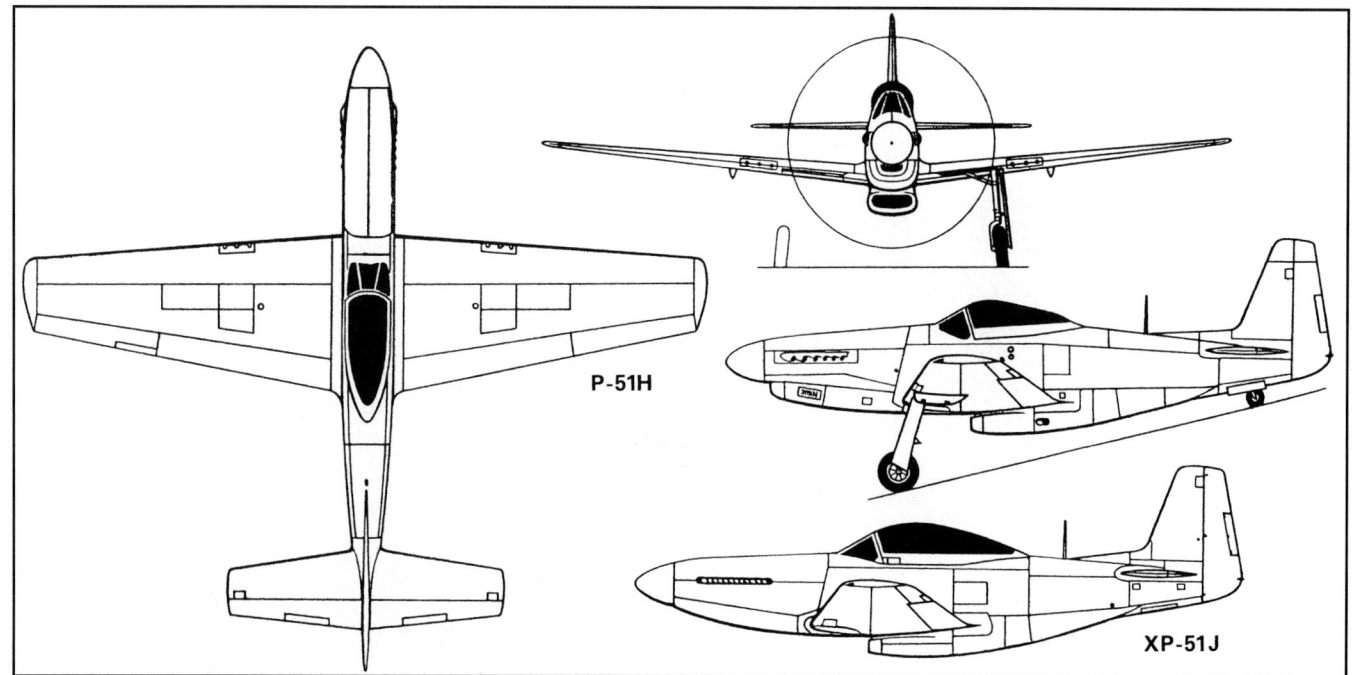

to carry a 500lb (227kg) bomb under each wing, hydraulically operated dive brakes in each wing and a change of gun armament to what would later become the definitive six Browning MG53 50-calibre machine guns in the wings.

It's probably ironic to see a fighter aircraft being 'downgraded' to a dive bomber (the days of which were numbered anyway), but it does indicate the USAAF's lack of appreciation of the Mustang's true potential at that time. Nevertheless, the 500 A-36As were delivered between September 1942 and March 1943 and served with some distinction in North Africa and the Mediterranean, despite their troublesome air brakes being locked shut most of the time and the operational penalties which resulted. The A-36A's main claim to fame was that it was the first version of the Mustang to see combat service with the USAAF.

The final Allison powered version of the Mustang to appear was the P-51A, 310 of which were ordered by the USAAF for delivery to the RAF under Lend-Lease as the Mustang II. Only 50 were eventually delivered to Britain from late 1942, the remainder serving with the USAAF mainly in the China-Burma-India theatre on a mixed bag of ground attack, reconnaissance, patrol and interception roles.

The P-51A was powered by the improved 1,200hp (895kW) V-1710-81 engine which gave the aircraft a top speed of 390mph (627km/h) at 20,000 feet. Fixed armament was reduced to four 0.50 inch machine guns (with a total of 1,260 rounds of ammunition) although provision for the carriage of a single 500lb (227kg) bomb under each wing was retained. Of importance was the incorporation of the plumbing necessary to support 75 or 150 (for ferry flights) US gallon (284/568 litres) underwing drop tanks, the first Mustang

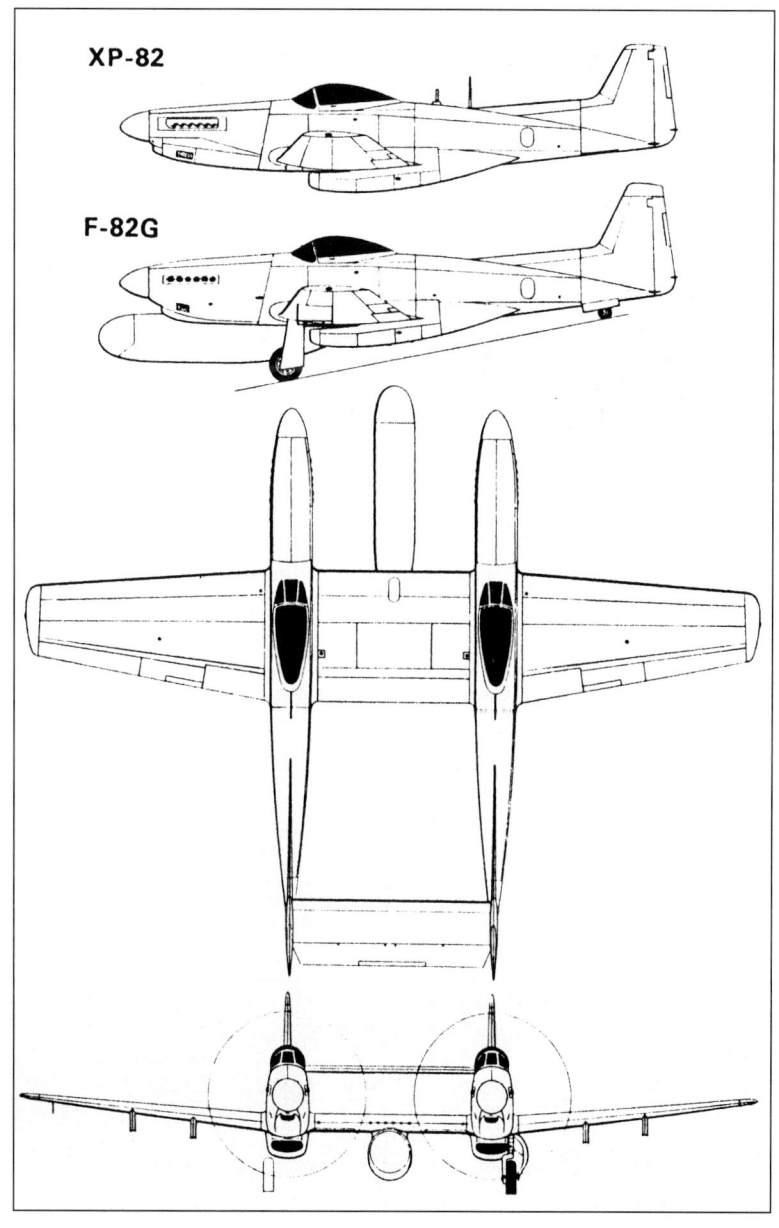

The first Mustangs to carry the official US P-51 designation were 150 Mk.IAs ordered for the RAF under Lend-Lease. Of these, 57 were diverted to the USAAF as the P-51 or F-6A as they were fitted with cameras. The designation P-51-1 was also sometimes used. Note the four cannon armament.

variant to have this feature and one which later played such a vital role in the war over Germany.

With standard internal tankage of 180 USgal (681 litres) the P-51A had a range of 750 miles (1,207km); two 75 USgal (284 l) external tanks increased this to 1,250 miles (2,011km) and on a ferry mission with two 150 USgal (568 l) tanks the aircraft's range exceeded 2,000 miles (3,218km). Field modifications also allowed the fitting of three rocket launch tubes under each wing – the Mustang's potential versatility was finally starting to be appreciated.

Included in the P-51A's production total of 310 were 35 aircraft fitted with two F.24 cameras. These were designated F-6B.

Merlin the Magician

The Allison engined Mustang's inadequacies at anything higher than medium altitudes might have relegated it to tactical reconnaissance or other low level roles for the remainder of its career if people in both the USA and Britain had not considered the 'what if' idea of installing the Rolls-Royce Merlin engine (in its two-stage/two-speed supercharged '60 series' form) in the Mustang's undoubtedly fine and efficient airframe.

The Merlin was already being built under licence in the USA by the Packard company as the V-1650 for installation in some versions of the Lancaster, Canadian Hurricane and Mosquito, so why not the Mustang? It was obvious that no matter how wonderful the Mustang's airframe was, to exploit its potential properly required much greater performance at altitude.

A proposal for re-engining the Mustang was put to the British Air Ministry in May 1942, the idea was immediately approved and six Mustang Is were delivered to Rolls-Royce for conversion between May and August of that year. Of these, five were converted. The first Merlin 61 engined Mustang (AL975 and designated Mustang Mk.X) flew on 13 October 1942, and the contrast was immediately apparent, the Merlin

The A-36A dive bomber – unofficially known as the 'Invader' – was the first version of the aircraft ordered specifically for the USAAF. It was also the first Mustang variant to see combat with the USAAF and served with some distinction in North Africa and the Mediterranean.

The final Allison powered Mustang was the P-51A or Mk.II in RAF service. Fitted with a more powerful version of the V-1710 engine and incorporating the significant addition of the necessary plumbing for underwing fuel tanks, the P-51A first flew in February 1943. This is 43-6004 Slick Chick, *the second P-51A used as an unarmed test aircraft at Wright Field, Ohio.*

and its 11ft 4in (3.17m) four bladed Rotol propeller increasing the aircraft's top speed to 422mph (679km/h) at optimum altitude after some fine tuning. Further increases were subsequently recorded and rate of climb was notably improved.

A slight diversion to explain the mysteries of the numerous Merlin variants may be desirable here. Early engines featured single-stage/single-speed superchargers, engines in the Merlin 20 series had two-speed/single-stage blowers, the '30 series' reverted to the original layout but with considerably more boost with optimisation for maximum power at low altitudes, while the 60-series and later Merlins were fitted with two-speed/two-stage superchargers.

Within that, the supercharger gear ratios could be changed to suit the role of the aircraft to which the Merlin was to be fitted. Therefore two-speed/two-stage Merlins were optimised for maximum performance at medium-high, high and low-medium altitudes. The Merlin 61 fitted by Rolls-Royce to the Mustang X developed 1,290hp (962kW) for takeoff, 1,565hp (1,167kW) at 12,250ft and 1,390hp (1,036kW) at 23,500ft and was a type of Merlin fitted to many Spitfire IXs.

The conversion of two Mustangs to Packard Merlin power in the United States occurred simultaneously, the first aircraft (41-37352 with a V-1650-3 engine and 11ft 2in/3.12m) diameter Hamilton-Standard four bladed propeller) taking to the air on the last day of November 1942, seven weeks after the British prototype had flown. Initially designated XP-78, the US Merlin-Mustang was soon officially known as the XP-51B. The American conversions differed from the British ones in several ways, including the deletion of the Mustang X's rather bulbous nose intercooler intake and moving that into an enlarged ventral scoop which incorporated both it and the main radiator. The XP-51B recorded a top speed of 453mph (729km/h) at 29,000 feet.

P-51B and P-51C

After testing of the prototypes over the northern hemisphere winter of 1942/43 in both countries, the first production P-51B Mustangs were de-

With the installation of the Packard Merlin engine, the Mustang was transformed into one of the great fighters of any era. The P-51B was the first production version with the new powerplant, deliveries to the USAAF beginning in June 1943.

The P-51B was named Mustang III in RAF service. This aircraft is carrying a British serial number (FX893), fin flash and camouflage but also USAAF 'stars and bars'.

livered in June 1943. These aircraft were very close to the XP-51B's specification and included either four or six 0.50 calibre machine guns with 1,260 rounds in total, the addition in all but the earliest examples of an 85 US gallon (322 litres) fuselage tank behind the cockpit and upgraded radio equipment.

The first USAAF unit to receive the P-51B was the 354th Fighter Group at Greenham Common, England, in November 1943. A part of the 9th Air Force, this unit immediately began escorting American bombers on their daylight raids against Germany.

P-51B production totalled 1,988 aircraft between June 1943 and February 1944 (of which some 274 went to the RAF as the Mustang III), the first 1,598 aircraft powered by the V-1650-3 engine and the remainder by the slightly more powerful but optimised for lower altitudes V-1650-7. With a maximum boost of +18 pounds, the V-1650-7 was rated at 1,490hp (1,111kW) for takeoff, 1,720hp (1,283kW) at 6,200 feet and 1,565hp (1,167kW) at 17,250 feet.

The P-51C was identical to the 'B' except it was built at North American's Dallas, Texas, plant rather than at Inglewood. Of the 1,750 P-51Cs manufactured, 636 went to the RAF (also as Mustang IIIs), many of them featuring the so-called 'Malcolm Hood', a sliding and bulged cockpit canopy which substantially increased visibility.

A photo-reconnaissance conversion of the P-51B/C was also produced, the F-6C, with the usual two F.24 cameras. Ninety-one conversions were completed.

Enter the D

The best known and most widely used version of all the Mustangs, the P-51D (NA-109), came about as a result of trying to permanently solve the aircraft's visibility problem. The solution was found in a sliding 'tear drop' canopy, which, in conjunction with cut down fuselage decking behind the pilot, gave superb all round visibility.

The P-51D also featured either Packard Merlin V-1650-3 or -7 engines along with the increased internal fuel capacity (265 USgal/1,003 litres) of the B and C models, standardisation on six 0.50 calibre Browning MG53-2 machine guns (with total ammunition increased to 1,880 rounds), a strengthened main wing spar to cater for additional underwing ordnance and, on all but the earliest examples, a fin leading edge fillet which compensated for the reduced fuselage side area resulting from the cut down decking.

The XP-51D prototype (43-12101, converted from a P-51B) first flew on 17 November 1943 and production amounted to 8,102 aircraft between February 1944 and the end of the war. Of these 6,502 were built at Inglewood and 1,600 at Dallas. Included in the production total were 271 for the RAF (as the Mustang IV), 146 completed at Dallas as F-6D photo-reconnaissance aircraft and ten aircraft converted to two-seat tandem TP-51D combat trainer configuration.

Almost identical to late model P-51Ds was the P-51K. This version featured an Aeroproducts propeller of 11ft 0in (3.07m) diameter and

The P-51D introduced another major breakthrough in the Mustang's design with its cut down upper fuselage decking and bubble canopy for greatly improved pilot vision. Deliveries began in early 1944. 44-13961 is an Inglewood built P-51D-5NA from the 4th Fighter Group's 336th Fighter Squadron.

The P-51K was similar to the D but with an Aeroproducts rather than Hamilton Standard propeller. All 1,500 were built at NAA's Dallas plant and both models were designated Mustang IV in British service. This is an RAAF aircraft of No 84 Squadron. (RAAF)

came about due to a shortage of the usual Hamilton-Standard unit. All 1,500 P-51Ks were built at Dallas of which 594 went the RAF (again as Mustang IVs) and 163 of the total were completed as F-6Ks.

Lightweights

As is always the case with aircraft, the Mustang's continued development had caused it to put on weight. To counter this, several lightweight experimental models were flown in 1944 and 1945. The first was the P-51F, which compared to the P-51D featured a lightened structure, thinner wings, reduced size wheel struts and brakes, the removal of two machine guns and the fuselage fuel tank and a the incorporation of a lightweight three bladed Aeroproducts propeller. All this reduced the tare weight by some 1,500lb (680kg) to around 6,600lb (3,000kg) and increased the maximum speed by 25mph (40km/h), but flight stability problems stopped the programme after only three prototypes had been built. First flight was in February 1944.

Two examples each of the P-51G (first flight August 1944) and P-51J (April 1945) were built, these were similar to the F but powered by a highly boosted 1,910hp (1,424kW) Merlin 14SM with five-bladed Rotol propeller and 1,700hp (1,268W) Allison V-1710-119, respectively. The J also had some streamlining of the cowling incorporated and was nine inches (23cm) longer than a standard Mustang.

The final Mustang production variant was the P-51H, which incorporated many of the weight saving innovations of the experimental models along with the reversion to six guns, an extended dorsal fin, a 50 US gallon (189 litre) fuselage fuel tank and a 2,218hp (1,654kW) war emergency rating (using +25lb boost) Packard Merlin V-1650-9 engine driving a four bladed Aeroproducts propeller. Top speed of this variant was a remarkable 487mph (784km/h) at 25,000 feet, 50mph (80km/h) faster than the P-51D.

Deliveries began in February 1945, and 555 were built. When hostilities ended, a further 1,845 were cancelled. Although entering service too late to see action in Europe, the P-51H did briefly serve in the Pacific in the final weeks of the war. Total production of the P-51 by North American Aviation reached 15,484 aircraft.

The P-51L was to be a Dallas-built version of the H with a direct fuel injected V-1650-11, but none of the 1,700 ordered had been built by the Armistice and the order was cancelled. The P-51M was identical to the H but built at Dallas and only one out of 1,628 on order had rolled out of the factory when peace came.

Twin Engined Diversion

The need for even greater range for the escorting of bombers across Europe and the Pacific resulted in development of the P-82 (later F-82) Twin Mustang, in concept two lengthened P-51 fuselages joined together by a new centre wing and tailplane.

The engineering involved was a little more complicated than that but the basic concept remained intact. The P-51D's Merlins were replaced with a pair of 1,600hp (1,193kW) Allison V-1710s in production versions, but the two XP-82 prototypes had Merlins. The first of these was flown on 15 April 1945. The P-82's fixed armament of six 0.50in machine guns was located in the leading edge of the new centre wing section and fuel capacity was substantially increased to allow a range of over 2,200 miles (3,605km).

Twin Mustang major production variants were the F-82E long range escort fighter for Strategic Air Command; and F-82F/G radar equipped night fighters for Air Defence Command. Following order cancellations with the end of the war, only 273 Twin Mustangs were built, serving with the USAF until 1953. Some F-82Gs saw combat in Korea, two of these credited with the first USAF 'kills' of the conflict, a pair of Yak-9s in June 1950.

Post War Activities

Although North American Aviation ceased production of the P-51 Mustang after VJ day, the type continued in widespread service with various air arms for many years after, most being equipped from USAF stocks. Australia's Commonwealth Aircraft Corporation (CAC) built 200 Mustangs

Several attempts were made at developing a 'lightweight' Mustang but only one achieved production. The first P-51H flew in February 1945 and deliveries began just as the war against Japan was reaching its conclusion. This view shows well the P-51H's lengthened and deepened fuselage.

based on the P-51D under licence between April 1945 and August 1951 but the list of other post war users was an extensive one: the Soviet Union, Italy, Canada, Sweden, Switzerland, Taiwan, New Zealand, France, the Philippines and Indonesia all taking delivery of Mustangs in the immediate post war period.

Numerous South and Central American countries also received P-51Ds under the terms of the Rio Pact; Bolivia, Cuba, Haiti, Guatemala, Uruguay, Dominica and El Salvador among them. Many of these countries retained their Mustangs until the early 1970s. One of them – El Salvador – used its aircraft in combat against Honduras other as late as 1969.

The incident was the so-called 'Football War', and came about as a result of fierce battles between players and spectators on and off the field during the soccer World Cup elimination playoffs between the two countries. Blood was shed over the roll of a soccer ball – ostensibly anyway – but the incident was really a manifestation of deeper rooted tensions between the two countries.

Mustangs covertly obtained from Sweden also fought for Israel during its 1948 war of independence, while in the Netherlands East Indies in 1948 and 1949 the type fought in the battles which would result in the creation of the Republic of Indonesia.

The Mustang came into its own once again during the Korean conflict of 1950-53. The range, endurance and airfield requirement shortcomings of the first generation of jets made them unsuitable for many missions and the Mustang (now designated F-51) was put to work once again not only by the Americans but also by the Australians and South Africans.

Cavaliers and Turboprops

After World War II, civilian interest in the Mustang increased as war surplus stocks became available. The type was ideally suited to the Bendix Trophy type point-to-point races which restarted after the war and the 'round the pylons' races which continue to this day in the form of events such as the Unlimiteds at Reno.

The 1946 Bendix Trophy race from Cleveland to California was won by famous aviator Paul Mantz, whose P-51D averaged a stunning 535.5mph (700.8km/h) over the 2,048 mile (3,296km) course – with the aid of a tailwind.

Since then Mustangs have been raced in standard, slightly modified and highly modified forms, the latter exemplified by the famous and ill-fated 'Red Baron' in which Steve Hinton set a world speed record for piston engined aircraft of 499mph

The distinctive form of the P-82 Twin Mustang with its two fuselages joined by a new wing centre section and tailplane. Developed as a long range escort fighter, the P-82 went on to perform that role and was also an effective night fighter. This is one of the XP-82 prototypes.

The final expression of the Mustang and a long way removed from the original. The turboprop powered and heavily armed Piper Enforcer was intended as a low cost COIN (counter-insurgency) aircraft but never found a customer.

(803km/h) in 1979. The 'Red Baron', was powered by a 3,800hp (2,834kW) Rolls-Royce Griffon 57 engine driving contra-props.

It took another Mustang to set a new record. This time it was Frank Taylor, whose Merlin powered P-51 (with the engine producing over 3,000hp/2,237kW at enormous boost) recorded 517mph (832km/h) in 1983.

The use of the Mustang as a two seat executive aircraft was probably not high on the North American design team's list of operational requirements when they designed the original NA-73 in 1940, but that's exactly the role a company called Trans-Florida Aviation envisaged for it in the late 1950s.

Two seater Mustangs were not a new idea, field modifications of P-51Ds first being performed in 1944 by removing the fuselage fuel tank and installing a seat instead. North American Aviation delivered 10 such aircraft in the same year as the TP-51D after modifying them on the production line, and in 1951 the Tempco Aircraft Corporation modified 15 more aircraft under the designation TF-51D. The Tempco conversion was more elaborate than the earlier ones in that a set of controls and instruments were provided for the rear seat and the canopy size and profile were modified.

Trans-Florida Aviation was formed in 1957 by David Lindsay, who originally had set out to make his company a primary source of spare parts for the many military and civil operators of the Mustang around the world. He purchased large amounts of Mustang spares and Merlin engines from the USAF and set up business also offering a TF-51D for conversion training and pilot checkout. His company also supplied refurbished armed Mustangs to several South American nations.

From there the idea of an executive two seat Mustang evolved with increased fuel capacity, extensive avionics and a comfortable cockpit with a high standard of sound proofing. The basic P-51 was stripped, rebuilt and 'zero timed', and FAA Type

A Cavalier Executive Mustang, one of several post war refurbished models developed by Trans-Florida Aviation for both civil and military use. Note the second seat in the area previously occupied by radio equipment.

Approval was obtained in February 1959.

These Mustangs were dubbed 'Cavalier' and five models were eventually offered with varying fuel capacities thanks to the incorporation of wing tip tanks and various combinations of extra internal wing tanks.

The Vietnam war revived interest in COIN or counter-insurgency aircraft and Trans-Florida (now called Cavalier Aircraft Corporation) developed a Mustang based aircraft to fill that need in 1967. Called the Cavalier Mustang II, this latest version of a basic design now more than a quarter of a century old used the P-51D airframe with wings strengthened to carry a variety of underwing stores up to a total of 4,000lb (1,814kg). Although successful in trials, none were ordered.

The next step was a turboprop version of the aircraft, dubbed the Mustang III. The first version, flown in October 1968, was powered by a 1,600shp (1,197kW) Rolls-Royce Dart 510 from a Capitol Airlines Vickers Viscount but two others were powered by a 2,445shp (1,823kW) Lycoming T55-L-9. Any resemblance to the original Mustang was by now becoming fairly vague – even the familiar ventral scoop had disappeared.

Cavalier sold the Mustang III's production rights to Piper in 1971, which as the PA-48 Enforcer entered it in the USAF's PAVE COIN competition, one intended to find a cheap aircraft to supply to smaller air forces under the USA's Military Assistance Program. By now there was little connection between the Enforcer and the Mustang with less than ten percent component part commonality and the addition of not only the turboprop engine but also an ejection seat, very large tip tanks and a total of ten underwing hardpoints capable of carrying an ordnance load of 5,680lb (2,576kg).

Despite attracting some attention, the Enforcer never achieved production although two more with further major structural and aerodynamic modifications were built under a USAF evaluation contract awarded in 1981, but as late as 1984 Piper was still offering the aircraft to smaller nations.

That marked the end of the Mustang's career as a potential combat aircraft. Even before that, the Mustang had become a highly prized warbird, with the world's flying population gradually increasing as more restorations were performed. In 2001, over 230 were regarded as airworthy and many of these were being regularly operated.

MUSTANG PRODUCTION

North American Aviation

Model	Inglewood	Dallas	Total
NA-73X	1	-	1
Mustang I	620	-	620
XP-51	2	-	2
P-51/Mustang IA	148	-	148
A-36A	500	-	500
P-51A/Mustang II	310	-	310
XP-51B	2	-	2
P-51B	1988	-	1988
P-51C	-	1750	1750
P-51D	6502	1600	8102
XP-51F	3	-	3
XP-51G	2	-	2
P-51H	555	-	555
XP-51J	2	-	2
P-51K	-	1500	1500
P-51M	-	1	1
Totals	**10,635**	**4,851**	**15,486**

F-6A: 57 included in P-51/Mustang IA total.
F-6B: 35 included in P-51A/Mustang II total.
F-6C: 71 included in P-51B total and 20 in P-51C total.
F-6D: 146 included in P-51D (Dallas) total
F-6K: 163 included in P-51K total.
TP-51D: 10 in 1944 included in P-51D total.
TF-51D: 15 in 1951 by Tempco converted from F-51Ds.

Commonwealth Aircraft Corporation

CA-17 Mustang Mk.20	80
CA-18 Mustang Mk.21	26
CA-18 Mustang Mk.22	28
CA-18 Mustang Mk.23	66
Total	**200**

North American F-82 Twin Mustang

XP-82	2
XP-82A	1
P-82B	20
F-82E	100
F-82F	91
F-82G	45
F-82H	14
Total	**273**

MUSTANG DESCRIBED

MUSTANG DESCRIBED

The P-51D production line at Dallas with T-6s bound for the Soviet Union in the background. (NAA)

The following is a reproduction of the report on the Mustang prepared by the general manager of Australia's Commonwealth Aircraft Corporation, Lawrence Wackett following his study of various types of fighter aircraft for licence production in Australia for the Royal Australian Air Force.

Wackett spent the first half of 1943 in the USA and Britain looking at different aircraft and his detailed report on the Mustang gives a good insight into the aircraft's physical characteristics and manufacturing points of interest.

Wackett makes his preference for the Mustang quite clear early in the report's preliminary remarks by stating: "It was very soon ascertained that the choice of a high altitude fighter would lie between the Spitfire VIII (which entered service with the RAAF later in 1943) and the P-51 Mustang, both with the Merlin 61 engine.... in making the final selection between the Spitfire and the Mustang, it was apparent that the Mustang, while being the best production job, had a good margin of superiority in the most important characteristic of speed.

"Its climb, however, was somewhat inferior but it was evident that this was being continually bettered by progressive reductions in gross weight, so that by the time production could be established, it was likely to be almost equivalent in climb to the Spitfire [this was in fact never achieved by the P-51D] while still holding its increased margin of speed. It was possible, therefore, to select the Mustang with every confidence."

The key issue seems to have been the Mustang's relative ease of manufacture over the Spitfire as well as superior speed, and as history records, Australia went on to become the only country outside the USA to build the aircraft.

CAC was a privately owned company which had only been formed in 1936 in an attempt to establish a viable Australian aircraft industry. Its first aircraft – the Wirraway – was a licence built development of the North American NA-16-2K general purpose trainer and the association with NAA continued into the 1950s and '60s with a locally produced version of the F-86 Sabre.

The report – which is reproduced here almost in full – was written in June 1943, just as the Merlin powered P-51B was entering service and five months before the XP-51D prototype was first flown.

Introductory:

At the time of writing, June 1943, it can be claimed that the North American Mustang, Model P-51D is the world's best fighter. Up to quite recently it was proper to regard the Spitfire as the world's best fighter, and it can also be said that the Spitfire has been the world's best fighter since the outbreak of war until now. There is no doubt whatsoever that the Spitfire was the best development in light of the knowledge available at the time of its design.

The fact that it is possible to claim that the Mustang is now the best example of a high performance fighter is due to the fact that it has been designed to improve on the Spitfire in the light of further experience and knowledge which has accumulated during the last three years. In the first place, the Mustang and the Spitfire use the same engine and approximate to the same gross weight. They have rates of climb which will become almost identical as the weights tend to become equal. At first the Mustang was heavier and had a lesser rate of climb. Progressively, however, the Mustang is being lightened until now it is only about 5 per cent heavier than a Spitfire similarly equipped.

It is in regard to speed that the superiority of the Mustang is most marked, and speed, being the most important of all characteristics in a fighter, is the feature which, other things being nearly equal, makes the Mustang what it is. To attain the 30mph and greater superiority of speed it has been necessary to adopt fundamentally different design features in the Mustang. The wing section is of the new laminar flow type, and the wing skins are of thick metal which enables a smooth surface to be produced, and this smooth surface is maintained under all conditions of flight. It is sufficiently thick not to wrinkle in flight.

Then again, there are no departures from a smooth aerodynamic shape over the front half of the aircraft. The air scoop for the radiators is on the underside of the body and well aft. The outflow from the oil cooler, the main cooling radiator and the intercooler are so placed that they do not disturb the airflow over any other part of the aircraft. The disturbances at the junction of the wing to the fuselage are relatively lower than in the Spitfire. The result is that the aircraft, while being a little heavier, is always, and under all conditions, about 30mph better than the Spitfire, which is itself as good as or better than any other known aircraft in regard to speed.

The great feature of the Mustang, and the one which must not be reduced by any military requirement, is its superiority of speed. This superiority of speed can be translated into superiority of climb in combat because of the greater kinetic energy possessed by the faster moving aircraft. If the aircraft can be zoomed up during a fighting manoeuvre it will have enhanced climb for a few thousands of feet, and this, for all practical purposes, means that it has greater tactical rate of climb than the steady climbing curve indicates.

Closeup detail of an early Mustang's cockpit and sideways hinging canopy. The empty space behind the pilot's seat of this P-51A would normally be occupied with radio equipment. (NAA)

The Power Unit:

The fundamental feature of a fighter aircraft is its powerplant. While fighting is confined to heights not exceeding 30,000 feet, which is the limitation imposed by the ability of the pilots to withstand the effects of reduced atmosphere pressure even with a full supply of oxygen, it is only necessary to provide a powerplant with a rated height less than 30,000 feet. A greater rated height would require a pressure cabin for the pilot and lead to a fundamentally new design of fighter, necessarily larger and heavier [the pressurised Spitfire VII belied this philosophy to a large extent].

The use of a 2-stage mechanical supercharger in the Rolls-Royce Merlin 61 engine provides the necessary supercharging in the most convenient manner. Compared with other supercharging arrangements which have been developed, the Rolls-Royce design is much to be preferred for the following reasons:-
(1) The mechanical details of the supercharger are simpler; having fewer parts it is also more compact than any other arrangement now available.
(2) The use of liquid cooled intercooling eliminates the bulky installation of ducts, which feature is particularly difficult to arrange in a small fuselage such as is possible with an in-line engine.
(3) The control of the supercharger is not an additional responsibility for the pilot in that it is quite automatic.
(4) No additional difficulties arise in screening the exhaust flames at night. This is particularly difficult with an exhaust turbo installation.
(5) The installation is the least vulnerable of all such installations, it being conceded that the in-line engine is fundamentally more vulnerable than an air cooled engine, but would be even more so with an exhaust turbo installation.

Finally, the development of the Rolls-Royce in-line engine has been carried to a greater stage of advancement than any other engine. It seems capable of delivering greater power for a given frontal area than any other engine, and seems capable of doing so without any serious difficulties continually arising with cooling problems. However, its one drawback is its vulnerability, but this can be accepted for high altitude operation particularly as it enables the attainment of high speeds and this feature is itself the greatest safeguard against vulnerability.

Construction and Manufacture of the Wings:

The Mustang has a straight taper wing of 37 feet span, and total area of 233sq ft. The taper ratio is about 0.5 from a root chord of 104 inches. The

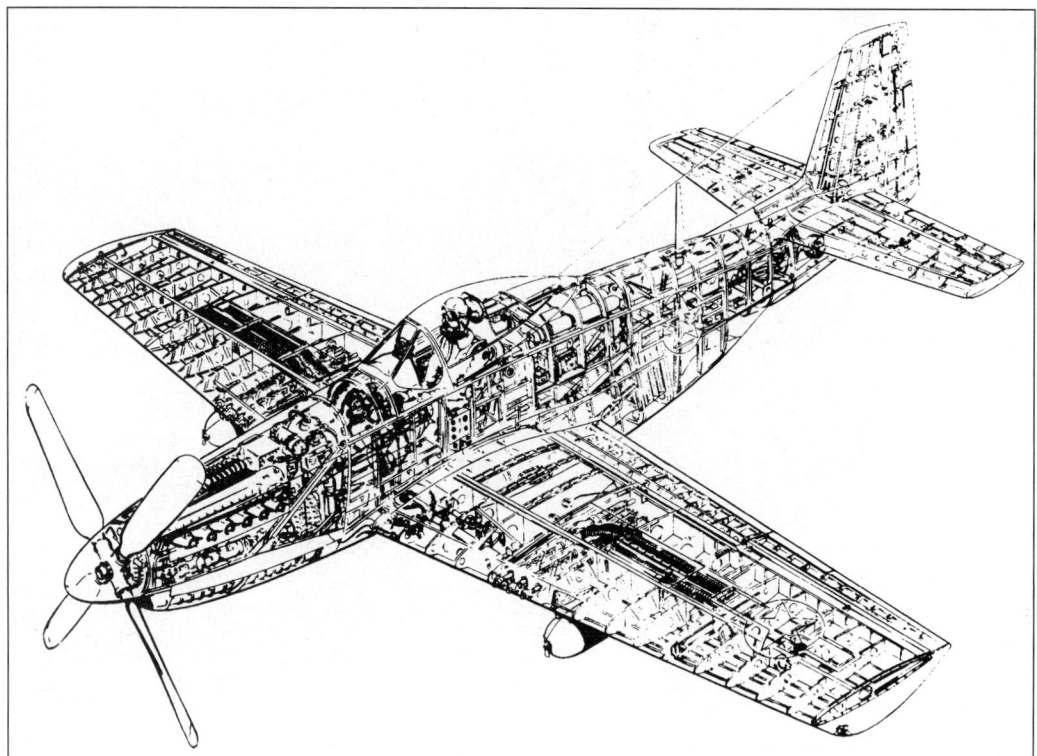

A cutaway drawing of a P-51D shows the aircraft's salient airframe and equipment features. (NAA)

wing is made in two halves joined at the centre line, and is set with a dihedral of 5 degrees and a washout of incidence from root to tip of 1.5 degrees. The wing section is NACA Low Drag type known as laminar flow section. There are two spars of simple design produced by flanging up the edges of a tapered web plate and reinforcing the flanges by angle members bent from sheet material and rivetted in place. Both the web plates and angle stiffeners are stepped down in thickness and size at intervals to produce a tapered beam spar.

The production of the correct depth of spar is ensured by starting with web plates longer than required and after flanging in the brake press, placing the taper channel in a jig and trimming for length while located in the taper jig. The web sections are assembled in a jig and joined by rivetted joining plates. At the same time the reinforcing angle flanges are rivetted on. Some vertical web stiffeners are and some fittings are also rivetted on in the spar jig.

In the case of the rear spar, all the hinge bracket castings for the ailerons and flaps are also attached in the spar jig. In some places extrusions are used for flange reinforcements, particularly on the top of the front spar which has a heavy bar of dural rivetted into the angle section. In the web there are a few flanged lightening holes and also holes for the guns to pass through.

Before construction of the wing can proceed, several sub-assemblies must be made. These consist of sections of the skin and the leading edge each built up with their stringers and former ribs on separate jigs. The wing is finally assembled by bringing together two large sub-assemblies which have been built up from smaller sub-assemblies attached to each of the spars respectively.

The rear spar has attached to it the portion of the wing behind the ammunition box and all the wing structure beyond out to the wing tip.

The front spar is attached to the wheel well structure, the large magnesium alloy casting carrying the undercarriage, the top of the wing tank compartment and all of the leading edge.

The design of the wing provides for two petrol tanks either side of the centre joint and extending out to the undercarriage location. This box-like section contained between the front and rear spars and the very stiff top skin is closed on the lower side by a tank door, and forms the main torsional structure of the wing up to the very stiff rib directly behind the undercarriage mounting casting. At this point the torsional stiffness is transferred to the structure comprising the leading edge and the front spar, and this torsional structure extends right out to the wing tip.

The torsional transfer is made by very thick dural plates which reinforce the skin both top and bottom, above and below the large casting carrying the undercarriage. Inside of the undercarriage, the region in front of the front spar comprises the wheel well, which is closed on the underside by a hydraulically operated door. In order to house the wheel the undercarriage is arranged to swing forward slightly so that the wheel tyre clears the spar web. This means that the chord must be increased near the wing root to provide space to accommodate the wheel. It seems probable that this increase in chord in this region had produced aerodynamic advantages in the form of reduced wing root fillet interference.

Outside of the undercarriage the space between the wing spars is first devoted to the housing of the guns, and then still further out to holding the ammunition boxes. These two compartments have removable top doors.

In the main wing jig where the two large sub-assemblies are brought together, all the skin joints are completed and the structure finally closed by a roll on strip which is progressively rivetted on. There are four large openings in the completed wing. The tank door, being a vital structural member, is attached by screws and anchor nuts. The wheel well door is a very strong hinged door which is opened and closed by hydraulic strut. The gun compartment opening is closed by two doors, one completely removable, and the other hinged at the rear and arranged to lock the removable door when closed. Finally there is the door to the ammunition compartment which is hinged at the front edge and held by DZUS fasteners.

The wing tip consists of a short length of wing structure of normal construction, to which is attached a formed tip section. The tip section is produced of drop hammer panels and welded, and is attached by screws and anchor nuts. The whole wing tip structure is finally attached to the main wing structure by screws and anchor nuts.

The two wings join together at the centreline of the aircraft by a strong joint, and the two wings are assembled together as a unit before being attached to the fuselage. To enable the fuselage to be attached to the wing, very strong channel members and forgings are built on to the very heavy skin structure of the upper surface of the wing, and give four strong points for bolted attachment.

The skins of the Mustang are very thick, being 0.080in at the inner end and never thinner than 0.040in at the tip. All the rivetting is flush with drilled countersinking, which results in a remarkably smooth and true surface which does not show any crinkles even under 3g loading.

During the assembly of the subsections of the wing, and during final assembly, many additional fittings are built in as convenient. Gun mounting castings, blast tubes, landing light in leading edge, and electrical fittings also on the rear spar, mountings for aileron control brackets, trim and tab controls.

The aileron control is entirely behind the rear spar and carried on the web of the spar. The controls to the port and starboard ailerons respectively are entirely separate, and are operated by separate push-and-pull rods directly connected to the rock shaft levers of the central flying control. The rods each operate a large pulley mounted on the face of the rear spar and carry cables to a similar but smaller pulley, also on the face of the rear spar and located opposite the inner end of the aileron.

The aileron control lever on the inner end of the aileron is directly attached to the pulley, being universally jointed and moving with a unique conical motion which is very effective and very neat, giving as it does a differential movement of aileron angle in relation to stick movement.

The control of the trim tab is on one aileron only, but there are tabs on both ailerons. The starboard acts as a servo balance only, whereas the port combines servo balance with trimming.

Both ailerons are completely skinned with metal, and finish with a sharp trailing edge in conformity with the laminar flow wing section. This construction is torsionally stiff and is a safeguard against aileron twist at high speed; also, it permits the control to be applied on the inner, ie the thickest end. The means of balancing the aileron is new and unusual, and has only very recently been introduced after a long series of trials to improve the aileron control. Adverse criticism of the aileron control has been levelled at Mustang for a very long time, and it is only by the introduction of this special balance that satisfactory results have been achieved.

The aileron balance consists of a plate-like extension on the leading edge of the aileron and on its aerodynamic centreline. This plate extends into a cavity in the wing immediately ahead of aileron. The cavity is entirely behind the rear spar because the aileron hinge line is set well back on brackets.

A flexible fabric diaphragm is attached to the rear spar web face and to the leading edge of the balancing surface, and seals the airflow from the top to the bottom of the wing through the hinge gap. The plate balance carries a heavy front edge which serves to provide the mass balance. The scheme is discontinuous around the centre hinge, and some leakage is tolerated at this point. The effective result is that the aileron can be very closely balanced when the air loads are very high at high speed. The stick loads remain light at high speeds, and the danger of overbalance which sometimes results with exposed horn balances is avoided. The effects of variation of hinge gap widths, which are difficult to control during manufacture, are avoided by sealing the gap.

The laminar flow wing does not permit the use of satisfactory split flaps so that we find aileron type flaps being used, and as these are completely covered with metal they are torsionally stiff and can be

This underside shot of a P-51D – complete with D-Day stripes – shows details of the control surfaces, radiator and undercarriage doors. Also shown is how easily the airframe became streaked with oil.

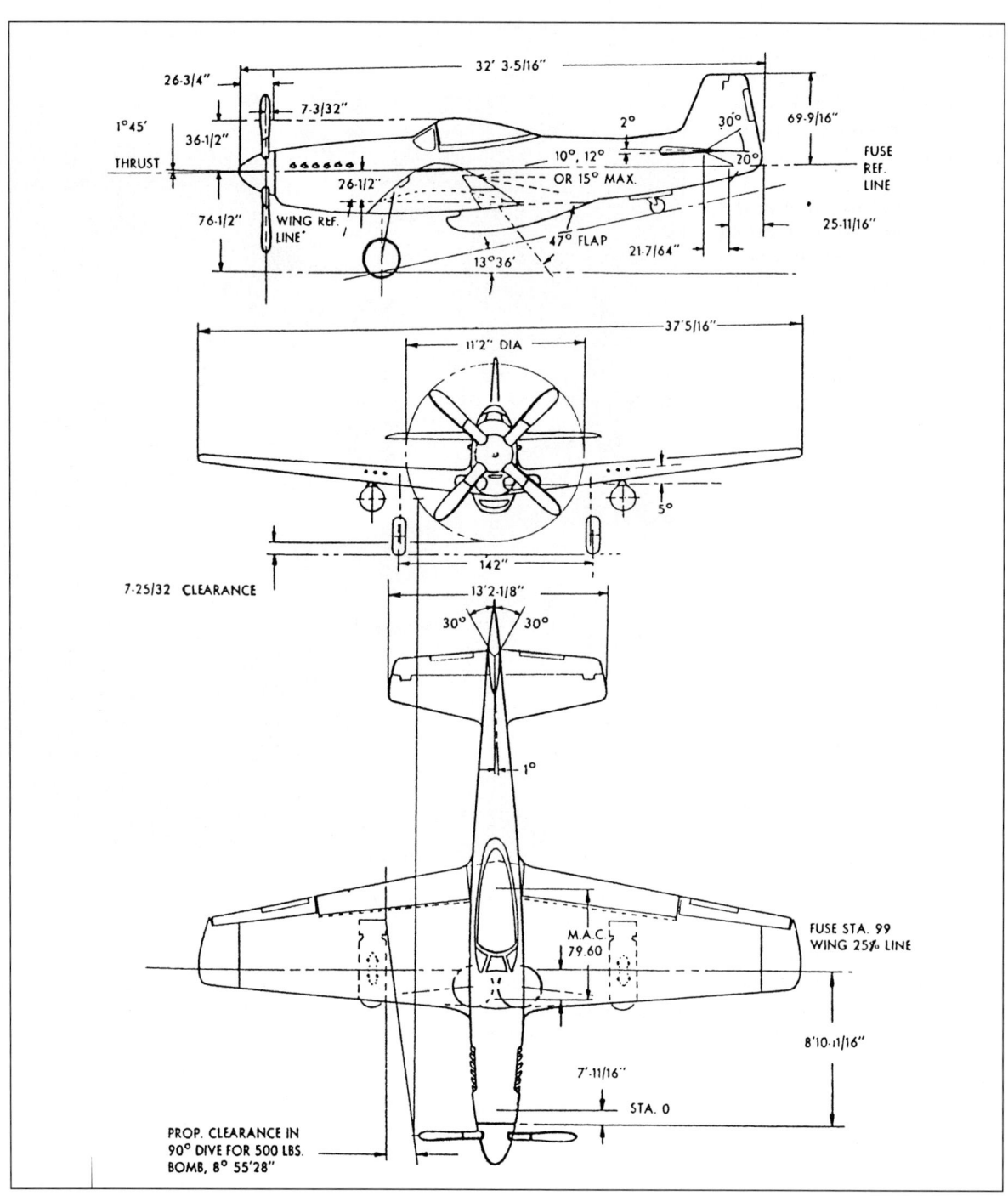

P-51D Mustang geometric data.

operated by a control at the innermost end. This feature greatly simplifies the hydraulic operating system for the flaps. This type of flap does produce a marked change of trim in operation but this has been found reasonable to control. The flaps terminate opposite the fuselage sides and do not continue to the centre line under the fuselage as this region is occupied by the radiator scoop.

The main flying control is mounted directly on the wing surface over the bolt angle joint at the centre. This control consists of a for and aft rock shaft in bearings mounted on the wings. At the front end there is a horn bracket casting similar to that used on the Wirraway, and this carries the control column. To the lower end of this column is attached the elevator control rod, which passes rearward through the hollow rock shaft to attach to a double ended lever to which the elevator control cables are attached.

This same lever is mounted loose on the cross shaft which transmits the force of the flap operating jack to the flaps. The shaft itself is carried on bearings on the lower longerons. The rear end of the rock shaft carries the two levers to which the aileron control push rods are attached. Transverse movement of the control column is transmitted by means of the rock shaft, which passes directly under the pilot's seat to operate the ailerons. By this neat arrangement there are no aileron or elevator control wires visible in the pilot's cockpit.

At the front of the wing and on the upper surface on either side of the centre joint are mounted two hydraulic jacks operating vertically to open

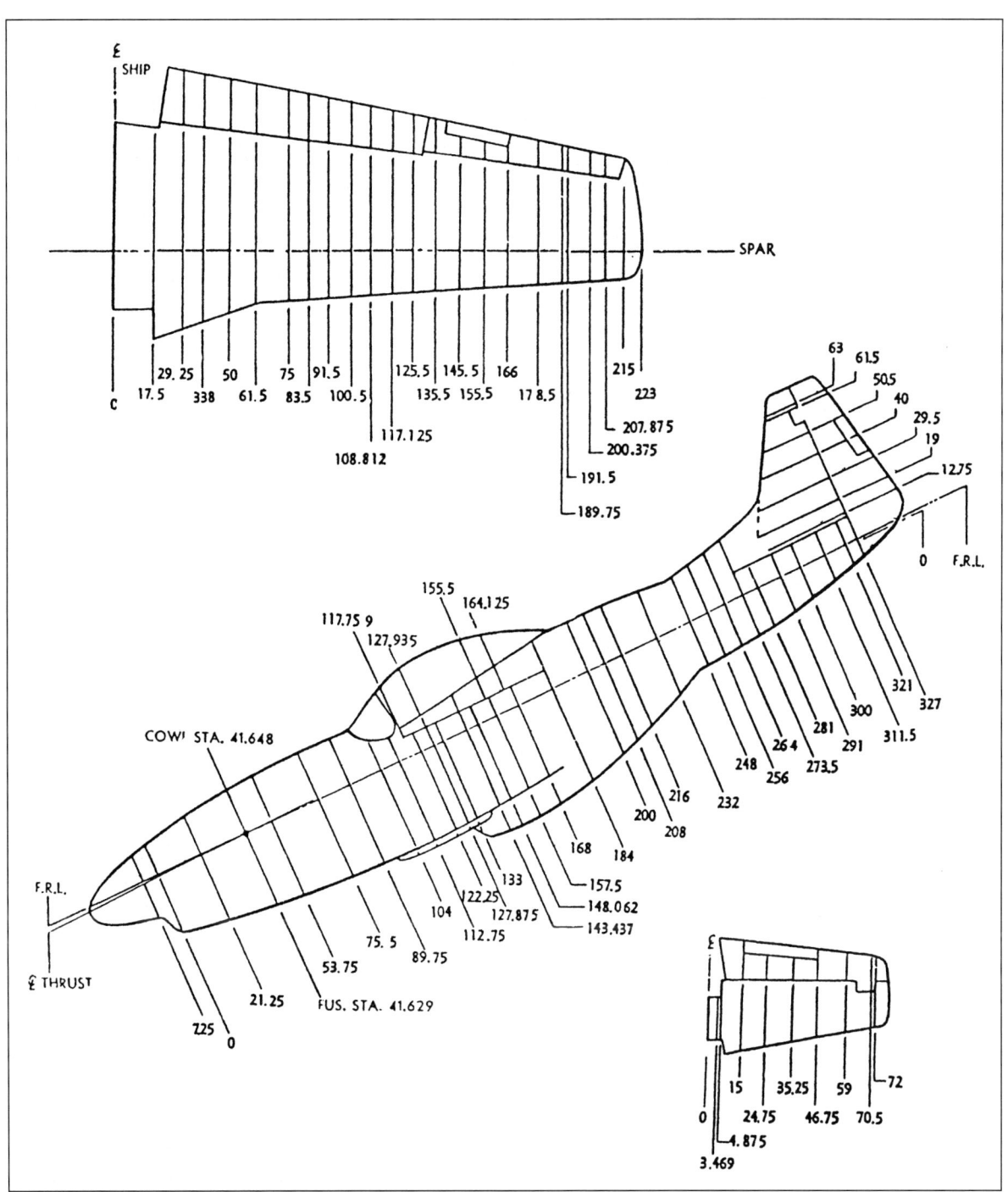

P-51D Mustang stations diagram.

and close the wheel well doors in proper sequence with operation of the folding of the undercarriage. The operating jacks for folding the undercarriage are mounted on the front face of the front spar and are accessible through the open wheel wells.

The undercarriage struts are locked in the down position by hydraulically operated lock plungers located in the main hinge casting. Each leg carries a large door which effectively seals the gap in the wings into which the leg retracts, and this door registers and seals with the hydraulically operated door already mentioned as being hinged to the wheel well opening.

The self sealing fuel tanks are two in number, and one is contained in each wing on either side of the centre joint. The cellular construction is of Firestone practice, and wholly flexible and without interior structure. Mushroom headed bolts are built into the top and bottom surfaces, and serve to attach these to the top and bottom surfaces of the wings and prevent collapse due to lack of internal support.

The tanks hold 90 American gallons each, and are very long and shallow, extending from the centre line of the aircraft out to the undercarriage mounting in the wings. Seeing that the inner ends of the tanks lie under the pilot's cockpit it is possible to arrange fuel gauge indicators directly on the tanks so that they can be read directly through apertures in the floor of the cockpit, which is, of course, the upper surface of the wing.

Electrically driven petrol pumps by Thompson Products are mounted entirely within the petrol holding

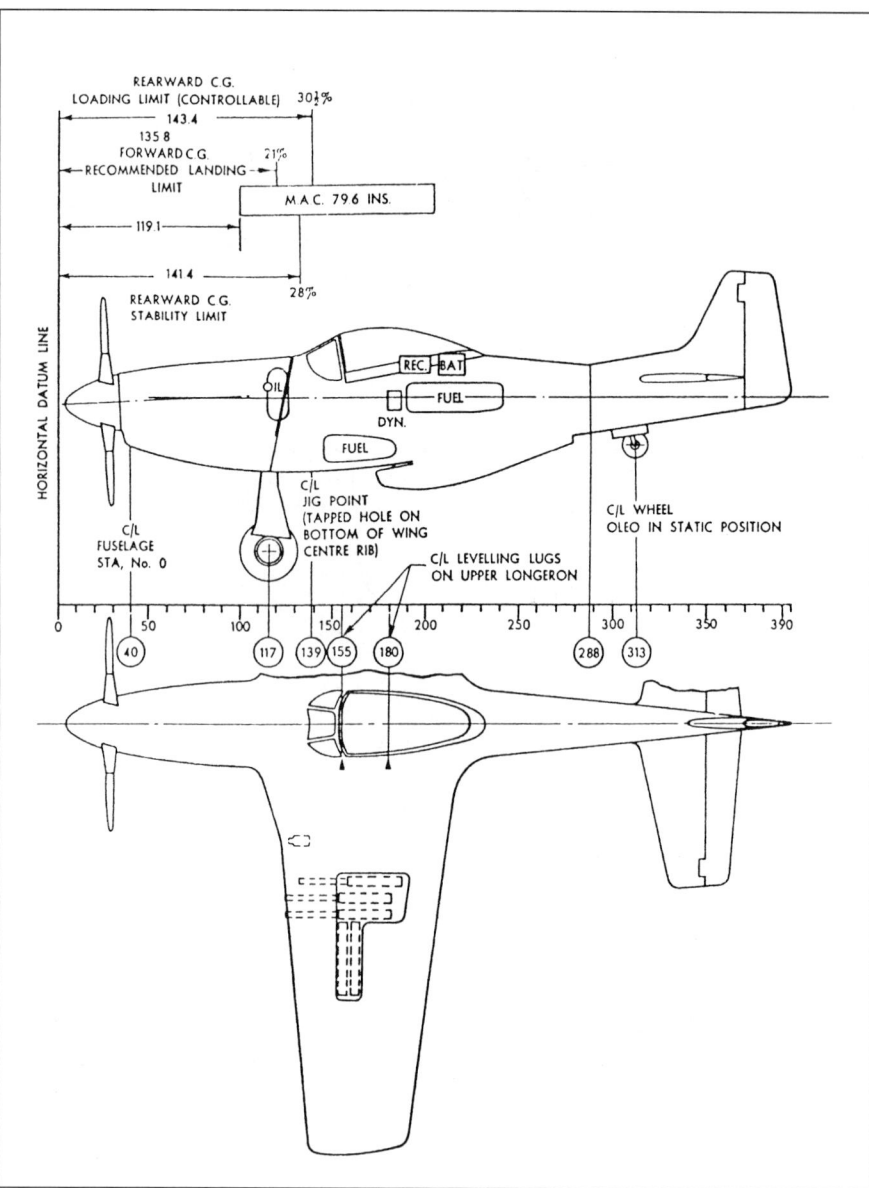

This weight and balance diagram from the CAC Mustang overhaul manual shows the location of some items including the troublesome (from a centre of gravity point of view) fuselage fuel tank. (HDHV)

stances, forms the top part of the rear fuselage

Following the lead given by the Japanese in their Zero fighter, and followed later by the Germans with their Focke-Wulf fighter, the British are now universally convinced that rearward vision for the fighter pilot is of vital importance, and that the turnover truss can be dispensed with as not being worthwhile. The desire for good rear vision has been met with the 'tear drop' type of cockpit enclosure now being adopted for all new fighters under development.

The new Mustang P-51D will include a 'tear drop' cockpit enclosure, and there will be no turnover truss. These changes will mean a considerable alteration to the top of the fuselage, and an altogether new type of cockpit enclosure which will be produced from a single piece of moulded plastic sheeting and will have no obstruction to the rearward view.

The armour plate behind the pilot is well shaped to assist rearward vision, and is also curved forward over the pilot's head so as to protect the top of the head from downward shooting up to fully 20 degrees.

As the turnover truss was normally built into a bulkhead directly to the rear of the pilot, and as this bulkhead is an important structural member carrying the fuselage attachments to the rear spar of the wing, it will be referred to as the turnover truss frame for the purposes of the description which follows, although it must be borne in mind that the actual structure to carry the turnover load will be eliminated in the P-51D, and certain structural members which are determined by the turnover truss stressing loads have been lightened in consequence.

The turnover truss frame is built on a flat jig from channel extrusion struts mounted as an inverted V on a built up sheet metal cross beam. At the bottom ends of the extrusion struts are two castings which serve to attach the fuselage to the rear spar of the wing by bolts. The turnover truss frame is mounted into the fuselage structure by two double webbed fuselage ribs which are built integrally with the frame and are rivetted to the fuselage sides during final assembly of the fuselage.

The fuselage sides are built up in frame jigs from two sub-assemblies, one front and one rear, which are

cells and are attached to a flange connection on the bottom of the deepest section of the tank. Electric leads to the pump motor and also the discharge pipe pass through this flange.

The tooling used for the assembly of the wings is all very simply constructed of large diameter steel tubing, and structural sections built up by electric welding. Accurately made location blocks and cramps are welded on where necessary. All jigs are made torsionally rigid so as to stand on the floor by three point locations. Frequent minor earthquakes in California make this necessary and there is the further advantage that jigs may be removed without loss of internal alignment and accuracy.

A feature which is peculiar to North American construction is the use of high shear rivets of steel, which are inserted in duralumin structures and secured by dural collars swaged over the shanks which are grooved to hold these collars. This scheme results in a great reduction in the number and size of dural rivets which would normally be used at locations of high shear stress.

Construction and Manufacture of the Fuselage:

The present model Mustang P-51B has a turn-over truss behind the pilot and the customary type of cockpit enclosure, which comprises a wind shield, a sliding cover and a streamlined rear portion which, in most in-

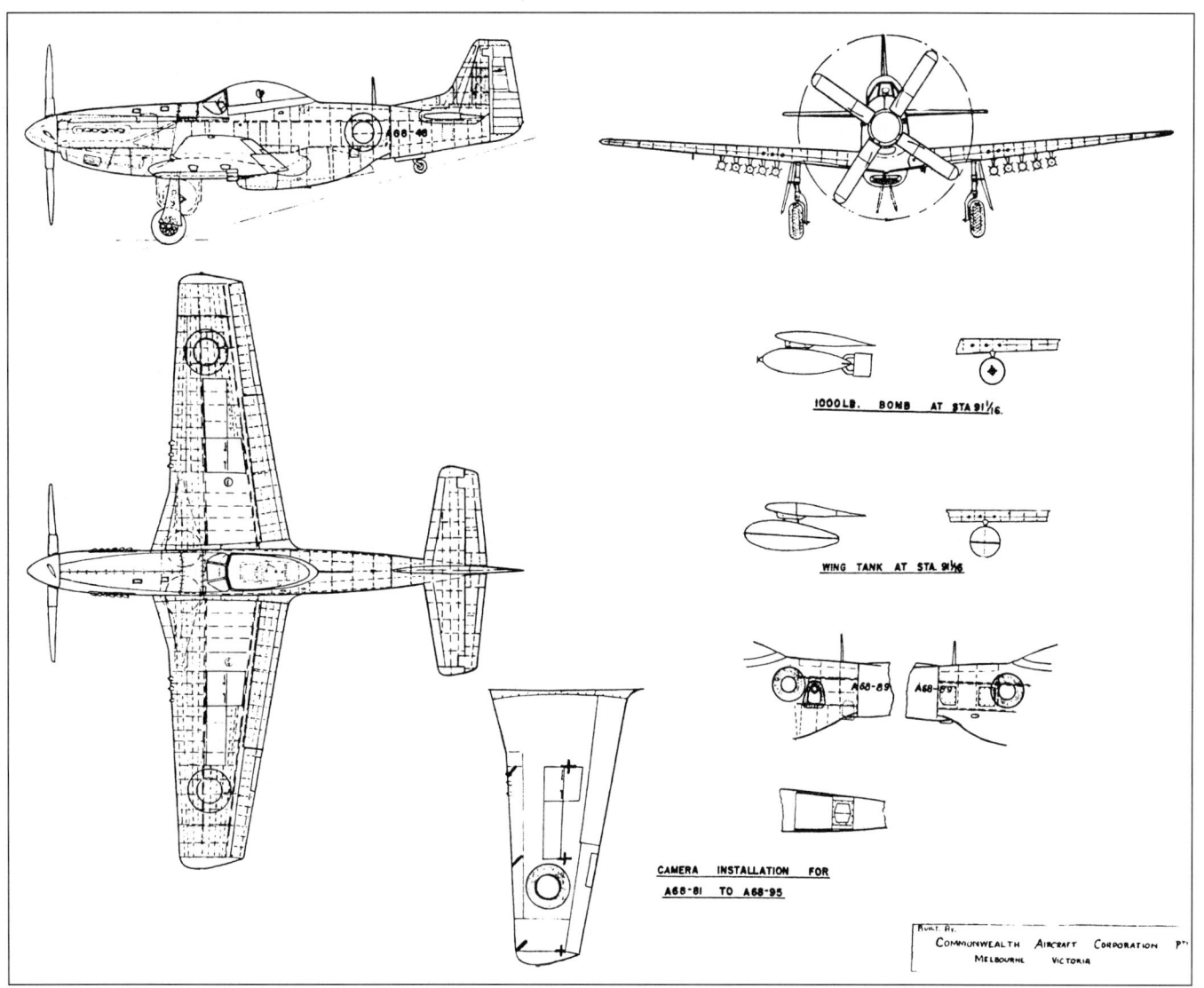

General arrangement and detail drawings for the CAC Mustang including scrap views of the bomb, drop tanks and camera installations. (HDHV)

brought together in another jig in which the jointing operation is carried out by splicing the longerons, the stringers and the side skins.

The front portion of the fuselage side comprises a top and bottom longeron of heavy H section extrusion with vertical sheet metal ribs between, and covered with a flush rivetted skin which is nowhere thinner than 0.40in.

At the front end of each longeron is bolted a heavy dural fitting produced from bar stock or by forging, and these form the attachments for the engine mount bolts. The attachment to the front spar of the wing is made by a bar stock fitting on the lower longeron, which fitting is built into a strong double rib which carries the load into the side skin and up to the top longeron. The skin in this region is 0.80in thick. Further aft the longerons are milled to taper rapidly, and are spliced to T section extrusions which form continuations of the longerons into the rear portion of the fuselage sides.

The lower longeron is finally made as a sheet metal channel. The ribs are mostly of flanged up sheet metal, some with L section extrusions as stiffeners, and there are a few other ribs of L section extrusions in special places.

In the splicing jig for the front and rear portions of the fuselage sides, a motor driven router was mounted to trim the top edge of the fuselage sides at the line of the attachment of the curved top deck, which joins the top of the fuselage sides in the final assembly jig. In the P-51D with teardrop cockpit enclosure, the top deck of the fuselage is much wider than, and of flatter arch than the type used on the P-51B. This also requires narrower fuselage sides trimmed down to the top longeron line or thereabouts.

These changes had not been made at the time of inspection, and it is certain that arrangement of the motor router for trimming will be altered considerably, or possibly could be eliminated for small scale construction. Trimming could quite easily be done by hand.

The front portion of the fuselage which is built up from the two sides, the turnover truss frame, the top deck and the floor sections, ends at a frame just ahead of the stabiliser to tailplane join. At this station a bolt angle joint is made with an entirely separate structure comprising the rear end of the fuselage.

To build up the front portion, a sub-assembly must be made of the top deck, which is simply a curved skin rivetted to arch form ribs. The floor structures, which are flat, close the bottom of the fuselage between the bottom longerons from the rear end to the turnover truss frame. The floors consist of three sub-assemblies. The rear section, a built up flat floor with many stiffeners, extends for about half the length.

Then there is a step-up beam of built up construction, which joins the rear edge of the front section of the floor which is directly over the location of the radiator. This front section of the floor has many stiffeners and forms the shelf on which the radio is mounted.

Just ahead of the rear bolt angle flange and at the point of junction with the rear longerons, there are two forgings which mount the transverse lift tube and also form strong points to splice the lower longerons to the tail section.

The construction of the tail section requires quite a number of sub-assemblies and fittings, for besides making a bolt angle joint to the rear fuselage there are mountings for the tail wheel and tail plane, and the stern frame.

The first jig for the tail section holds the two lower longerons and the curved lower skin which is rivetted to sheet metal arch ribs. The front and rear bulkheads are stiffened with L section extrusions, and are incorporated with the longerons and bottom skins together with two torque resisting boxes which mount either side of the hole through which the tail wheel retracts.

Several fittings are rivetted in, such as the hinge casting for the tail wheel unit, and the mounting for the rudder control bell crank, on which the rudder cables terminate and final operation of the rudder is effected by a push rod through the stern frame. In addition, there is a sheet metal built up box bracket to carry the tail wheel steering pulley brackets.

The tail section is finally assembled on another jig in which the side ribs are erected in place and the top deck sections and side skins are rivetted in place. The top deck carries the top longerons on which there are four fittings for the tail plane attachment bolts.

In the tail section there is a mounting for the tail wheel retracting hydraulic jack and some electrical wiring. The tail section is attached to the rear of the fuselage at an early stage along the final assembly line.

Returning to the continued assembly of the rear fuselage, there is the attachment of the rear duct below the rear section of the floor. This duct is directly aft of the radiator which is mounted suspended to the lower longerons. The lower duct is quite a complicated structure, giving a clean airflow controlled by a hinged door while maintaining a good aerodynamic fairing for the radiator block into the rear of the fuselage on the underside. This means that there is an internal sheet metal duct and an external fuselage skin which are assembled together with sheet metal former ribs involving several sub-assemblies.

The hinged door also has an inside and outside skin which are assembled on former ribs and completed with a front hinge and an attachment for an operating rod. This rod is actuated by a hydraulic jack which is mounted on a sheet metal beam across the rear of the fuselage directly above the location of the door. This beam is built in the rear fuselage during final assembly and before the tail section is bolted in place.

At the front end of the fuselage, several operations are performed by the aid of drill jigs. The locations of the wind shield attachment bolts are drilled; holes are drilled for the mounting of the rudder pedal unit assembly, and the instrument panel mounting. These units come together and provide mutual bracing and a mounting for the electrical control box.

Finally, all the above mentioned units are incorporated in the fuselage under final assembly, together with many other items of equipment which are brought forward at this location on the assembly line.

Such items are brackets for oxygen bottles just above the rear floor; and immediately aft of the turnover truss frame there is the cross tube which has bearings on the lower longerons and crank connections for the flap operating jack (also mounted in the rear fuselage) and the push-and-pull rods to the flaps themselves. This cross tube carries, loose at its midpoint, the double-ended lever which provides the junction of elevator control wires to the push-pull rod to the control column.

Mention has already been made of the rear duct for the radiator and the radiator itself. To conduct air into the radiator, a very elaborate front duct structure is necessary, and this is built on to the lower side of the fuselage, under the radio shelf, and directly aft of the attachment of the fuselage to the rear spar of the wing.

To provide efficient cooling with low drag, it is necessary to scoop air at high velocity, and expand this air gradually so as to reduce its velocity, and allow it to pass through the radiator at reduced velocity in sufficient volume to dissipate heat at the required rate to maintain the correct operating temperature of the coolant over a wide range of power output. This control is effected by the hydraulically operated door in the rear duct. As the radiator is partitioned to provide cooling both the cylinders and the supercharger intercooler, as separate coolant circuits, the one control door suffices for these two circuits.

For the oil, a separate radiator is provided, but this is arranged to draw its cooling air from the main scoop by means of a branch sub-duct on the lower side. Control through the oil cooling radiator is provided by a separate small hinged door to the under side and operated with a small hydraulic jack.

Construction of the scoop with its expanding bifurcated ducts to main and oil radiators, and conforming as it does to the smooth aerodynamic shape of the fuselage at its junction with the wing, results in an elaborate sheet metal structure with a large number of drop hammer formed panels.

The internal and external skins are assembled together with a large number of former ribs, requiring several sub-assemblies to be made before these are finally brought together to produce the whole unit. When completed, the final scoop structure is made a detachable unit so that it can be removed from the front of the radiator for accessibility to this important unit.

Construction and Manufacture of the Engine Mounting:

Whereas the design and construction of the wings and fuselage are not fundamentally different from that which may be used for a radial engined fighter, the engine mounting structure of the Mustang is quite different from that which may be used for a radial engine. It is quite unlike that used in many other inline engined fighters.

Two views of a CAC Mustang on the ground showing the aircraft's general characteristics. In both shots the flaps and undercarriage doors are fully down, a sure sign the aircraft has been on the ground for a reasonable amount of time, allowing hydraulic pressure to bleed off.

Basically, the engine mounting structure comprises two large cantilever beams, one on each side of the engine. These beams are attached to the lower longerons at their rear ends and extend forwards to the very front of the engine. Each beam is supported near the middle of its length by a diagonal brace which connects to the top longeron.

At the point of junction of the diagonal brace with the beam, the latter has its maximum depth which amounts to about 10 inches, and from this point both to the front and to the rear, the beam tapers to a point. Roughly speaking, each beam is of an elongated diamond shape in side elevation. To conform with tapering shape of the fuselage towards the nose, each beam is given an inward bend in plan.

To complete the engine mount structures so as to form a cradle to support the engine, two large built up arch form beams are inserted between the beams and bolted rigidly to them. The largest of these inverted arch cross beams is located near the point of maximum depth, and the other is located at the forward end. The actual engine attachments consist of four groups of shock absorbers located under each of the four feet on the engine crankcase, and these shock absorbers are bolted to the beams at the points of junction with the arch form cross beams.

The whole engine mount structure is fabricated from extrusions and sheet metal plates, and requires a large number of accurately made jigs for the correct forming, drilling and assembly of each of the units and of the mounting as a whole.

It is clearly obvious that a great deal of labour could be saved if the large beams at least, and possibly the two arch cross beams as well, were produced as dural forgings. Inquiry at North American Aviation revealed that they agreed with this contention, but could not adopt the suggestion because of the critical situation in the USA in regard to the production of forgings. It has been noted that for the German Messerschmitt, which is an inline engined fighter, the engine mounting consists in the main of two large forgings for side beams.

With the availability in Australia of a very large hammer which is being only lightly loaded, the opportunity is open to effect a very great economy in manpower by redesigning the engine mounting to use forgings for the side beams and cross beams. This is particularly desirable because the engine mounting of the Mustang constitutes a very major portion of the fabrication of the airframe, and the tooling required for the existing built up structure is very extensive and constitutes a very big percentage – probably over 25% – of the really difficult tool making required for the entire airframe.

The description given hereafter refers to the existing engine mount only.

The top and bottom members of the beams, together with the diagonal brace, consist of H section dural extrusions. They are fabricated separately, bent and milled where necessary to take the end fittings.

To form the main beams, the top and bottom flange members are assembled in a jig, and rivetted to a number of formed sheet metal vertical struts which tie them together. The side web plates are profiled and drilled in a jig and then rivetted to the sides of the beam in another jig. At the same time the necessary fittings produced from heavy bar stock are bolted into the two ends.

Simultaneously, the arch form cross beams are assembled, drilled, rivetted and bolted together in separate jigs from components which have been pre-fabricated elsewhere in the machine shop and sheet metal shop. Finally, the whole is placed in a large assembly jig and completed while holding the four attachments to the longerons accurately by bolting to a base plate on which are locations corresponding to the fuselage attachment points.

At the same time, the locations of the engine feet shock absorbers are drilled, and these themselves consist of machined sockets in solid dural to house a group of 3 cylindrical rubbers for each of the front engine feet.

The front arch form cross beam is built up into a unit with a large magnesium casting which forms the carburettor air entrance and joins to the sheet metal duct itself, which passes through an aperture in the cross beam web and continues along directly under the engine to finally join with the carburettor elbow just ahead of the firewall bulkhead.

The Engine Cowling:

Because of its intimate association with the engine mounting, it is well to consider the engine cowling in continuation of the engine mount structure.

Bolted to the engine mounting are several sheet metal sections, which serve as the formers to maintain the shape of the engine cowling and to which the engine cowling as attached by DZUS fasteners. These members will be called cowling supports. There is a long one on each side running full length from front to rear. Another support, bent into a semi-circular shape, passes under the engine and is bolted to the main arch form cross beam.

There are many sections of cowling, and almost all of them require forming on a stretching press, as three-dimensional curvature is necessary to obtain the correct aerodynamic exterior shape.

There are two main pieces jointed along the centre line which form the top cowling extending from the firewall to the front diaphragm ahead of the engine. The lower edges of these pieces of cowling are reinforced with stainless steel and cut away for the exhaust ports where necessary. There are two lower sections of cowling, one front and one rear, joining on the cross cowling support. At each side and just below the exhaust pipes there is a section of cowling which runs full length from firewall to front diaphragm.

At the front diaphragm immediately ahead of the engine, all cowling terminates flush with the propeller spinner. At this position the radiator header tank is mounted, together with a piece of armour plate, and on the lower side below the propeller shaft there is the casting which forms the carburettor air intake.

The air intake passing along the engine crankcase has a large removable section directly under the rear of the engine, to permit access from underneath to filters, oil pumps and other engine accessories. There is a proposal to incorporate an air filter in a portion of the carburettor duct.

The Engine Installation:

The Rolls-Royce Merlin 61 engine is supplied complete with its accessories mounted in convenient positions which facilitate the installation. The problem of cooling for the inline engine is really much simpler than with the radial air cooled, in that there is no problem of airflow round the cylinders. The heat is transferred by the liquid coolant to the radiator, which is arranged to have a section for cooling of the liquid cooler which cools the intercooler. The problem then becomes one of plumbing.

The design of the header tank has required special development, as there is little space available, and this has necessitated that the shape of the tank be such to utilise what space is available between the rear of the airscrew spinner and the front of the engine. The tank is therefore of horseshoe shape in elevation and fits over the propeller reduction gear housing.

The different metals present in the coolant circuit have been the cause of electrolyte corrosion and this has been greatly increased by the presence of air which circulates with the hot coolant. It is necessary to have an airspace in the header tank to allow for expansion, and it is therefore not possible to exclude air entirely. The header tank is sealed, and a valve is provided to blow off at 35lbs per sq inch, which pressure is automatically built up as the liquid heats up.

In order to extract the air from circulation and reduce its effects to a minimum, two centrifugal air extractors are arranged in the header tank in the outflow from the top of the cylinder blocks.

In order to reduce corrosion to a minimum, it has been necessary to anodise the interior of the header tank and of all the piping in the circuit. This procedure has involved the adoption of special methods in the anodising department to obtain a satisfactory anodic deposit on the inner surfaces.

The result of Lawrence Wackett's investigations into a new fighter for the RAAF – one of the 200 Mustangs built under licence in Australia.

In the engine installation, precautions have been taken to counter the effects of icing of the carburettor. When temperature indications are given that icing conditions exist, the supply of intake air via the front intake duct is entirely cut off by a guillotine-like shutter, which is incorporated in the air intake pipe about 18 inches back from its front opening.

When this shutter is closed, the engine draws its main air supply from the inside of the engine cowling through a spring loaded flap which is sucked open. When this occurs, the engine is deprived of all ram effect and gives a reduced output. The air which is drawn in is warmed by contact with the warm engine. The cut-off valve is provided with a manual control.

In addition to the flap valve, there is a special hot air intake, manually operated, which draws hot air from the region of the rear cylinder exhaust pipe outlet.

For a rapid takeoff in cold weather, there is an arrangement for injecting petrol into the oil supply and so reducing its viscosity so that oil circulation takes place quickly. The petrol so injected is evaporated off via the breather as soon as the oil warms up.

In the oil tank itself there is a baffled compartment provided with flap valves which will trap oil in the compartment during inverted flight. A special jointed end is provided for the oil intake pipe in the bottom of the oil tank, which, operating by acceleration, enables the suction supply to be maintained for short periods. No such arrangement is provided in the petrol tanks, as it has been found that the engine will run for 20 seconds on the fuel in the pile lines. This is sufficient for service manoeuvres.

Cockpit heating is arranged by scooping air from behind the radiator, and there is manual control in the cockpit to control cabin temperature. A similar supply of cool air is taken from in front of the radiator, and this is also controlled manually.

MARKS and MODELS

North American NA-73X

Fresh from the factory, the NA-73X prototype photographed in October 1940 at the time of its first flight.

Type number: NA-73X.
First flight: 26 October 1940 (NX19998).
Service entry: Not applicable.
Powerplant: One 1,150hp (857kW) Allison V-1710-F3R (V-1710-39) vee-12; Curtiss three bladed constant-speed propeller of 10ft 6in (3.20m) diameter. Fuel capacity 180 USgal (681 l) in two wing tanks.
Dimensions: Wing span 37ft 0in (11.28m); length 32ft 3in (9.83m); height 12ft 2in (3.71m); wing area 233sq ft (21.65m^2).
Weights: Max loaded 8,633lb (3,916kg).
Armament: Provision for two 0.50in Browning machine guns in lower nose with 400rpg and four 0.30in Browning machine guns in wings with 500rpg; not fitted in aircraft.
Performance: Max speed 382mph (615km/h) at 13,700ft; initial climb 2,300ft (700m)/min; service ceiling 32,000ft; max range 750 miles (1,207km).
Production: 1.

Notes: North American Aviation's first high speed fighter design, what became the Mustang resulted from a feeling of unease by many within the British Government and military about the situation in Europe following Hitler's rise to power in Germany. Some felt that war was inevitable, with the result that an expansion of the Royal Air Force was put in place.

Part of that expansion was the acquisition of aircraft from the USA in order to supplement British production. Sir Henry Self's British Direct Purchasing Commission (DPC) visited the USA during 1938 and ordered Lockheed Hudsons and North American BC-1 (AT-6A) advanced trainers, an early version of the famed Texan/Harvard family.

As related in more detail in the opening chapter, Britain approached North American Aviation in late 1939 regarding the possibility of building additional Curtiss P-40 fighters (already on order from the parent company), but in January 1940 NAA proposed a new and advanced design of its own utilising the same Allison powerplant as the P-40 but promising improved performance due to the use of laminar flow wings and a low drag ventral radiator housing.

Britain gave the go-ahead for the new aircraft – company designation NA-73X – on 10 April 1940 and a formal contract was issued on 29 May. As per the stringent requirements of the contract, the prototype NA-73X was designed, built and flown in a very short time, just 122 days elapsing between these events.

Carrying the civil registration NX19998, the prototype first flew on 26 October 1940 from Mines Field, Inglewood, California with highly experienced freelance test pilot Vance Breese at the controls. Breese made several more flights in the aircraft during November 1940 before handing it over to project pilot Paul Balfour. His first flight resulted in the aircraft being badly damaged when it flipped onto its back during a wheels down forced landing in a ploughed field short of the runway. Incorrect tank selection had resulted in fuel starvation.

The crash had no diminishing effects on the RAF's enthusiasm for the aircraft as its potential had already been shown. The name 'Mustang' was officially bestowed on it by the British on 9 December 1940. The NA-73X was reflown on 11 January 1941 and retired on 15 July 1941 after completing 45 flights.

P-51 Mustang I/IA

Mustang I AG633 XV-E of No 2 Squadron RAF.

Type numbers: Mustang I – NA-73/83; P-51/Mustang IA – NA-91.

First flights: Mustang I – 23 April 1941 (AG345). XP-51 – 20 May 1941 (41-038). Mustang 1A – 29 May 1942.

Service entry: Mustang I (RAF) – February 1942. Mustang IA (RAF) July 1942. P-51 (USAAF) April 1943.

Powerplant: P-51/Mk.I/IA – one 1,150hp (857kW) Allison V-1710-39 vee-12; Curtiss three bladed constant-speed propeller of 10ft 6in (3.20m) diameter. Fuel capacity 180 USgal (681 l) in two wing tanks.

Dimensions: Wing span 37ft 0in (11.28m); length 32ft 3in (9.83m); height 12ft 2in (3.71m); wing area 233sq ft (21.65m^2).

Weights: P-51 – empty 6,550lb (2971kg); loaded 8,800lb (3,992kg).

Armament: P-51/Mk.IA – four 20mm cannon in wings. Mk.I – two 0.50in machine guns in nose; two 0.50in and four 0.30in machine guns in wings.

Performance: P-51 – max speed 387mph (622km/h) at 15,000ft; max cruise 307mph (494km/h); initial climb 2,600ft (792m)/min; time to 25,000ft 16.0min; service ceiling 31,350ft; range 750 miles (1,207km).

Production: 620 Mk.I, 148 P-51/Mk.1A.

Notes: The RAF placed a contract for 320 North American NA-73s in May 1940, their acceptance subject to the aircraft proving to be satisfactory. As the Mustang I, a further 300 were subsequently ordered (as the NA-83) for a total of 620 and the aircraft was formally ordered into production for the RAF on 20 September 1940, less than a week after the Battle of Britain had reached its peak. Part of the contract was that two aircraft (the 4th and 10th airframes) would be delivered to the US Army Air Corps (US Army Air Force from June 1941) for testing, these later designated XP-51. These aircraft were not part of the RAF contract but additional airframes.

The Mustang I differed only in detail from the prototype: it had armament installed, the carburettor air scoop on the top of the engine cowling was lengthened, the radiator intake area enlarged, a three piece armoured windscreen was fitted in place of the original single piece unit, the ailerons were modified to improve their responsiveness and British radios and other equipment was fitted.

The first Mustang I (AG345) flew on 23 April 1941 and was retained by North American for testing. The first aircraft shipped to Britain was AG346, arriving in late October. No 26 Squadron RAF based at Gatwick was the first to receive the new aircraft from January 1942. Trials quickly revealed the Mustang's speed and handling virtues, although as was the case with all Allison engined Mustangs, performance fell off badly above about 13,000 feet.

This meant the aircraft could not be used as a day fighter in Europe as most combat took place higher than that, but at lower altitudes it was a match for anything including the Focke-Wulf Fw 190. It also proved to be an ideal army co-operation aircraft due to its low altitude performance and heavy armament, and it was in this role – and tactical reconnaissance with an oblique camera fitted in the cockpit behind the pilot – that it was used, equipping 14 UK based RAF squadrons.

Mustang I AG357 (the 13th built) wearing RAF prototype markings and carrying a load of underwing rocket projectiles.

US interest in the Mustang was slow to develop. The first of the two XP-51s flew in May 1941 but it wasn't until after Pearl Harbour that 57 Mustang IAs (see below) were diverted from British orders as the P-51, of which 55 were fitted with cameras as the F-6A, although the P-51 designation remained the official one. The camera installation involved an oblique F.24 behind the pilot's head and a vertical F.24 in the lower rear fuselage.

The USA named its early Mustangs 'Apache', but the British appellation was formally adopted with the arrival of the Merlin engined P-51B in late 1942.

The Mustang IA differed from the original mainly in having four 20mm cannon in the wings in place of the original eight nose and wing machine guns. It was supplied to Britain under the terms of Lend-Lease, this requiring that the aircraft be first purchased by a US agency and then transferred to the destination country and therefore had to be given a US designation. The first Mustang IA flew in May 1942 and deliveries began two months later.

The USAAF's P-51/F-6As (sometimes also known as the P-51-1) entered operational service in April 1943 when the 12th Air Force's 68th Observation Group in North Africa began flying armed reconnaissance missions over the Mediterranean from Tunisia

A P-51 Mustang in USAAF markings clearly showing its armament of four 20mm cannon. In RAF service this model was called the Mustang IA.

A-36 Mustang

The first of 500 A-36A dive bombers for the USAAF (42-83663), first flown on 21 September 1942.

Type number: NA-97.
First flight: 21 September 1942 (42-83663).
Service entry: April 1943.
Powerplant: One 1,325hp (988kW) Allison V-1710-87 vee-12; Curtiss three bladed constant-speed propeller of 10ft 9in (3.28m) diameter. Internal fuel 180 USgal (681 l) in two wing tanks; provision for two 75 USgal (284 l) underwing drop tanks.
Dimensions: Wing span 37ft 0in (11.28m); length 32ft 3in (9.83m); height 12ft 2in (3.71m); wing area 233sq ft (21.65m^2).
Weights: Empty 6,100lb (2,767kg); max loaded 10,700lb (4,853kg).
Armament: Two 0.50 Browning machine guns in lower nose and four in wings; two 500lb (227kg) bombs under wings.
Performance: Max speed (clean) 368mph (592km/h) at 14,000ft, 356mph (573km/h) at 5,000ft or 310mph (499km/h) at 5,000ft with bombs; service ceiling 25,100ft; max range with drop tanks 1,600 miles (2,575km).
Production: 500.

Notes: The first Mustang variant ordered directly by the USAAF was not a fighter but the A-36A dive bomber/ground attack aircraft. It featured a strengthened structure, underwing shackles for a pair of 500lb (227kg) bombs, the more powerful V-1710-87 engine, reversion to machine gun fixed armament (all 50-calibre Brownings), a modified radiator inlet design and slotted air brakes in the upper and lower wing surfaces to keep speed under control in the vertical dive used during dive bombing attacks.

The USAAF ordered 500 A-36As in April 1942 (company designation NA-97), the first of which was flown on 21 September 1942. The A-36A followed the P-51 to North Africa, joining the 12th Air Force, but was just too late to see action there. However, the 27th Fighter Bomber Group's three squadrons (the 522nd, 523rd and 524th) did begin operations over Sicily from June 1943 and were joined the following month by the 86th FBG.

These units were extensively used in the Sicily and Salerno landings before moving to mainland Italy and remained equipped with the A-36A until mid 1944. No official name was applied to the A-36A with the result that the units operating them adopted the appellation 'Invader'. Another A-36A operator was the 311th FBG in the India/Burma theatre, which used its aircraft in the conventional fighter-bomber role. One A-36A was delivered to Britain for evaluation while several RAF squadrons in the Mediterranean and North Africa 'borrowed' some aircraft for tactical reconnaissance and bomber escort duties.

The A-36A proved to be a successful fighter-bomber, its USAAF operating units between them flying over 23,000 sorties for the loss of 177 aircraft to enemy action. A-36A pilots also shot down 84 enemy aircraft.

A-36A EW998/42-83685 delivered to the RAF in March 1943 for evaluation. This shot shows the aircraft's upper and lower wing air brakes in the open position.

P-51A Mustang II

43-6005, the third P-51A Mustang II, flown in early 1943.

Type number: NA-99.

First flights: P-51A – 3 February 1943 (43-6003). Mustang II – 13 February 1943 (FR890).

Service entry: P-51A (USAAF) March 1943.

Powerplant: One 1,200hp (895kW) Allison V-1710-81 vee-12; Curtiss three bladed constant-speed propeller of 10ft 9in (3.28m) diameter. Internal fuel capacity 180 USgal (681 l) in two wing tanks; provision for two 75 USgal (284 l) or 150 USgal (568 l) underwing drop tanks.

Dimensions: Wing span 37ft 0in (11.28m); length 32ft 3in (9.83m); height 12ft 2in (3.71m); wing area 233sq ft (21.65m^2).

Weights: P-51A – empty 6,850lb (3,107kg); normal loaded 8,600lb (3,900kg); max loaded with external fuel 10,600lb (4,808kg).

Armament: Four 0.50in machine guns in wings with 280rpg outboard and 350rpg inboard; provision for two 100lb (45kg), 250lb (113kg), 325lb (147kg) or 500lb (227kg) bombs under wings; field modification developed for six underwing rocket launcher tubes.

Performance: Max speed 390mph (627km/h) at 20,000ft, 380mph (611km/h) at 15,000ft, 340mph (547km/h) at 5,000ft; max climb 2,300ft (700m)/min; time to 20,000ft 9.1min; service ceiling 31,000ft; range (internal fuel) 750 miles (1,207km) or 1,250 miles (2,010km) with 75 USgal drop tanks.

Production: 310.

Notes: The final Allison engined Mustang, the P-51A (NA-99) was powered by the V-1710-81 engine with improved supercharger, fitted with a larger diameter propeller and had a reduced fixed armament of four 0.50 inch machine guns in the wings. The aircraft's usefulness as a fighter-bomber was enhanced by the incorporation of the A-36A's underwing bomb racks, while modified fuel system plumbing allowed the carriage of underwing fuel tanks.

The USAAF ordered 310 P-51As of which 50 were delivered to the RAF, in part to make up for the 57 P-51/Mustang IAs which had earlier been diverted to the USAAF. The first P-51A (43-6003) flew on 3 February 1943 and deliveries began the following month, initially to the USAAF's 311th Fighter Bomber Group in India which replaced two of its three A-36A equipped squadrons with the new model. Thirty-five P-51As were converted to F-6B photo-reconnaissance aircraft with camera installations similar to that of the P-51/F-6A.

P-51A production ended in the northern hemisphere summer of 1943, by which time the Merlin engined P-51B was beginning to roll off NAA's Inglewood assembly line in large numbers. A total of 1,579 early model Mustangs powered by the Allison V-1710 engine was built, of which 763 were delivered to the original customer, the RAF.

A pair of operational USAAF P-51As with 43-6237 in the foreground. This final Allison engined Mustang version entered USAAF service with the 311th FBG in India during March 1943.

Mustang Mk.X

AL975 was the first Mustang X conversion to fly, on 13 October 1942 and fitted with a Rolls-Royce Merlin 65 engine. This aircraft and the following prototype conversions quickly proved that a Merlin powered Mustang would be a formidable fighter.

Type number: Not applicable.
First flight: 13 October 1942 (AL975).
Service entry: Not applicable.
Powerplant: One 1,705hp (1,271kW) Rolls-Royce Merlin 65 vee-12; Rotol four bladed propeller of 10ft 9in (3.28m) or 11ft 4in (3.45m) diameter. Internal fuel capacity 180 USgal (681 l) in two wing tanks.
Dimensions: Wing span 37ft 0in (11.28m); length 32ft 3in (9.83m); height 12ft 3in (3.71m); wing area 233sq ft (21.65m²).
Weights: Loaded 9,100lb (4,128kg).
Armament: Not applicable.
Performance: Max speed 433mph (697km/h) at 22,000ft, 406mph (653km/h) at 10,000ft, 360mph (579km/h) at 2,000ft; max climb 3,560ft (1,085m)/min; time to height 3.9min to 10,000ft 8.3min to 20,000ft, 14.3min to 30,000ft; service ceiling 38,500ft.
Production: 5 conversions from Mustang I.
Notes: With the altitude performance of the Allison powered Mustang found to be wanting, the expedient of fitting the efficient airframe with the Rolls-Royce Merlin 60-series engine with a two-speed/two-stage supercharger at a stroke solved that problem and created one of the best engine/airframe combinations of the war.

Development of the idea was carried out simultaneously in Britain and the USA, the first of five Mustang I conversions performed by Rolls-Royce (AL975) flying on 13 October 1942. Four other conversions followed: AM208 (first flight 13 November 1942), AM203 (13 December 1942), AL963 (21 January 1943) and AM121 (7 February 1943). All were fitted with Merlin 65 engines and Rotol four bladed propellers, initially a standard Spitfire IX unit and subsequently a purpose built propeller.

The concept for the Merlin-Mustang had its origins after a late April 1942 test flight of an Allison powered Mk.I by Ronnie Harker, a Rolls-Royce test pilot. Harker's 30 minute sortie in the Mustang at the Air Fighting Development Unit (AFDU) at Duxford demonstrated to him the aircraft's fine handling qualities and low altitude performance, but also its rapid decline in performance at higher altitudes. As a result, Harker recommended that fitting a Merlin to the Mustang would transform its performance and an initial report was issued in early June 1942.

This covered performance estimates for a Mustang with the two-speed/single-stage Merlin XX (as installed in the Avro Lancaster) and two-speed/two-stage Merlin 61 which was fitted to the new Spitfire IX. Estimates for the Merlin 61 version included a maximum speed of 432mph (695km/h) at optimum altitude, more than 40mph (64km/h) faster than the standard aircraft. The decision was made to convert an initial three (later five) Mustang Is to Merlin 65 power, this engine similar to the Spitfire IX's Merlin 61 but with revised supercharger gear ratios and a different carburettor. The conversions were carried out at Rolls-Royce's Hucknall facility.

The Rolls-Royce Merlin installation in the Mustang incorporated a deep chin intake under the nose which combined both the carburettor intake (moved from the top of the cowling as the Merlin had an updraught rather than downdraught carburettor) and the intercooler radiator, while the ventral radiator initially remained as before.

Early testing revealed some problems with the engine installation and criticism of directional stability resulted in the fitting of a small dorsal fin to some of the prototypes. Various modifications were incorporated as testing continued but the performance estimates were proven to be valid. Some of the Mustang X prototypes were subsequently used to test the high altitude Merlin 70 and later Merlin 113 engines.

The idea of converting some 500 of the RAF's Allison powered Mustangs to Merlins was briefly considered, but the availability of the P-51B from US production meant this was unnecessary. Across the Atlantic, North American had also installed Merlins into Mustangs and it was this configuration that would achieve production in very large numbers.

AM203 was the third Mustang X conversion to fly, taking to the air for the first time in December 1942. Note the undernose intercooler/carburettor intake, this unique to the Mk.X conversions.

P-51B/C Mustang

The prototype XP-51B with Packard V-1650-3 Merlin engine and first flown on 30 November 1942. The US Merlin installation differed from the British one in that it featured the definitive underfuselage intercooler/radiator configuration.

Type number: XP-51B – NA-101. P-51B – NA-102/104. P-51C – NA-103.
First flight: XP-51B – 30 November 1942 (41-37352). P-51B – 5 May 1943 (42-106429). P-51C – 5 August 1943 (42-102979).
Service entry: P-51B – June 1943.
Powerplant: One 1,595hp (1,189kW) Packard V-1650-3 Merlin vee-12 or 1,720hp (1,283kW) V-1650-7; Hamilton Standard four bladed constant-speed propeller of 11ft 2in (3.40m) diameter. Internal fuel capacity 184 USgal (696 l) in two wing tanks plus 85 USgal (322 l) tank in rear fuselage; provision for two 75 USgal (284 l), 110 USgal (416 l) or 150 USgal (568 l) drop tanks under wings.

Dimensions: Wing span 37ft 0in (11.28m); length 32ft 3in (9.83); height 12ft 2in (3.71m); wing area 233sq ft (21.65m^2).
Weights: P-51B – empty 7,450lb (3,379kg); normal loaded 9,800lb (4,445kg); max loaded 11,200lb (5,080kg).
Armament: Four or six 0.50in machine guns in wings with total 1,260 or 1,880 rounds; provision for two 1,000lb (454kg) bombs under wings.
Performance: With V-1650-3 – max speed 440mph (708km/h) at 30,000ft, 424mph (682km/h) at 15,000ft; max climb 3,900ft (1,189m)/min; time to 20,000ft 6.9min, time to 30,000ft 12.5min; service ceiling 41,800ft; range (internal fuel) 850 miles (1,368km); range with 75 USgal

Production P-51B-1NA 43-12201. The P-51B entered USAAF service in June 1943 and was delivered to the RAF as the Mustang III.

The P-51C was identical to the P-51B but manufactured at North American's Dallas plant rather than Inglewood. Deliveries began in August 1943.

drop tanks 1,240 miles (1,995km); range with 110 USgal drop tanks 1,440 miles (2,317km); range with 150 USgal drop tanks 1,600 miles (2,575km).

Production: 1,988 P-51B (including 71 F-6C) and 1,750 P-51C (including 20 F-6C).

Notes: The USA was informed of Rolls-Royce work on the Merlin engined Mustang X through the USAAF Assistant Air Attache in London, Major Thomas Hitchcock. He noted the results being achieved by Rolls-Royce and as production of the Merlin in the USA by Packard had begun in the second half of 1941, a proposal for a similar test programme to be undertaken in the USA was developed.

Major Hitchcock's proposal was taken to USAAF chief, General Henry 'Hap' Arnold, and on 25 July 1942 the USAAF contracted North American to install Packard-Merlins in two P-51 Mustangs, initially under the designation XP-78 and then XP-51B.

The American installation differed from the British one in that although the carburettor intake was relocated to under the nose in a neat and compact intake, the bulkier supercharger intercooler was housed within an enlarged and highly efficient ventral radiator. The result was not only a much nicer looking aircraft but also a considerable reduction in drag compared to the British conversions.

The first XP-51B (41-37352) conversion with a 1,595hp (1,189kW) Packard V-1650-3 Merlin driving a four bladed Hamilton Standard propeller flew on 30 November 1942. Although the XP-51B's maiden flight (conducted by Bob Chilton) was cut short by clogged radiator cooling vents causing engine overheating, early tests quickly revealed the potential of the new airframe/engine combination with a maximum speed of about 450mph (724km/h) at optimum altitude quickly achieved.

As a result, the P-51B was ordered into production for the USAAF as the first Mustang variant to be built in quantity for the service. Deliveries began in June 1943. The P-51B was built at North American's Inglewood (California) factory, joined from August 1943 by the similar P-51C from the company's Dallas, Texas, facility.

Seventy-one camera equipped tactical reconnaissance conversions of the P-51B were performed (plus 20 based on the P-51C) as the F-6C, while the RAF received 274 P-51Bs and 636 P-51Cs under Lend-Lease as the Mustang III, many of them fitted with the bulged 'Malcolm Hood' canopy for improved pilot visibility.

Early aircraft had a four machine gun fixed armament which was subsequently increased to six and the more powerful V-1650-7 engine appeared later in the production run. All but the very first batch of P-51Bs were fitted with an additional fuselage fuel tank of 85 USgal (322 litres) capacity, this usually limited to carrying only 65 USgal (246 l) as a full tank caused stability problems by moving the centre of gravity too far aft. This in combination with underwing drop tanks gave the P-51B prodigious range for a single engined fighter.

The P-51B/C served mainly with the USAAF's UK based 8th Air Force as a long range escort fighter. The first operation was to Kiel in December 1943 and in March 1944 the first mission to Berlin and back was performed, escorting B-17s and B-24s. They also served in the Mediterranean and China-Burma-India theatres as well as equipping RAF and Commonwealth squadrons in Britain, Europe and Italy. The Mustang went on to play an ever increasing role in the bomber offensive over Europe and by 1945 equipped all but one of the 8th AF's fighter escort groups.

P-51D/K Mustang

The P-51D with bubble canopy represented another step forward in the Mustang's development. The two aircraft in the foreground are both from the 'Dash-5' production batch, one without the dorsal fin fillet and one with. These aircraft are from the Eighth Air Force's 361st Fighter Group based in England.

Type numbers: P-51D – NA-106/109/111/122/124. P-51K – NA-111.

First flight: XP-51D – 17 November 1943 (43-12101).

Service entry: March 1944.

Powerplant: One 1,720hp (1,283kW) Packard V-1650-7 Merlin vee-12; Hamilton Standard four bladed constant-speed propeller of 11ft 2in (3.40m) diameter on P-51D, Aeroproducts four bladed propeller of 11ft 0in (3.35m) diameter on P-51K. Internal fuel capacity 184 USgal (696 l) in two wing tanks plus 85 USgal (322 l) tank in rear fuselage; provision for two 75 USgal (284 l), 110 USgal (416 l) or 150 USgal (568 l) drop tanks under wings.

Dimensions: Wing span 37ft 0in (11.28m); length 32ft 3in (9.83); height 12ft 2in (3.71m); wing area 235sq ft (21.8m^2).

Weights: P-51D – empty 7,635lb (3,463kg); clean combat weight 10,100lb (4,581kg); max loaded 12,100lb (5,488kg).

Armament: Six 0.50in machine guns in wings with 400rpg (inboard) and 270rpg (middle and outboard); up to 2,000lb (907kg) bombs or six 5in (12.7cm) rocket projectiles under wings.

Performance: Max speed 437mph (703km/h) at 25,000ft, 413mph (665km/h) at 15,000ft, 395mph (636km/h) at 5,000ft; max climb 3,475ft (1,059m)/min; time to 20,000ft 7.3min; time to 30,000ft 12.6min; service ceiling 41,900ft; range (internal fuel) 950 miles (1,529km) at 25,000ft; max range with drop tanks 1,650 miles (2,655km).

Production: 8,102 P-51D (including 146 F-6D and 10 TP-51D) and 1,337 P-51K (including 163 F-6K).

Notes: Accounting for the bulk of Mustang production, the P-51D and closely related K represent the 'quintessential' Mustang and dominated USAAF fighter operations over Europe in the last year of the war, flying tactical missions as well as the all important escort of bombers to targets deep in Germany. The P-51D also operated extensively in the Pacific, escorting B-29s to Japan from Iwo Jima starting in February 1945 and visiting Tokyo for the first time two months later.

The P-51D differed externally from the P-51B/C by virtue of its cut down rear fuselage decking and sliding 'teardrop' canopy. This resulted from the analysis of combat reports by pilots flying the earlier models and although they were almost unanimous in their praise for the aircraft's performance and flying qualities, the need for improved visibility, especially to the rear, was a common complaint.

The British developed and bulged 'Malcolm Hood' was fitted to some P-51B/Cs but helped only a little, so the decision was made to incorporate a teardrop canopy with 360 degrees vision. Two P-51Bs (43-12101 and 43-12102) were allocated for conversion to prototypes for the new variant. Referred to at the time as the XP-51D, the first of them flew on 17 November 1943.

Most production P-51Ds were powered by the Packard Merlin V-1650-7 engine as fitted to later P-51B/Cs (some early aircraft had the less powerful V-1650-3) and the D also standardised on a six gun fixed armament with the weapons mounted upright rather than on their sides to alleviate an ammunition belt feed jamming problem. Internal and external fuel capacity options were as per the P-51B/C, and on all but the earliest examples, a fin fillet was fitted to compensate for the reduced fuselage side area caused by the cut down rear fuselage decking.

Another small external difference was the incorporation of wing roots which were extended slightly forwards to produce a more definite 'kink' in the leading edge, this also resulting in a small wing area increase.

P-51D production was initiated at Inglewood (as the P-51D-NA) in January 1944 followed by the Dallas plant (P-51D-NT) the following July. Successive production blocks introduced mainly minor equipment, instrumentation and radio modifications. Operational equipment improvements included introduction of the K-14 gyroscopic gunsight (a US licence built version of the British

A late war photograph of a P-51D with canopy open and direction finding (DF) loop installed immediately behind the radio mast. The P-51D entered USAAF service in March 1944 and became the most numerous of all Mustang variants with over 8,100 built.

Ferranti unit) which performed the necessary deflection shooting calculations for the pilot and therefore substantially raised the standard of gunnery accuracy by the average pilot.

Variants included 146 P-51D-NTs completed as photo-reconnaissance F-6Ds and ten TP-51D tandem two seater conversion trainers completed in 1944. These featured dual controls with the second (rear) seat installed where there had previously been radio equipment and the fuselage fuel tank.

The closely related P-51K was built only at Dallas and differed from the D in having an Aeroproducts propeller instead of the usual Hamilton Standard unit. This came about due to a feared shortage of Hamilton Standard propellers as P-51D production accelerated to very high levels.

The Aeroproducts propeller differed from the Hamilton Standard unit in several ways including being of slightly smaller diameter and featuring hollow steel blades. This saved about 50lb (23kg) of weight but production delays were incurred when vibrations resulting from blade imbalance caused some minor incidents. As a result, the original contract for 1,500 P-51Ks was the only one placed as a shortage from Hamilton Standard did not eventuate. Of the P-51K production tally, 163 were converted to camera equipped F-6Ks.

The RAF received 271 P-51Ds and 594 P-51Ks under Lend-Lease as the Mustang IV. The P-51D began to supplement the Bs and Cs in Europe from June 1944 followed by the P-51K later in the year. By the end of 1944, 14 of the USAAF Eighth Air Force's Fighter Groups were equipped with either P-51Ds or Ks.

The United States Air Force became an independent service in September 1947 and in June 1948 all USAF fighter designation prefixes changed from 'P' for 'Pursuit' to 'F' for 'Fighter'. Therefore the P-51D became the F-51D and the photo-reconnaissance F-6 Mustangs were redesignated as RF-51s.

Many Mustangs continued to serve with USAAF/USAF units in the post war years including some P-51Bs until 1949 as the F-51B. The F-51K remained in limited service until 1951 while the F-51D flew for a few years after that with Air National Guard and Air Reserve units. The F-51D was the first USAF fighter to serve in the Korean War, operated by three Fighter-Bomber Groups from the second half of 1950.

P-51K-10NT Mustang 44-11998. The K was similar to the P-51D apart from its different propeller. All 1,500 were built at Dallas. Both models were dubbed Mustang IV by the RAF.

P-51F/G/J Mustang

Type number: NA-105.
First flights: XP-51F – 14 February 1944 (43-43332). XP-51G – 10 August 1944 (43-43335). XP-51J – 23 April 1945 (44-76027).
Service entry: Not applicable.
Powerplant: XP-51F – one 1,720hp (1,282kW) Packard V-1650-7 Merlin vee-12; three bladed Aeroproducts propeller. XP-51G – one 1,910hp (1,424kW) Rolls-Royce Merlin 145; five bladed Rotol or four bladed Aeroproducts propeller. XP-51J – one 1,720hp (1,282kW) Allison V-1710-119; three bladed Aeroproducts propeller. Fuel capacity 205 USgal (776 l) in two wing tanks.
Dimensions: XP-51F/G – wing span 37ft 0in (11.28m); length 32ft 3in (9.83); height 12ft 2in (3.71m); wing area 233sq ft (21.65m²). XP-51J – length 32ft 11in (10.03m).
Weights: XP-51F – empty 5,635lb (2,556kg); loaded 9,060lb (4,110kg). XP-51G – loaded 8,885lb (4,030kg). XP-51J – loaded 9,141lb (4,146kg).
Armament: Four 0.50in machine guns in wings.
Performance: XP-51F – max speed 466mph (650km/h) at 29,000ft; range (clean) 650 miles (1,046km). XP-51G – max speed 472mph (760km/h) at 20,750ft.
Production: 3 XP-51F, 2 XP-51G, 2 XP-51J.

Notes: Although the Mustang's speed performance was as good as any other fighter and its range unsurpassed, North American's engineers were looking at ways to improve its rate of climb and agility to a level similar to that of the lighter Spitfire while at the same time further increasing speed. Development therefore began of lightweight versions of the aircraft incorporating considerable internal redesign and equipment changes.

The first was the XP-51F (first flight February 1944) which featured a lightened and simplified structure, the use of plastics in some secondary structures, a simplified hydraulic system, a new and thinner laminar flow wing section, redesigned fuselage, revised ventral intake, main undercarriage legs with much smaller diameter wheels and brakes (which in turn allowed removal of wing root chord extensions), deletion of two guns, removal of the dorsal fin fillet and fuselage fuel tank (slightly larger wing tanks were installed), a recontoured canopy and a lightweight three bladed Aerostructures propeller. The P-51D's V-1650-7 Packard Merlin was retained.

The XP-51F's tare weight was reduced by a substantial 2,000lb (907kg) compared to the P-51D and maximum speed increased by nearly 30mph (48km/h). Despite this, the lightweight Mustang programme in its uncompromised forms was terminated partly due to ongoing directional stability problems but also because it was discovered that the aircraft were more difficult to maintain and unsuitable for operations from rough airfields.

Three XP-51Fs were built and a rethink of the concept led to the production P-51H incorporating compromises between reduced weight, performance and operational practicalities.

The XP-51G (first flight August 1944) was similar to the F but powered by a highly boosted Rolls-Royce Merlin 145 (RM.14SM) driving either a Rotol five bladed propeller or an Aeroproducts four blader. Two Gs were built and like the XP-51F, one example was sent to Britain for testing by the Aircraft and Armament Experimental Establishment (A&AEE) at Boscombe Down.

The third and final experimental lightweight Mustang was the XP-51J (first flight April 1945), basically similar to the F and G but featuring a slightly longer fuselage, reinstated dorsal fin fillet (to help the directional stability problem) and removal of the nose carburettor intake to the radiator ducting in a further attempt to reduce drag.

Two XP-51Js were built, powered by a 1,720hp (1,282kW) Allison V-1710-119 with two-stage supercharger and water injection, this a new generation version of the engine which had originally powered the Mustang. Performance estimates included a maximum speed of 491mph (790km/h) but the troublesome engine could not be run at full power so this was never achieved.

The Allison engine was selected for the XP-51J as a hedge against the British cancelling the Packard Merlin licence agreement when the war ended.

The first lightweight Mustang to fly was XP-51F 43-43332 in February 1944 with a simplified structure, the use of plastics in some secondary areas, three bladed propeller, reduced armament and fuel capacity and other lightening features.

The XP-51G first flew in August 1944 and was powered by a highly boosted Rolls-Royce Merlin 145 engine turning out over 1,900hp (1,416kW). Like the other experimental lightweight models and despite its maximum speed of 472mph (760km/h), the G was found to be unsuitable for operations and did not achieve production.

P-51H Mustang

Although based on the experimental XP-51F, the P-51H incorporated some compromises to the lightweight ideal to make it suitable for operational service. Its empty weight was nevertheless some 600lb (272kg) less than the P-51D and its highly boosted V-1650-9 Merlin provided prodigious performance capabilities. 44-64164 was the fifth P-51H. (NAA)

Type number: NA-126.
First flight: 3 February 1945 (44-64160).
Service entry: Mid 1945.
Powerplant: One 2,218hp (1,654kW) emergency rating with water injection Packard V-1650-9 Merlin vee-12; Aeroproducts four bladed constant-speed propeller. Internal fuel capacity 210 USgal (795 l) in two wing tanks plus 50 USgal (189 l) fuselage tank; two 75 USgal (284 l) underwing drop tanks.
Dimensions: Wing span 37ft 0in (11.28m); length 33ft 4in (10.16m); height 13ft 8in (4.16m); wing area 235sq ft (21.8m^2).
Weights: Empty 7,040lb (3,193kg); loaded (clean) 9,500lb (4,309kg); max loaded 11,500lb (5,216kg).
Armament: Six 0.50in machine guns in wings; max 2,000lb (907kg) bomb load or ten 5in (12.7cm) rocket projectiles under wings.
Performance: Max speed 487mph (784km/h) at 25,000ft, 463mph (745km/h) at 15,000ft; max climb 5,350ft (1,630m)/min; time to 30,000ft 12.5min; service ceiling 41,600ft; range (clean) 850 miles (1,368km); range with drop tanks 1,160 miles (1,867km).
Production: 555.
Notes: The final P-51 Mustang variant to achieve production, the P-51H was based on the experimental XP-51F, incorporating some of the weight saving features of that and the other 'lightweight' models but with some compromises to make the aircraft suitable for production and service. Nevertheless, the P-51H had an empty weight some 600lb (272kg) below that of the P-51D.

Compared to the XP-51F, the P-51H featured a lengthened and slightly deeper fuselage with a raised cockpit and smaller canopy, fixed armament reverted to six machine guns (with the ammunition belts loaded via pre packed removable boxes), a taller fin and rudder was fitted from the 21st aircraft, the ventral radiator was deeper and a fuselage fuel tank was installed.

One of the P-51H's major features was its V-1650-9 engine, highly boosted, capable of running on 150 octane fuel and fitted with water/methanol injection to produce a maximum war emergency rating of 2,218hp (1,654kW). An automatic constant-speed Aeroproducts four bladed propeller was installed.

The first P-51H flew on 3 February 1945. Orders for 2,000 were placed for production at Inglewood but only 555 were built and the remainder cancelled after VJ Day. The last was handed over in November 1945. The P-51H never saw combat in World War II because the conflict ended as aircraft were being delivered to their squadrons, mainly in the Pacific. One P-51H was delivered to the RAF for evaluation.

The P-51M was intended to be the Dallas built version of the H, differing only in having a V-1650-9A engine without water injection. Orders were placed for 1,628 aircraft but only one had been flown before the war ended and the contracts were cancelled.

The P-51L was also intended to be built at Dallas, this similar to the H but featuring a V-1650-11 engine with direct fuel injection. All 1,700 orders were cancelled on VJ Day before the first aircraft had been flown.

Arguably the fastest piston engined fighter to enter regular service, the P-51H flew with the US Air Force, Air Reserve and Air National Guard in the early post war years until replaced by jets.

P-51H production amounted to 555 aircraft as the last of the US built Mustang line (discounting the P-82 Twin Mustang). Service entry was in mid 1945 and the final example was handed over in November 1945.

CAC Mustang

Type numbers: CA-17, CA-18.
First flights: CA-17 – 30 April 1945 (A68-1).
Service entry: June 1945.
Powerplant: Mks.20/21/22 – one 1,720hp (1,283kW) Packard Merlin V-1650-7 vee-12 piston engine. Mk.23 – one 1,655hp (1,234kW) Rolls-Royce Merlin 70; four bladed Hamilton Standard constant-speed propeller of 11ft 2in (3.40m) diameter. Max internal fuel capacity 269 USgal (1,018 l); provision for two 75 or 110 USgal (284 or 416 l) underwing drop tanks.
Dimensions: Wing span 37ft 0in (11.28m); length 32ft 3in (9.83m); height 12ft 2in (3.71m); wing area 235sq ft (21.8m^2).
Weights: Mk.21 – operational empty 7,863lb (3,567kg); normal loaded 9,500lb (4,309kg); max overload 10,500lb (4,763kg).
Armament: Six 0.50in machine guns in wings with 400rpg (inboard) and 270rpg (others); two 500lb (227kg) bombs or six 5in rockets under wings.
Performance: Max speed 437mph (703km/h) at 25,000ft, 395mph (636km/h) at 5,000ft; max climb 3,475ft (636m)/min; time to 20,000ft 7.3min; service ceiling 41,900ft; range (internal fuel) 950 miles (1,529km); range with drop tanks 1,650 miles (2,655km).
Production: 80 Mk.20, 26 Mk.21, 28 Mk.22 and 66 Mk.23, total 200.
Notes: The Royal Australian Air Force was a major user of the North American P-51D/K Mustang, operating a total of 499 from 1945, including 200 built under licence in Australia by the Commonwealth Aircraft Corporation (CAC). These were the only Mustangs manufactured outside the United States.

The decision to manufacture the Mustang in Australia was made in April 1944 after an extensive evaluation of available types including the Supermarine Spitfire, which had been in RAAF service 'at home' since 1942 and with British based squadrons since 1941. Relative ease of manufacture and range were major factors in the decision in favour of the Mustang.

Initial orders covered 690 aircraft but with the end of the war the need for them reduced (especially as nearly 300 North American built aircraft had been delivered), this resulting in just 200 being built at a leisurely pace with production stretched out to help keep CAC's workforce employed in the lean post war years.

Local production was preceded by the arrival of a P-51D 'pattern' aircraft in 1944, although this was used for extensive ground testing and didn't fly in Australia until April 1945, just before the first CAC CA-17 Mustang Mk.20 took to the air. All CAC Mustangs were based on the P-51D with minor modifications, the 200 comprising 80 Mk.20s (built up from sets of imported components); 26 CA-18 Mk.21s (the first wholly Australian built version); 28 CA-18 Mk.22 tactical reconnaissance versions with two F.24 cameras in the rear fuselage (one vertical and one oblique); and 66 CA-18 Mk.23s with a Rolls-Royce rather than Packard Merlin.

The CA-18 Mustang models had some modifications incorporated compared to the original CA-17s, these including larger diameter brake discs (10in/254mm instead of 7in/178mm), a moulded laminated wooden seat in place of the previous magnesium alloy sheet and tube unit, a Mk.IID rather than Mk.IIL gyroscopic gunsight and a different gun camera in the port wing leading edge.

The first batch of 80 Mk.20s had been handed over to the RAAF by July 1946 but it would be another year before deliveries of the next group started. The last CAC Mustang (a Mk.22) was delivered in August 1951. A handful of CAC Mustangs flew with the P-51Ds of No 77 Squadron in the Korean War in 1950-51 but most equipped Australian based squadrons and then the RAAF's five Citizen Air Force squadrons. The last of these was disbanded in June 1960.

Australia was the sole source of Mustang production outside the USA with 200 built by the Commonwealth Aircraft Corporation for the RAAF between 1945 and 1951. A68-84 was a camera equipped CA-18 Mustang Mk.22 delivered in July 1947.

CAC CA-17 Mustang Mk.20 A68-67, delivered in March 1946. The first 80 CAC Mustangs were built up from sets of imported P-51D components.

F-82 Twin Mustang

P-82B Twin Mustang 44-65169 from the initial production batch delivered from August 1945. The P-82B was the only Merlin powered Twin Mustang variant, most aircraft powered by Allison V-1710s. This photograph shows 44-65169 after conversion to a P-82C night fighter prototype with radar housed in a large nacelle under the centre section. The forward end of it can just be seen behind the lower edge of the port engine cowling.

Type numbers: NA-120/123/144/149/150.
First flight: XP-82 – 15 April 1945 (44-83886).
Service entry: August 1945.
Powerplants: F-82E/F/G – two 1,600hp (1,193kW) dry/1,930hp (1,439kW) with water/methanol injection Allison V-1710-143/145 vee-12s; Aeroproducts four bladed counter-rotating propellers of 11ft 0in (3.35m) diameter. Internal fuel capacity 576 USgal (2,180 l) in four wing tanks; provision for two 310 USgal (1,173 l) underwing drop tanks.
Dimensions: F-82G – wing span 51ft 7in (15.72m); length 42ft 2½in (12.86m); height 13ft 10in (4.22m); wing area 417sq ft (38.8m²). F-82E – length 39ft 1½in (11.92m).
Weights: F-82E – empty 14,914lb (6,765kg); normal loaded 24,864lb (11,278kg). F-82G – empty 15,997lb (7,256kg); loaded (clean) 21,819lb (9,897kg); max loaded 25,891lb (11,744kg).
Armament: Six 0.50in machine guns in centre wing section with 400rpg; up to 4,000lb (1,814kg) bombs or rockets under wings.
Performance: F-82G – max speed 456mph (734km/h) at 21,000ft; cruising speed 288mph (463km/h); initial climb 3,770ft (1,149m)/min at combat weight; service ceiling 38,900ft; combat radius 1,015 miles (1,633km) at 25,000ft with drop tanks; max range 2,240 miles (3,605km).
Production: 2 XP-82, 1 XP-82A, 20 P-82B, 100 P-82E, 91 P-82F, 45 P-82G and 14 P-82H, total 273.
Notes: Despite the P-51 Mustang's exceptional range for a single engined fighter, a requirement existed in 1944 for an escort fighter with even greater range so that Allied bombers could be accompanied to the farthest reaches of the Third Reich, Czechoslovakia, Poland and Northern Italy. Greater range was also required in the Pacific, this leading to development of the P-82 (F-82 from June 1948) Twin Mustang. Too late to see service in World War II, the Twin Mustang was subsequently developed into a night fighter and saw combat in Korea.

On the surface, the design allowed a substantial increase in fuel capacity by simply joining two lengthened Mustang fuselages with a new centre wing and tailplane. The engineering involved was a little more complicated than that, but the basic concept remained. The command pilot was housed in the port fuselage section and a second pilot in the starboard. Six 0.50in machine guns were mounted in the new centre section and ordnance could be carried under the wings. Counter-rotating propellers were fitted.

Two XP-82 prototypes with Packard Merlin engines and one XP-82A with Allison V-1710s were ordered, the first XP-82 flying on 15 April 1945 and the others later in the year. The USAAF ordered 500 Merlin powered P-82Bs but the contract was cancelled in early 1946 after only 20 had been built. Two were converted to P-82C and D night fighter prototypes with SCR720 radar in a large nacelle under the centre section and the starboard cockpit was modified to house a radar operator.

Subsequent production models were all Allison powered: the F-82E long range escort fighter which served with Strategic Air Command 1948-50 and the radar equipped F-82F and G night fighters operated by Air Defence Command between 1947 and 1953. The designation F-82H was applied to nine Fs and five Gs 'winterised' on the production line for operations in Alaska.

Three F-82G squadrons operated in Korea, two aircraft of the 68th FS credited with the destruction of a pair of Yak-9s on 27 June 1950, the first USAF 'kills' of the Korean War.

Rear view of a Twin Mustang showing the two fuselages and the new tailplane joining them. The propellers were counter-rotating to negate the effects of torque.

Cavalier Mustang

Trans-Florida Aviation (later Cavalier Aircraft Corporation) had some success selling its refurbished Mustangs to both the military and civil markets. This pair were from a batch of nine supplied to Bolivia in 1967-68. Here they carry USAF markings before delivery. 67-14866 (top) was a TF-51D with lengthened canopy.

Powerplant: Executive Mustang – one 1,720hp (1,282kW) Packard V-1650-7 Merlin vee-12; Hamilton Standard four bladed propeller of 11ft 2in (3.40m) diameter. Fuel capacities: 750 – 184 USgal (696 l) in two wing tanks; 1200 – 280 USgal (1,060 l) in four wing tanks; 1500 – 310 USgal (1,173 l) in four wing tanks; 2000 – 376 USgal (1,423 l) in wing and tip tanks; 2500 – 484 USgal (1,832 l) in wing and tip tanks.
Mustang II – one 1,810hp (1,350kW) Rolls-Royce Merlin 620; fuel capacity 404 USgal (1,529 l) in wing and tip tanks.
Dimensions: Wing span 37ft 0in (11.28m); length 32ft 3in (9.83m); height 12ft 2in (3.71m) or 13ft 8in (4.16m); wing area 235sq ft (21.8m^2).
Weights: 2000 – empty 7,500lb (3,402kg); max loaded 10,500lb (4,763kg).
Armament: Mustang II – six 0.50in machine guns in wings with total 2,000 rounds; six underwing hardpoints for max 4,000lb (1,814kg) ordnance including bombs and rocket pods.
Performance: 2000 – max speed 457mph (735km/h) at 30,000ft; max cruise 424mph (682km/h) at 30,000ft; normal cruise 370mph (595km/h) at 25,000ft, economical cruise 316mph (508km/h) at 20,000ft or 260mph (418km/h) at 10,000ft; initial climb 2,550ft (777m)/min; service ceiling 42,000ft; max range 2,000 miles (3,219km).
Notes: In 1944, North American Aviation converted 10 P-51Ds to tandem two seat trainers (as TP-51Ds) with dual controls by placing the second seat where the fuselage fuel tank and radio gear had previously been. In 1951 the concept was taken a step further when the Tempco Aviation Corporation modified a further 15 aircraft as TF-51Ds for Air National Guard units, this conversion involving more comprehensive controls and instrumentation for the rear seat, which was raised slightly and necessitated the installation of a reprofiled canopy.

Many air forces operated Mustangs in the post war era, a fact which didn't escape the notice of David Lindsay, who formed Trans-Florida Aviation in 1957 to become a primary source of spares for all Mustang users. Trans-Florida purchased large quantities of P-51D spares and Packard Merlin engines from the USAF. Lindsay also noted the increased use of Mustangs in sport and private flying, seeing another potentially lucrative source of business.

Trans-Florida also purchased a TF-51D for demonstrations and conversion training of customers for the range of two seat rebuilt Mustangs it was offering for sale to private buyers. Called 'Cavalier' these Mustangs were in effect remanufactured by Trans-Florida and 'zero timed' after being completely stripped with military equipment removed, worn or time expired parts replaced and electrical and hydraulic systems renewed. Leather seats were installed, as were heating and passenger oxygen systems plus new instrument panels incorporating appropriate avionics. The V-1650-7 engines and Hamilton Standard propellers were also overhauled.

Several models were offered under the generic name Executive Mustang, the designations reflecting the aircraft's maximum design range according to fuel capacity. The Cavalier 750 had only the standard P-51D wing tanks while the 1200 and 1500 had additional tanks in the wings. The standard model was the Cavalier 2000 with wing tanks plus two 96 USgal (363 l) wingtip tanks, while the Cavalier 2500 had these plus larger wing tanks.

FAA Type Approval for the Executive Mustang was granted in February 1959 and the company was turning out a handful annually by 1961. By then, the list price of a Cavalier 2000 was $US32,500 without radio. One customer was North American Aviation itself, which purchased a Cavalier Mustang for legendary fighter pilot and World War II ace Bob Hoover to fly at air shows.

The civil market for the Cavalier was necessarily

The sole piston engined Cavalier Mustang II conversion, developed for the counter-insurgency (COIN) role with six underwing hardpoints to carry up to 4,000lb (1,814kg) of ordnance. No buyers were found but the concept was further developed into the turboprop powered Turbo Mustang III and Enforcer.

limited, the company soon turning its attention to the military potential of the aircraft, refitted with armament (including underwing racks for ordnance) and reverting to the normal P-51D fuel tank configuration including the use of drop tanks. A taller P-51H type fin was usually fitted to military Cavaliers plus at least two of the civil models, while all had provision for a second seat.

The company's efforts were rewarded in February 1967 when the USAF ordered a batch of F-51Ds for supply through the Military Assistance Program (MAP) to South American countries already operating Mustangs. Trans-Florida Aviation changed its name to Cavalier Aircraft Corporation later in 1967 and ultimately rebuilt 17 F-51Ds for supply through MAP, these given new USAF serials.

Nine went to Bolivia (including a single TF-51D with full dual controls) and six to El Salvador. Two more were ordered by the USAF in 1968 for use as chase aircraft on the Lockheed AH-56A Cheyenne attack helicopter programme. These lacked armament and had the wingtip tanks of the civil Cavalier 2000 and 2500 models.

The Vietnam War revealed the need for an inexpensive ground attack and counter insurgency (COIN) aircraft, Cavalier further developing the Mustang for this role. A prototype of what was called the Mustang II first flew in December 1967. A single seater, the new variant featured the tall fin, tip tanks, a substantially strengthened wing to carry up to 4,000lb (1,814kg) of ordnance on six underwing hardpoints and a more powerful Rolls-Royce Merlin 620 taken from a Canadair North Star transport.

Despite representations to the USAF and others, no buyer was found for the Mustang II and Cavalier instead turned its attention to improved turboprop powered versions, resulting in development of the Turbo Mustang III and Enforcer as described in the next entry.

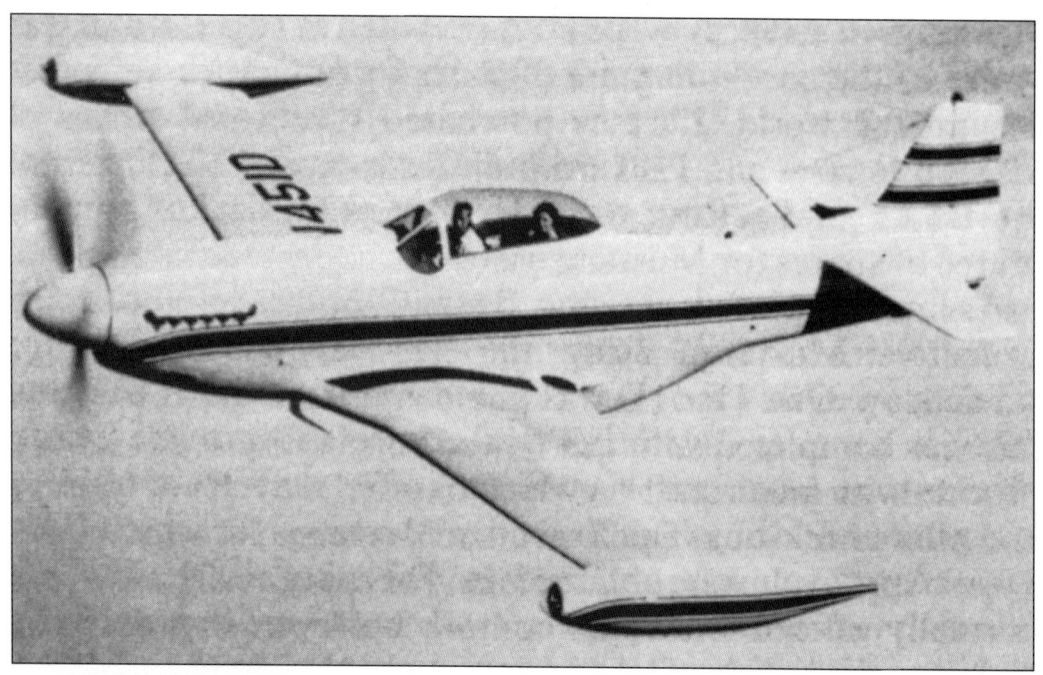

A civil Cavalier complete with TF-51D style extended canopy, dual controls and wingtip fuel tanks.

Cavalier Turbo Mustang III and Piper Enforcer

The single seater Cavalier Enforcer prototype photographed after the programme had been taken over by Piper in late 1971. Power was provided by a Lycoming T55 turboprop. By now, the aircraft had little in common with its Mustang origins. No sales were made.

First flights: Turbo Mustang III – 1968 (N6167U). Enforcer – 29 April 1971 (N202PE).

Powerplant: Turbo Mustang III – one 1,740ehp (1,297kW) Rolls-Royce Dart 510 turboprop; four bladed Rotol propeller of 10ft 0in (3.05m) diameter. Enforcer – One 2,445shp (1,823kW) Lycoming T55-L-9 turboprop; Aeroproducts four bladed propeller of 11ft 6in (3.50m) diameter. Internal fuel 184 USgal (696 l) in two wing tanks plus 240 USgal (908 l) in two wingtip tanks; provision for four 110 USgal (416 l) and two 70 USgal (265 l) underwing drop tanks; max total fuel 1,004 USgal (3,800 l)

Dimensions: Enforcer – wing span over tip tanks 41ft 4in (12.60m); length 34ft 2in (10.41m); height 13ft 1in (3.98m); wing area 257sq ft (23.9m²).

Weights: Turbo III – empty 6,816lb (3,092kg); max loaded 13,700lb (6,214kg). Enforcer – empty equipped 7,885lb (3,577kg); max loaded 14,000lb (6,350kg).

Armament: Turbo III – six 0.50in machine guns in wings with total 2,000 rounds; six underwing hardpoints for max 4,000lb (1,814kg) ordnance including bombs and rocket pods. Enforcer – 10 underwing pylons for max 5,680lb (2,576kg) ordnance including bombs, rocket pods and 30mm gun pods.

Performance: Turbo III – typical transit speed 345-380mph (555-611km/h); loiter speed 150mph (240km/h); combat radius with max warload and 1hr 25min loiter over target 172 miles (278km); loiter time over target 57 miles (92km) from base with 2,000lb (907kg) warload 5hr 30min. Enforcer – max speed 362mph (583km/h); cruising speed 253mph (407km/h) at 15,000ft; initial climb 2,500ft (762m)/min; service ceiling 25,000ft; combat radius with two gun pods 460 miles (740km).

Production: 1 Turbo Mustang III conversion, 4 Enforcers.

Notes: Although Cavalier had found no market for its dedicated ground attack and counter-insurgency (COIN) Mustang II development of the F-51D (see previous entry), it nevertheless pushed ahead with a turboprop version powered by a Rolls-Royce Dart, taken – complete with cowling and propeller – from a United Air Lines Vickers Viscount airliner. Flown in 1968 as the Turbo Mustang III (with the civil registration N6167U), the prototype was otherwise similar to the Mustang II.

Cavalier offered the aircraft to meet the USAF's AX attack aircraft requirement (eventually filled by the Fairchild A-10) but despite some moderate interest being shown, none was ordered. Of interest is the fact that another Dart-Mustang conversion was performed in Australia during 1971-72, again using a powerplant from a Viscount. This privately performed conversion of an ex RAAF CAC built aircraft was very similar to the Cavalier effort, but while completed, it was never flown in the new configuration. It was subsequently restored to standard.

With the USAF looking for an aircraft to meet its Pave Coin project for a low cost aircraft for supply to third world nations, Cavalier began work on a much more ambitious turboprop Mustang. Called, the Enforcer, it was powered by a Lycoming T55 turboprop driving a cut down four bladed propeller from a Douglas Skyraider. The Enforcer

Sovereign 2 – Mustang 53

Piper revived the Enforcer programme in the early 1980s and built two more aircraft as the PA-48 under a USAF evaluation contract. Once again, no sales were forthcoming. N481PE was the first of the further redesigned duo to fly, in March 1983.

design was originally intended to retain as many Mustang components as possible but in reality the aircraft was very much a new design. It was able to carry a substantial warload on 10 underwing pylons, had large wingtip fuel tanks and an ejection system for the pilot.

Two prototype conversions were built. The first – a two seater (registered N202PE) – flew in April 1971 followed quickly by a single seater, N201PE. The first aircraft was lost in July 1971 when it crashed after the elevator separated from the tailplane as a result of flutter. The pilot ejected safely.

Realising it had insufficient capital to properly develop the Enforcer, Cavalier sold the rights to the aircraft to Piper later in 1971. Evaluation by the USAF confirmed the Enforcer's performance estimates but the service was only moderately enthusiastic about the concept. Piper continued to promote the aircraft over the next few years, and despite support from some in the US Congress, no orders were placed.

The Enforcer got another chance in the early 1980s following continued pressure from Congress. In September 1981 it was announced that Piper had been awarded a $US11.8m contract to build two more prototypes for a two year evaluation. Piper allocated the company model number PA-48 to these aircraft which had many changes over the original pair of Enforcers. These included a longer fuselage, larger tailplane, modified ailerons, the introduction of hydraulically boosted controls and a myriad of engineering and structural modifications. As a result, commonality with the P-51 was no more than about 10 per cent.

The two PA-48 Enforcer prototypes (both single seaters) flew on 9 April and 8 July 1983 as N481PE and N482PE, respectively. They were evaluated, but once again no orders were forthcoming. Both aircraft were placed into storage following completion of the USAF's trials, Piper meanwhile having made some further attempts to sell the Enforcer to smaller nations.

A formation of Mustangs from the 339th Fighter Group's 505th Fighter Squadron plays for the camera. The photograph was taken in the northern hemisphere spring of 1945, just as the war in Europe was ending. (via Neil Mackenzie)

MUSTANG CHRONOLOGY

1938-40

The men largely responsible for the design of the Mustang (from left): Larry Waite, vice president in charge of engineering Raymond Rice, and chief designer Edgar Schmued.

January 1938: With Nazi Germany's military capabilities constantly expanding and its threat to Europe increasing, many within the Royal Air Force and British Government start to realise that war with Germany is becoming more likely. At an RAF Air Staff meeting, the Chief of Air Staff (ACM Sir Cyril Newall) points out that the various expansion schemes proposed for the service to this date would leave it with only nine weeks' reserve should war break out and the aircraft manufacturing industry would be caught short.

March 1938: RAF Expansion Scheme L is settled on after German troops entered Austria and caused the British Cabinet under Prime Minister Neville Chamberlain to finally wake up to the fact that positive action was required. Scheme L involved a rapid expansion of the RAF's strength, taking it to 12,000 aircraft in two years should war break out with the emphasis on fighter production.

To help put this into perspective, in March 1938 the first flight of the production Supermarine Spitfire I was still two months away and squadron service wouldn't start until August. The Hawker Hurricane programme was more advanced with two squadrons equipped by March 1938 and 11 of by the end of the year.

April 1938: With war looking more likely, the decision is made to purchase some aircraft for the RAF and Royal Navy from the USA in order to ease the strain on the British industry and to ensure the expansion plan is met. The British Purchasing Commission is established under Sir Henry Self.

The BPC visited the USA in April 1938 with ordering training aircraft its priority. Two types were required, a single engined advanced trainer and a multi engined aircraft for pilot and navigation training. The first requirement was met by placing an order for 200 North American NA-16s (Harvard in RAF service), while it was decided that the multi engined requirement would be met by the British Avro Anson. Britain eventually received nearly 4,800 Harvards of various models.

The BPC had evaluated the Lockheed L.14 12-14 seat commercial transport to meet the latter requirement and the company had proposed a bomber version. Suitably impressed, the British ordered an initial 200 in June 1938 to meet an RAF Coastal Command maritime reconnaissance bomber requirement.

September 1938: The Munich Crisis, and the RAF was still in a critically weak position to defend itself with only six Spitfires and 100 Hurricanes in service with RAF Fighter Command.

15 March 1939: German troops enter Prague, Czechoslovakia is dismembered.

3 September 1939: The start of World War II when Britain, France, Australia and New Zealand declare war on Germany as a consequence of the latter's invasion of Poland two days earlier.

4 November 1939: Neutral USA placed an embargo on the export of military equipment with the outbreak of war but on this date opened a loophole for the benefit of the British and French. The 'Cash and Carry' clause introduced to the US Statute of Neutrality permits Britain and France to purchase aircraft and other arms providing they leave American shores in the holds of ships owned by the purchasing country.

A joint Anglo-French Purchasing Board was also established and immediately started placing orders with US manufacturers, this having the effect of not only helping meet British and French needs but also of starting to gear up US industry for large scale production. By the end of 1940, Britain had ordered no fewer than 11,000 aircraft from the USA, including French contracts taken over after that country's collapse in June 1940.

December 1939: With a desperate need for fighters, Britain begins negotiations for the purchase of 1,740 Curtiss P-40 Hawks (Kittyhawk in RAF service), this aircraft falling short of meeting the RAF's specific requirements but it was at least available and regarded as the best fighter in US service at the time. Further, it proved to be reliable and was also capable of undertaking ground attack missions.

Britain had already ordered Curtiss fighters, the earlier model P-40 (British name Tomahawk) both in its own right and subsequently taking over the aircraft ordered by France, these not delivered before the country fell. Deliveries began in late 1940 and overall, the RAF received nearly 900.

As the Curtiss production line was already fully occupied to meet the USAAC's needs and delivery of the RAF Kittyhawks would be later than desired, the BPC approached North American Aviation to see if it would be willing to build the P-40 under licence for the RAF.

1938-40

The aircraft Britain asked North American Aviation to manufacture under licence for the RAF, the Curtiss P-40D Kittyhawk. NAA came up with a better idea. The RAF and Commonwealth received large numbers of the Curtiss fighter anyway, this P-40D Kittyhawk I belonging to No 450 Squadron RAAF in the Western Desert. (RAAF)

January 1940: Britain's proposal that North American might establish a Curtiss P-40 production line in order to circumvent delivery delays to the RAF drew a predictably lukewarm response from the manufacturer, company president James H 'Dutch' Kindelberger seeing NAA as a design centre in its own right and not merely a sub-contractor and builder of others' designs. He also regarded the P-40 as being outmoded.

NAA therefore proposed that it should build a completely new and more advanced design for the RAF, powered by the P-40's Allison V-1710 engine. Following discussions between the company and the British Direct Purchasing Commission, NAA's design team starts work on the new fighter, albeit without a contract at this stage but with the intention of 'selling' the idea to the British. The team is led by chief engineer Raymond Rice and chief designer Edgar Schmued.

US Government approval for the plan was necessary and given – despite the USA's neutrality – on condition that two examples of the new fighter were provided at no cost for evaluation by the USAAC.

February 1940: NAA president 'Dutch' Kindelberger and vice-president Leland Atwood travel to London for a design conference with British Air Ministry representatives to show some preliminary drawings and concepts. Although the company had no previous experience with designing high performance aircraft, some innovative features were apparent, such as the laminar flow wing section to minimise induced and profile drag and an underfuselage radiator through which passing air was expanded and accelerated before ejecting through a controllable rear flap.

The result was some additional propulsive force, although the plumbing necessary to connect the radiator and engine was relatively complicated and – as discovered later – vulnerable to ground fire. The design was genuinely advanced and impressed the Air Ministry officials at the meeting.

When designing the new fighter's aerofoil section, North American obtained data from the National Advisory Committee for Aeronautics (NACA) which had developed the laminar flow concept, and purchased wind tunnel data from Curtiss for $US56,000. The latter occurrence has subsequently prompted some to suggest that what became the Mustang was only a rehash of a Curtiss design – namely the unsuccessful XP-46 – but this is completely false. The XP-46 did not have laminar flow wings and took to the air for the first some four months after the prototype North American fighter.

Other issues were also discussed at the London meeting, among them armament fit. NAA had originally proposed either four 0.50in machine guns or a mix of two

1938-40

NORTH AMERICAN AVIATION

North American Aviation was a dominant player in the US military industry during the 1940s and 1950s due to a series of innovative and successful designs. Formed in 1928, NAA initially operated as a holding company for other aviation concerns such as Curtiss, Sperry and the airline TWA and had no aircraft designs of its own, instead funding these other companies and their designs.

NAA was reorganised in 1933 when it came under control of James H ('Dutch') Kindelberger, formerly chief engineer at Douglas Aircraft. Joining Kindelberger was John Leland 'Lee' Attwood, the two men establishing the manufacturing division of North American Aviation at the old Curtiss-Caproni plant at Dandalk, Maryland.

The revamped NAA's first design was the model GA-15 two seat observation monoplane of 1935 powered by a 975hp (726kW) Wright R-1820 Cyclone radial engine. Ordered for the US Army Air Corps as the O-47, 239 were built. Most were based in the USA where they were used for training and general duties, although some saw limited service in the early weeks of the Pacific war.

NAA followed the O-47 with the aircraft which really made the company, the NA-16 family of military trainers which evolved into the hugely successful T-6 Texan/Harvard series of advanced and combat trainers. USAAC contracts for the early models allowed NAA to build the factory with which it is most readily associated, at Inglewood, California, located on the perimeter of Mines Field, or what is now Los Angeles International Airport.

The NA-16/T-6 family was built in huge numbers as it became the standard trainer of its type with many allied nations during World War II, armed versions seeing combat with some. North American alone built more than 15,000, to which must be added 755 built in Australia as the CAC Wirraway and over 2,600 Harvards by Noorduyn Aviation in Canada for the Royal Air Force, Royal Canadian Air Force and USAAF.

The company developed from there, producing two of the classic combat aircraft of World War II, the B-25 Mitchell medium bomber and the P-51 Mustang fighter. The end of the war saw several manufacturers which had previously been leading lights in the design and manufacture of military aircraft – notably fighters – fall by the wayside in that area. NAA was not one of them thanks to the F-86 Sabre and F-100 Super Sabre.

At its peak during World War II, NAA employed some 91,000 workers and during the war years built more than 42,000 military aircraft, or 14 per cent of all US production.

The name North American remained at the fore until the early 1970s when its aircraft became known as 'Rockwells' following the merger of NAA and the Rockwell Corporation in 1967, initially operating under the brand name 'North American-Rockwell'. Rockwell was acquired by Boeing in 1996.

In the meantime, the company had continued producing successful designs mainly for the military market: the B-45 Tornado bomber of 1947; T-28 Trojan trainer (successor to the Texan); T-2 Buckeye jet trainer for the US Navy; AJ Savage composite powered large naval bomber and reconnaissance aircraft; T-39 Sabreliner military and civil light jet transport (one of the first bizjets); A-5 Vigilante advanced supersonic naval bomber; XB-70 Valkyrie Mach 3 experimental strategic bomber; the extraordinary X-15 rocket powered research aircraft which achieved a speed of Mach 6.72 and an altitude of 354,200 feet (107,960m), and the B-1 Lancer swing wing bomber.

The aircraft that helped transform North American Aviation from a small player into a large one – the T-6 Texan/Harvard family of advanced trainers. Over 15,000 were built in the USA plus a further 1,600 in Canada and 755 in Australia as the Wirraway, the aircraft becoming the standard Allied advanced trainer of the war. These are South African Harvards in post war service.

1938-40

Before the Mustang, North American's only attempt at a fighter design had been the NA-50/P-64 series, a single seat armed derivative of the NA-16/T-6 trainer family. First flown in 1939, the aircraft was built in very small numbers with seven sold to Peru and six operated by the USAAF as trainers.

0.50in and two 0.30in guns, as on the Curtiss P-40. Britain's fighter armament philosophy at the time revolved around eight machine guns (as on the Hurricane and Spitfire), NAA consequently designing an installation with two 0.50in Browning MG 53s in the lower nose plus two more 'fifties' and four 0.30in Browning MG 40s in the wings.

10 April 1940: Britain gives a preliminary go ahead for development of the new fighter proposed by North American Aviation with the signing of a letter-of-intent for 320 aircraft. The company designation NA-73X is applied to the design, which is funded entirely by the manufacturer.

24 April 1940: A telegram is sent by Britain to NAA's Chief of Engineering, Raymond Rice, telling him to go ahead with the NA-73X's detailed drawings. This in effect is the formal go ahead for the aircraft to be designed and built within a specified four months. The effort involved working double shifts in order to meet deadlines. An all night effort saw a detailed general arrangement and weight study completed by the next day.

4 May 1940: Britain approves the preliminary design of the NA-73X.

5 May 1940: Production of detail design drawings begin.

Apart from the Mustang and Texan, North American's other major contribution to the Allied cause in World War II was the B-25 Mitchell medium bomber, more than 9,800 of which were built. This is a B-25D in RAAF service. (Colin Hill)

Sovereign 2 – Mustang 59

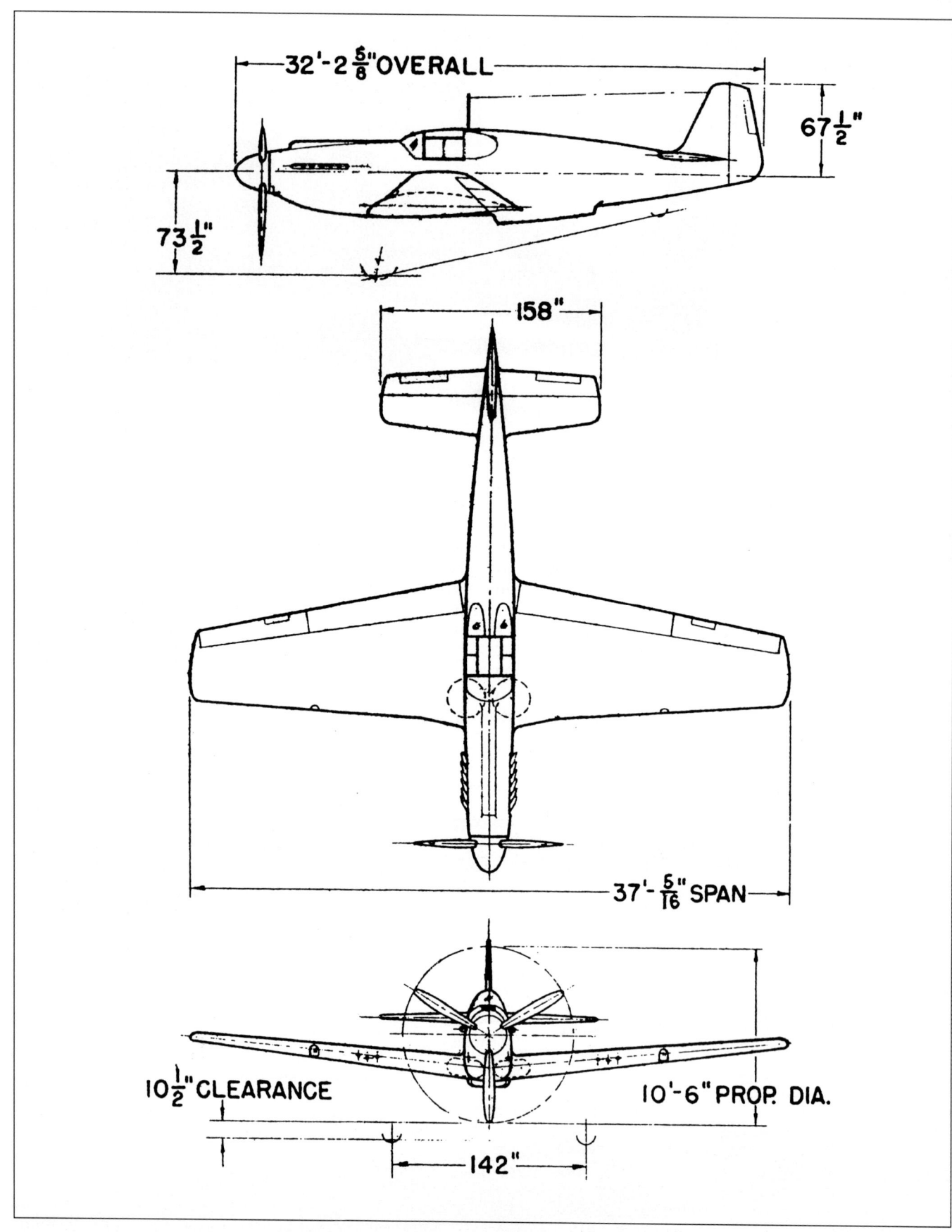

A 1940 North American Aviation drawing of the NA-73X as proposed, showing the aircraft's principal dimensions and overall configuration.

1938-40

THE ALLISON V-1710

It's strange how history treats some things. There can be two items of equipment which are very similar in concept and role and are contemporaries, yet one of these items can end up being the one that captures most of the glory, even though both might play a vital part in their area of history.

In aviation the Supermarine Spitfire and Hawker Hurricane are examples, the former grabbing most of the 'good PR' following the Battle of Britain (and retaining it ever since) despite the fact that the less glamorous Hurricane did most of the work through shear weight of numbers.

In the area of World War II powerplants, the Rolls-Royce Merlin and Allison V-1710 hold similar positions. Almost identical in size, general concept and early execution, the Merlin went on to grab most of the kudos despite the V-1710 being used in 9,594 Bell P-38 Airacobras, 3,303 Bell P-63 Kingcobras, 13,738 Curtiss P-40 Warhawks/Kittyhawks, 10,036 Lockheed P-38 Lightnings, 1,579 North American P-51 Mustangs and 251 F-82 Twin Mustangs.

Apart from a period in 1943 when the P-38H Lightning's Allison suffered turbocharger and cooling problems which resulted in restrictions on the use of maximum power, the V-1710 had a reputation as a solid and reliable powerplant which proved itself in every theatre of operation. The Merlin was also regarded as reliable and always seemed to steal the limelight in the field of liquid cooled vee-12 engines of the era and beyond. Perhaps it was because the Merlin was the powerplant of the two Allied fighters regarded as the best of the war by most, the Spitfire and later model Mustangs.

It is in the case of the P-51 where the V-1710 suffers in the eyes of many enthusiasts. Everyone knows that installation of the Merlin with 2-speed/2-stage supercharger transformed the Mustang, giving it the high altitude performance that could not be delivered by the single-speed and low altitude rated Allison on the first Mustangs. What this fails to recognise was that in 1940, this was the state-of-the-art for this type of powerplant. Even the Spitfire only had a 1-speed/1-stage supercharger at that time.

Rolls-Royce went on to develop the Merlin's power output and by introducing ever improving supercharger technology and with it the ability to 'tailor' different Merlin variants to suit specific requirements of altitude performance. Allison went a different way, introducing V-1710 variants with upgraded superchargers later, and in the interim increasing its power mainly by the use of turbochargers.

Design and development of the V-1710, like the Merlin a 60 degree vee-12, began in 1930, the initial V-1710-A of 1932 being unsupercharged and producing 750hp (559kW). The V-1710-B was similar but intended for airships and had a reversing capability, while development of the engine for fixed wing applications began in earnest in 1933 with the V-1710-C family with integral supercharger or exhaust driven turbocharger, depending on the subvariant. The C found application in the early model Curtiss P-40/B/C Hawk series and the prototype Lockheed XP-38.

The V-1710-D and E models were developed specifically for the mid engined Bell P-39 and P-63 fighters with an 8ft (2.44m) shaft extension and remote gearbox to drive the propeller.

The V-1710-F series powered the early Mustangs plus P-40s from the D onwards and the Lockheed P-38. Once again, supercharged and turbocharged versions were produced. The F models had some new features (10 per cent less frontal area and a raised propeller thrust line) and were intended to produce higher power outputs. The most powerful V-1710 to achieve regular production was the F30 (military designation V-1710-111) which turned out 1,475hp (1,100kW) at optimum altitude and was installed in the P-38L Lightning.

All V-1710s had similar main physical characteristics: capacity 1,710cu in (28.0 litres); cylinder bore 5.5in (139.7mm); piston stroke 6.0in (152.4mm); compression ratio 6.65:1; maximum engine speed 3,000rpm.

The versions installed in P-51 Mustangs were:

V-1710-39: (commercial designation V-1710-F3R); maximum power 1,150hp (857kW) for takeoff; 1,000hp (746kW) maximum continuous power at 2,600rpm at 10,800ft. Applications: NA-73X, P-51, Mustang I/IA.

V-1710-81: (commercial designation V-1710-F20R); maximum power 1,200hp (895kW) for takeoff; 1,125hp (839kW) at 18,000ft. Application: P-51A/Mustang II.

V-1710-87: (commercial designation V 1710-F21R); maximum power 1,325hp (988kW) at 3,000ft. Application: A-36A.

---

10 May 1940: Winston Churchill becomes British Prime Minister.

27-28 May 1940: The Allied evacuation from Dunkirk.

29 May 1940: Britain signs a formal contract for the purchase of 320 NA-73X fighters worth over $US15m. Contract conditions were demanding and included that due to the ever worsening war situation, the prototype must meet all specification goals and be flying within eight months. A maximum price of $US50,000 per aircraft was specified and as insurance against failure, NAA was required to obtain all current data on P-40 development including wind tunnel information.

22 June 1940: France surrenders to Germany.

July 1940: Rolls-Royce and Packard conclude arrangements for licence production of the Merlin in the USA, the agreement initially covering 1,500 engines with options on a further 10,000. Packard eventually built more than 55,000 Merlins as the V-1650.

10 July 1940: The Battle of Britain officially begins.

9 September 1940: After the expenditure of some 78,000 engineering man-hours, the NA-73X prototype is rolled out at North American's Inglewood plant, 127 days after approval of the preliminary design by Britain and 102 days after the purchase contract was signed. It would not

1938-40

The NA-73X prototype flew for the first time on 26 October 1940 with freelance test pilot Vance Breese at the controls.

be until 7 October that its Allison V-1710 engine was received for installation, the delay caused by the fact that as the aircraft was a private venture and not being developed under a US Government contract, such equipment was supplied on an 'as available' basis. The aircraft was also rolled out on wheels 'borrowed' from an AT-6 trainer.

20 September 1940: With the Battle of Britain less than a week past its peak, the NA-73X is formally ordered into production for the Royal Air Force. The initial order covering 320 aircraft, subsequently called the Mustang Mk.I, is later increased to 620. As required by the US Government when it gave NAA approval to design the aircraft for Britain, the contract specifies that two examples of the new fighter should be made available to the USAAC for testing and evaluation.

LAMINAR FLOW

The Mustang's laminar flow section wing has always been given part of the credit for the aircraft's performance, and incorporation of such a wing – which was innovative for its time – was one of several configurations studied when the aircraft was being designed.

The laminar flow concept revolves around the use of a symmetrical aerofoil (that is, the same curvature on both the upper and lower surfaces), with a thin leading edge and the wing's thickest section placed as far aft as possible. This means that boundary layer airflow adheres to the wing much further aft of the leading edge than conventional aerofoils (which have the upper surface more curved than the lower), thus 'laminating' layers of air on both surfaces to provide a smoother and more efficient airflow.

On a conventional aerofoil section, the boundary layer breaks up further forward on the wing surface, causing turbulence and therefore drag and reduced performance.

At the time the Mustang was being designed the concept was quite new and untried in a production situation. Those laminar flow wings which had been constructed were hand made, with their surfaces hand finished to ensure the integrity of the aerofoil shape. Hand finishing was obviously impractical in a mass production situation, so North American had to come up with a way of filling and sanding the forward part of the wing to ensure that laminar flow was maintained.

Fortunately, testing of NAA's methods in the wind tunnel at the California Institute of Technology proved it to be a practical proposition for mass production. To cover the possibility that the tests might fail, NAA also designed a wing of more conventional configuration which could be quickly substituted..... just in case.

In recent years, tests of the Mustang's wing have indicated that it never developed extensive laminar flow – at least not by more modern standards – and that its drag is no less than conventional wings of similar thickness and taper ratio.

Instead, most of the credit for the Mustang's performance is now thought to have resulted from a reduction in cooling system drag due to the efficient dynamics involved in its radiator design with smooth airflow at the intake and a progressively adjustable outlet.

It is interesting to note that the Merlin powered Mustang was about 30mph (48km/h) faster in level flight and at optimum altitude than the similarly powered but lighter Spitfire VIII and IX, which also featured a wing providing a considerably higher limiting Mach number. The Spitfire's twin underwing radiators have two-position exits – either fully open or partially closed, with no progressive adjustment available for different speeds. The result was turbulent airflow from the exit, a drop in efficiency and reduced speed.

1938-40

11 October 1940: The NA-73X prototype undergoes its first engine ground running tests, the engine having only been received four days earlier.

26 October 1940: First flight of the North American NA-73X prototype from Mines Field, Inglewood, California. Freelance test pilot Vance Breese is at the controls for the 22 minute sortie, conducted within gliding distance of the airfield. The aircraft carried the civil registration NX19998. Mines Field later became Los Angeles International Airport.

Breese was selected to perform the initial flight tests because even though NAA had test pilots on its payroll, none of them were *fighter* test pilots. Breese was a colourful, outspoken and famous pilot who was regularly employed by several manufacturers on a freelance basis – and for substantial sums of money

20 November 1940: On its fifth flight, the NA-73X is damaged when it flips onto its back during a forced landing in a ploughed field at the end of a test flight carried out by NAA pilot Paul Balfour. The engine had stopped due to fuel starvation, Balfour having failed to change tanks in time when the one he'd selected ran dry. It was his first flight in the aircraft. NX19998 would be out of action until the following January.

9 December 1940: The NA-73X is officially named 'Mustang' by the RAF.

December 1940: By now, Britain's dollar reserves had been almost entirely eaten up by the massive amount of equipment it had been purchasing from the USA. President Roosevelt had been aware of the situation for several months and had been working on a solution – the Lend-Lease Bill which was introduced in March 1941.

1 December 1940: The formation of Army Co-operation Command (ACC) within the RAF, its establishment resulting from the debacle of the British Expeditionary Force in France and observation of the close co-operation between German air and ground forces during the campaign.

This was of significance to the Mustang's early career in RAF service as it was to Army co-operation squadrons that the aircraft was first allocated. ACC remained in existence until June 1943 when it was disbanded as part of the reorganisation of tactical air power being undertaken in preparation for the invasion of France.

(left) Any euphoria associated with the NA-73X's performance and potential didn't last long. This is the scene at the end of the aircraft's fifth flight on 20 November 1940 when pilot Paul Balfour found himself having to make a forced landing following fuel starvation resulting from not changing tanks. The NA-73X was repaired and flew again in January 1941.

1941-42

Mustang I AG431, the 87th of 620 ordered for the RAF. The Mustang I equipped 14 UK based RAF Army Co-operation squadrons from early 1942. (via Neil Mackenzie)

10 January 1941: The Lend-Lease Bill is introduced into the US House of Representatives. The bills intended to give the President authorisation to "sell, transfer title to, exchange, lease, lend or otherwise dispose of.... any defence article" to any country whose defence the President deems "vital to the defence of the United States."

Payment or repayment for the goods might be "…. in kind or property, or any other direct or indirect benefit which the President deems satisfactory". In other words, it was a loose arrangement which President Roosevelt could use as he saw fit, at once satisfying his desire to help the British fight against Nazi Germany while at the same time technically preserving the USA's neutrality.

It also meant that should a country taking advantage of the benefits of Lend-Lease not be able to repay in hard cash (after having been invaded or left in ruin, for example), there was no question of reparations being demanded via the handover of territory or other national assets. With the Lend-Lease Bill, the USA did indeed fulfil Roosevelt's pledge to become "the arsenal of democracy."

11 January 1941: The NA-73X is reflown following repairs resulting from its accident the previous November. Flight test duties are taken over by Bob Chilton.

2 February 1941: Rommel arrives in North Africa.

11 March 1941: US President Franklin D Roosevelt signs the Lend-Lease Bill, allowing the supply of US war materials to allied nations for the duration of the war. As was the case with all aircraft supplied to Britain and others under Lend-Lease, the first batch of Mustangs approved under the scheme (150 Mk.IAs) were first purchased by the USAAC as P-51s before being transferred to the RAF. At the same time and for the same reasons, the Mustang I/IA's V-1710-F3R engine (a commercial designation) became the military V-1710-39.

23 April 1941: First flight of the first Mustang I for the RAF (AG345), the aircraft retained by North American for test duties. AG345 was flown by Louis Watt on this occasion but the overall flight test programme was under the direction of Bob Chilton.

AG345 was originally unpainted (apart from a black anti dazzle panel on the upper cowling) but later acquired RAF camouflage. It was also subsequently fitted with armament, landing lights in the wing leading edges, a gun camera, modified radiator inlet and a longer carburettor inlet on the upper cowling.

20 May 1941: First flight of the XP-51 (41-038), the fourth production airframe. The 10th airframe was also delivered to the USAAC as 41-039 for testing and evaluation, as per the purchase contract agreement. Both were new airframes, separate from the British order. The aircraft was initially called 'Apache' by the USAAC, the British name 'Mustang' not formally adopted until arrival of the P-51B in late 1942. The two XP-51s were evaluated at Wright Field, Dayton, Ohio but were apparently flown very little due to a combination of the workload associated with testing other types and – believe it or not – a lack of interest in the new North American fighter.

20 June 1941: As part of a major reorganisation of the United States Army Air Corps (USAAC) designed to give it greater unity and authority, the service is renamed the United States Army Air Force (USAAF).

1941-42

22 June 1941: Germany invades Russia.

July 1941: Britain orders 150 Mustangs under the terms of Lend-Lease (see 11 March entry) as the Mustang IA. Of these, 57 were retained by the USAAF as the P-51 or F-6A for the 55 of these fitted with cameras. The designation P-51-1 was also sometimes used for these aircraft.

15 July 1941: The NA-73X is retired after completing 45 flights.

August 1941: Bench testing of the first US built Packard V-1650-1 Merlin begins.

5 August 1941: The USA and Britain impose an embargo on the sale of raw materials to Japan.

24 October 1941: The first Mustang I (AG346) for the RAF arrives by sea at Liverpool from the USA, disassembled and crated. The aircraft was assembled at Speke by No 1 Aircraft Assembly Unit (which had been established to assemble Lockheed Hudsons shipped from the USA) and then tested by the Aircraft and Armament Experimental Establishment (A&AEE) at Boscombe Down. These trials revealed a maximum speed of 382mph (615km/h) at 13,000ft plus good manoeuvrability and general handling but a rapid drop in performance above that height due to the Allison V-1710 engine's only moderate level of supercharging.

The conclusion was made, therefore, that the aircraft was unsuitable for use as a day fighter in Europe but its low level performance and heavy armament made it suitable for re-equipping the RAF's Army Co-operation squadrons. In that role it would replace the Curtiss P-40 Tomahawk and Westland Lysander.

Comparative tests against the Spitfire V showed the American fighter was at least 28mph (45km/h) faster at all heights up to 20,000ft, but the Spitfire's rate of climb was superior – seven versus 11 minutes to 20,000ft – as was its turning ability. The Spitfire was also faster at high altitudes. On the issue of range it was no contest – the Mustang could travel two-and-a half times as far on its internal fuel capacity.

TACTICAL RECONNAISSANCE

Evaluation of the first Mustang Is to arrive in Britain in late 1941 quickly revealed the aircraft's relatively poor high altitude performance but also its effectiveness at lower levels. It was therefore decided to commit the RAF's early Mustangs to the armed tactical reconnaissance role, eventually equipping 14 RAF Army Co-operation Command squadrons and replacing the Curtiss P-40 Tomahawk and Westland Lysander.

To equip the Mustang for TacR duties, the aircraft were fitted with a single F.24 or K.24 camera mounted obliquely behind the pilot's head and pointing through the port side rear clear vision panel. The cameras took 5in (197mm) square photographs and were the same unit, the K.24 merely a US licence built version of the British F.24.

The camera was sighted by bringing the object to be photographed in line with a mark on the port wing, this eliminating the need for straight and level flying during the photographic pass and therefore reducing the risk of the aircraft being hit by anti-aircraft fire. This feature meant that the photographs could be taken from a reasonable distance away from a possibly well defended target or from an almost vertical bank and tight turn over the target.

A similar installation was devised for the USAAF's F-6A photo-reconnaissance aircraft, some of which also featured a vertical K.24 mounted in the lower fuselage immediately behind the ventral radiator.

December 1941: Mustang Is for the RAF were leaving North American's production line in increasing numbers by the end of 1941 and being shipped to Britain. Of the earlier arrivals, several were allocated to various test, training and evaluation duties: AG346 (as noted above) went to the A&AEE at Boscombe Down as did AG351, AG357 and AG359. AG356, AG360 and AG365 were sent

AG345, the first Mustang I for Britain before being painted in RAF camouflage. This aircraft first flew on 23 April 1941 and was retained by North American Aviation for tests and trials.

1941-42

RANGERS and RHUBARBS

In early 1941 the RAF's mood changed from defence to offence following the Battle of Britain. Early daylight offensive sweeps into Europe involving fighters were little more than cheeky displays of defiance, but they soon became organised and effective incursions into enemy occupied territory.

The RAF's first Mustangs were used exclusively in the tactical reconnaissance and army co-operation roles. An early type of sortie to be undertaken was specifically for the North American fighter due to its long range. From March 1942, RAF Mustang Is were sent out on *Lagoon* operations, these intended to seek out enemy shipping off the Dutch coast.

Other codenames given to offensive operations by fighters of any sort (not just Mustangs) were as follows, each with a specific purpose:

Circus: A bomber or fighter-bomber operation heavily escorted by fighters and intended mainly to entice enemy fighters into the air.

Sweep: A general term covering fighters flying offensive missions over enemy territory or the sea, with or without accompanying bombers.

Rodeo: Fighter sweep over enemy territory without accompanying bombers.

Ramrod: Similar to a circus but with the aim of destroying a specific target.

Rhubarb: Freelance fighter operations on a small scale attacking targets of opportunity. These were often conducted in bad weather so as to introduce an element of surprise.

Ranger: Two aircraft working together and flying at very low altitude to attack targets of opportunity, either in the air or on the ground. In the case of the RAF's Mustangs, these began in the middle of 1943.

A poor quality but interesting photograph showing the second of two XP-51s (41-039) retained by the USAAF for evaluation as per the original RAF contract but in addition to, not part of the RAF order. This was the tenth production Mustang airframe and along with 41-038 was based at Wright Field in Ohio but flown sparingly. Note the Wright Field logo on the side of the fuselage. (via Neil Mackenzie)

to the Air Fighting Development Unit (AFDU), while AG350 was the first Mustang I allocated to No 1 Operational Conversion Unit (OCU) at Old Sarum.

7 December 1941: Japan attacks Pearl Harbour, the Philippines, Hong Kong and Malaya. The Allies declare war on Japan the following day.

11 December 1941: Germany and Italy declare war on the USA.

January 1942: No 26 (Army Co-operation) Squadron based at Gatwick becomes the first RAF operational unit to receive the Mustang I (replacing P-40 Tomahawks) and the first of 14 UK based RAF Army Co-operation squadrons to fly the aircraft. For the tactical reconnaissance role, the Mustang Is were fitted with a single F.24 camera mounted obliquely in the cockpit behind the pilot.

15 February 1942: Japan captures Singapore.

March 1942: Nos 241 and 268 Squadrons RAF re-equip with the Mustang I. The latter unit immediately began *Lagoon* operations from its base near Newmarket, these

Early RAF Mustangs were shipped across the Atlantic to No 1 Aircraft Assembly Unit at Speke, near Liverpool, where they were bolted together in company with other aircraft sent from the USA. Mustang I AG349 (the fifth aircraft) shares the tarmac with a Hudson, two Bostons and a Kittyhawk.

1941-42

Mustang I AM148 of No 26 Squadron, the first RAF unit to operate the new fighter. Based at Gatwick, the squadron began receiving Mustangs in January 1942. It was a 26 Squadron Mustang which flew the type's first operational sortie, a reconnaissance over the French coast on 5 May 1942.

involving searching out enemy shipping off the Dutch coast.

April 1942: Nos 2, 4 and 613 Squadrons RAF re-equip with the Mustang I.

16 April 1942: The USAAF orders 500 A-36A dive bombers, the first Mustang variant ordered specifically for the service. The contract followed a period in which the USAAF/USAAC showed little interest in the Mustang as it was preoccupied with the testing of other types. Noting the results of what testing had been carried out, General H ('Hap') Arnold intervened, overruling an Air Materiel Command aircraft procurement recommendation and ensuring the Mustang was ordered for the USAAF.

30 April 1942: Rolls-Royce Service Liaison pilot, Ronnie Harker, flies Mustang I AG422 at the Air Fighting Development Unit as part of his general evaluation duties of service aircraft, whether or not they are powered by Rolls-Royce engines. After his 30 minute flight, Harker was impressed with the Mustang's manoeuvrability and low-medium altitude performance but was already familiar with the performance drop-off of the Allison V-1710 engine at higher altitudes.

Harker thought that the installation of the Merlin 60 series engine with two speed/two stage supercharger would do wonders for the aircraft's performance, stating in his report: "The point which strikes me is that with a powerful and good engine like the Merlin 61, its performance should be outstanding, as it is 35mph faster than a Spitfire V at roughly the same power...."

From there, development of the Merlin-Mustang began, this fully exploiting the aircraft's fine airframe and aerodynamics design and allowing it to be developed as a true fighter rather than being restricted to the tactical reconnaissance and other low level roles.

May 1942: Nos 225 and 229 Squadrons RAF re-equip with the Mustang I followed by six more – Nos 63, 169, 170, 308 (Polish), 400 (Canadian) and 414 (Canadian) – in June and July.

5 May 1942: The Mustang's first operational sortie when a camera equipped Mk.I from 26 Squadron RAF conducts a reconnaissance mission over the French coast. The aircraft was AG418 flown by Flg Off G Dawson, who took the opportunity to strafe some targets of opportunity during the flight.

6-8 May 1942: US forces in the Philippines surrender to Japan.

29 May 1942: First flight of the Mustang IA for the RAF, differing from the Mk.I in having four 20mm cannon in the wings replacing the original eight nose and wing machine guns. Deliveries of a planned 150 began two months later under the terms of Lend-Lease. Fifty-seven were diverted to the USAAF as the P-51, most of them fitted with cameras and given the designation F-6A and sometimes P-51-1.

30-31 May 1942: The first RAF '1,000 Bomber Raid' on Cologne. Most were Vickers Wellingtons and other twin engined types, the fleet scraped together from just about every available source including reserve and training units. Of the 1,047 aircraft which departed on the night raid, about 870 actually made it to their targets.

3 June 1942: After a period of correspondence between Rolls-Royce, the British Air Ministry, US Government agencies (through its enthusiastic and knowledgeable assistant military attache in London, Major Thomas Hitchcock), North American Aviation and other interested parties, approval is given for the conversion of five Mustang Is to Rolls-Royce Merlin power.

Enthusiasm for the project quickly developed on both sides of the Atlantic, a letter from Ray Dorey (manager of Rolls-Royce's Hucknall facility, where the conversions were performed) to Willoughby Lappin (the influential personal assistant to Rolls-Royce's general works

1941-42

A trio of Mustang Is from No 2 Squadron RAF, this unit re-equipping with the fighter in April 1942 while based at Sawbridgeworth. Note the camera port in the rear of the port side canopy, visible on shots taken from that side. (via Neil Mackenzie).

1941-42

The Mustang IA differed from the original Mk.I in having a four cannon armament instead of eight machine guns in the wings and nose. First flight was on 29 May 1942 and 150 were ordered for the RAF of which 57 went to the USAAF as the P-51 or F-6A when fitted with cameras. This photograph shows the oblique camera installation behind the cockpit.

manager and board member Ernest Hives) noting that the "Americans are red hot on this proposal....". Licence production of the Merlin by Packard was already well underway by then, although that of the Merlin 61 equivalent with two speed/two stage supercharger was still some months away.

3-4 June 1942: The Battle of Midway.

July 1942: Deliveries of the Mustang IA to the RAF begin.

16 July 1942: The RAF's first Mustang operational losses when two of No 26 Squadron's aircraft fail to return from a tactical reconnaissance in the Abbeville area of northern France.

25 July 1942: The USAAF contracts North American to install Packard Merlin engines in two P-51 Mustangs. The American Merlin-Mustang was originally given the designation XP-78 and then XP-51B.

August 1942: The USAAF orders its first Mustangs for the fighter role, placing a contract for 310 P-51As, essentially the A-36A without dive brakes or fuselage guns plus the V-1710-81 engine with a new supercharger which maintained power to higher altitudes. Fifty went to the RAF as the Mustang II.

August 1942: The USAAF's Commanding General, H ('Hap') Arnold, approves an order for 2,000 Merlin powered Mustangs on the basis of performance predictions, two months before the first Mustang Mk.X prototype had been flown and three months before the first XP-51B had taken to the air. The order was conditional upon these estimates being met and was confirmed at the end of 1942. To cater for the massive increase in Mustang production this order implied, North American established a new plant at Dallas, Texas to help meet the demand.

19 August 1942: The Mustang's first victory in aerial combat when Plt Off Hollis Hills (an American volunteer in the Royal Canadian Air Force) downs a Focke-Wulf Fw 190 during the ill fated Anglo-Canadian Dieppe landings. Hills was flying with No 414 (RCAF) Squadron

The fourth RAF Mustang I (AG348) is normally assumed to have ended up as the first of two XP-51s retained by the USAAF for evaluation. But it was the fourth production airframe (not RAF aircraft) which became the first XP-51 (41-038), while the tenth airframe became the other XP-51 (41-039). AG348 is pictured here in its RAF markings and is one of the ten Mustang Is which were shipped to the Soviet Union in May 1942.

Sovereign 2 – Mustang   69

1941-42

Mustang I AL975 was the first Mustang X conversion to fly with a Rolls-Royce Merlin 65 engine, on 13 October 1942.

within the RAF structure and later joined the US Navy to fly Grumman Hellcats. He became the first Mustang 'five kill' ace in June 1943.

Four Mustang squadrons were allocated to the Dieppe operation – Nos 26, 239, 400 (RCAF) and 414 (RCAF) – joining more than 60 squadrons of Spitfires, Typhoons, Hurricanes, Blenheims and Bostons with the intention (for the air battle) of coaxing all of the *Luftwaffe's* forces in France and the Low Countries into the air. The aircraft were placed under the operational control of Air Vice-Marshal Trafford Leigh-Mallory's No 11 Group and the outcome was disastrous with 106 RAF aircraft lost including ten Mustangs, five of them from No 26 Squadron.

The landings part of the Dieppe operation was intended to give commanders and their troops experience in landing on an enemy coast, and it was also the first large combined operation involving land, sea and air forces.

21 September 1942: First flight of the A-36A dive bomber Mustang variant for the USAAF (42-83663), this initially and unofficially known as the Invader.

27 September 1942: Acting on his own initiative, Flt Lt J Lewkowicz of No 309 (Polish) Squadron RAF flies his Mustang to Stavanger in Norway from Dalcross near Inverness in northern Scotland to prove that his fuel consumption/engine power settings/ground speed calculations that showed this was possible were correct. During the 700 mile (1,125km) round trip Flt Lt Lewkowicz attacked ground targets and took photographs in Norway.

On his return, Flt Lt Lewkowicz received a reprimand from senior officers for acting without orders and then congratulations from them on his achievement. As a result of that flight, RAF Mustang squadrons were allowed to attack more distant targets in Europe and more fully exploit the aircraft's range capabilities.

1 October 1942: A Mustang I becomes the first single engined RAF aircraft to fly over Germany, a reconnaissance over the Dortmund-Ems canal.

13 October 1942: First flight of the prototype Mustang Mk.X (AL975) with a 1,705hp (1,271kW) Rolls-Royce Merlin 65 engine. The aircraft was flown by Rolls-Royce's chief test pilot, Capt Ronnie Shepherd from the company's Hucknall facility. It was converted from a Mustang I by the engine manufacturer and fitted with standard Rotol four bladed propeller from a Spitfire IX. Four other conversions followed, all initially fitted with Merlin 65s – AM208 (first flight 13 November 1942), AM203 (13 December 1942), AL963 (21 January 1943) and AM121 (7 February 1943). From its seventh flight, AL975 was fitted with a purpose designed Rotol propeller of slightly larger diameter.

23 October 1942: Start of the Battle of El Alamein, the turning point in the North African campaign. From now and despite some setbacks on the way, the Allies begin to gradually gain the ascendency in the area.

October 1942: Scotland based No 225 Squadron RAF departs the United Kingdom for service in North Africa with a mixed complement of Mustang I/IIs and Hawker Hurricane IICs. The Mustangs remained on strength until August 1943, by which time Spitfire Vs had become the squadron's main equipment.

Closeup of the Merlin 65 installation in the Mustang X. The benefits of the new powerplant were immediately apparent.

North American NA-73X prototype N19998 in early 1941 following rebuild after its November 1940 accident.

Mustang I AG345, the first for the RAF, at the time of its first flight in May 1941 and before painting in RAF colours.

Mustang I AM148/RM-G of 26 Squadron RAF, August 1942.

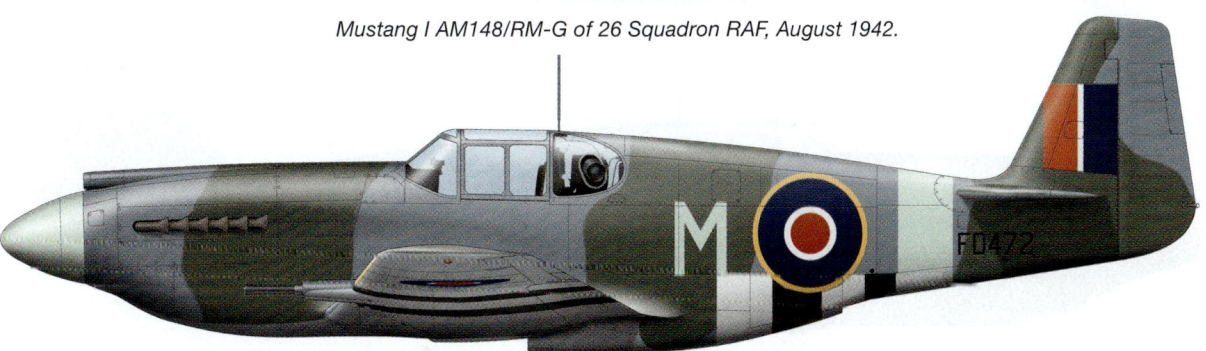

Mustang IA FD472/M of 168 Squadron RAF, June 1944 with D-Day stripes.

RAF Mustang I AG349 as displayed to the British press at the end of 1941.

Sovereign 2 – Mustang   71

Mustang I AG528 of 400 (City of Toronto) Squadron RCAF, UK mid 1943.

A-36A 42-84067 of the 527th FBS, 86th FBG USAAF, Italy 1944.

A-36A 42-83987 of the 532nd FBS, 27th FBG USAAF, Italy late 1943.

P-51 Mustang 41-37322 Mah Sweet Eva Lee *of the 154th Observation Squadron USAAF, Tunisia mid 1943.*

P-51A Mustang 43-6151 of the 1st Air Commando Group USAAF, Burma 1944.

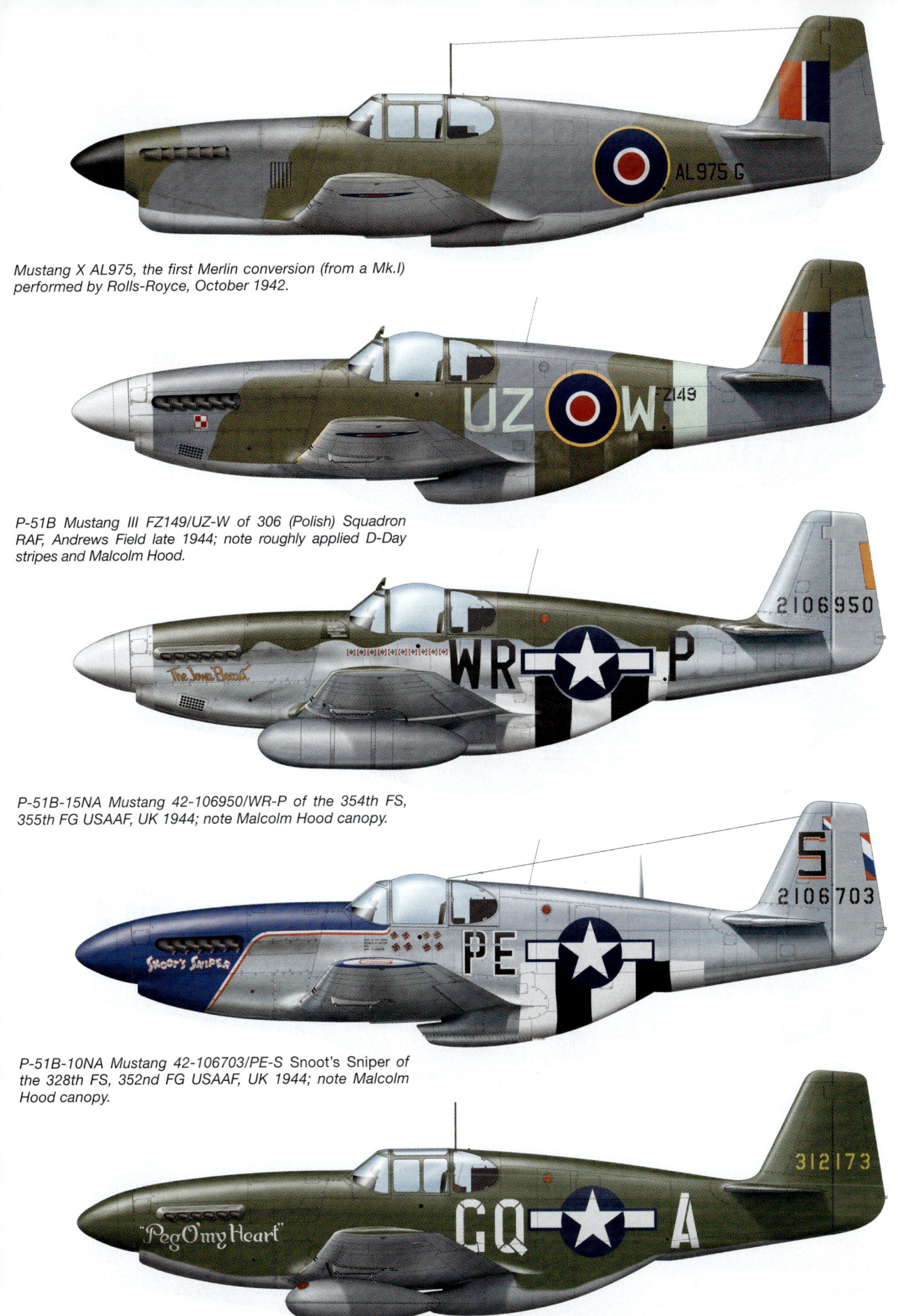

Mustang X AL975, the first Merlin conversion (from a Mk.I) performed by Rolls-Royce, October 1942.

P-51B Mustang III FZ149/UZ-W of 306 (Polish) Squadron RAF, Andrews Field late 1944; note roughly applied D-Day stripes and Malcolm Hood.

P-51B-15NA Mustang 42-106950/WR-P of the 354th FS, 355th FG USAAF, UK 1944; note Malcolm Hood canopy.

P-51B-10NA Mustang 42-106703/PE-S Snoot's Sniper of the 328th FS, 352nd FG USAAF, UK 1944; note Malcolm Hood canopy.

P-51B-1NA Mustang 43-12173/GQ-A Peg O'my Heart of the 355th FS, 345th FG USAAF, UK early 1944; aircraft of Lt George Bickell.

Sovereign 2 – Mustang

P-51C-10NT Mustang 42-103582/VF-Q of the 5th FS, 52nd FG USAAF, Italy 1944.

P-51B-15NA Mustang 42-106957 of the 26th FG USAAF, China 1944.

P-51C-5NT Mustang 42-103368/5M-G of the 15th TRS, 10th PRG USAAF, UK 1944; aircraft flown by Capt John Hoefker.

F-6C Mustang 44-10889/R7-N of Gr II/33 'Savoie' Armée de l'Air, France 1946; aircraft built as P-51C-10NT and converted to F-6C.

P-51D-5NA Mustang 44-13704/B7-H Ferocious Frankie of the 374th FS, 361st FG USAAF, UK mid 1944; flown by Maj Wallace Hopkins.

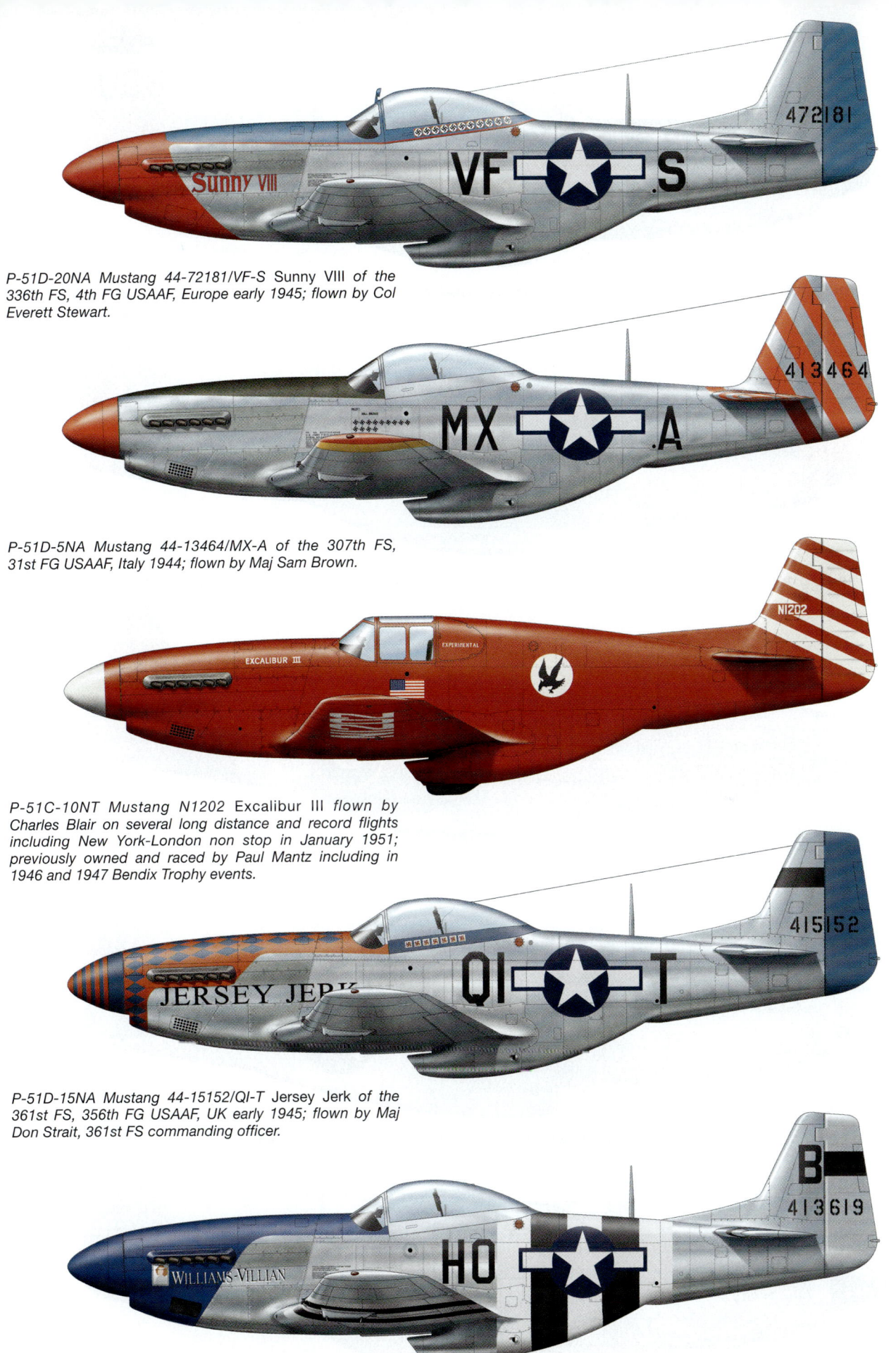

P-51D-20NA Mustang 44-72181/VF-S Sunny VIII of the 336th FS, 4th FG USAAF, Europe early 1945; flown by Col Everett Stewart.

P-51D-5NA Mustang 44-13464/MX-A of the 307th FS, 31st FG USAAF, Italy 1944; flown by Maj Sam Brown.

P-51C-10NT Mustang N1202 Excalibur III flown by Charles Blair on several long distance and record flights including New York-London non stop in January 1951; previously owned and raced by Paul Mantz including in 1946 and 1947 Bendix Trophy events.

P-51D-15NA Mustang 44-15152/QI-T Jersey Jerk of the 361st FS, 356th FG USAAF, UK early 1945; flown by Maj Don Strait, 361st FS commanding officer.

P-51D-5NA 44-13619/HO-B Williams-Villain of the 487th FS, 352nd FG USAAF, UK mid 1944; flown by Lt Harry Barnes.

Sovereign 2 – Mustang   75

P-51D-10NA Mustang 44-14626 of the 118th TRS, 23rd FG USAAF, China January 1944; flown by Lt Col Edward McComas.

P-51K-5NT Mustang 44-11622/G4-C Nooky Booky IV of the 362nd FS, 357th FG USAAF, Belgium early 1945; flown by Maj Leonard 'Kit' Carson.

P-51K Mustang IV KH695/YT-E of 65 Squadron RAF, UK April 1945.

P-51H Mustang 44-64573 of the Maryland Air National Guard 1955.

RF-51K-5NT Mustang 44-11913 Tulie Scotty & ? of the 45th TRS USAF, Kimpo, South Korea 1951.

P-51D-25NT Mustang 45-11412 Butchie *of the 12th FBS, 18th FBW USAF, Korea 1952.*

CAC CA-18 Mustang Mk.22 A68-82 of 3 Squadron RAAF, Canberra 1948.

CAC CA-18 Mustang Mk.23 A68-123 of 77 Squadron RAAF, Korea 1950.

P-51D Mustang NZ2419 of 2 Squadron RNZAF, New Zealand February 1953.

F-51D Mustang FAD1917 of the Fuerza Aérea Dominicana, Santiago May 1982.

Modified Mustang unlimited category racer Dago Red *in the mid 1980s; set a new speed record of 517.079mph (832.135km/h) over 15km in 1982.*

Highly modified Mustang unlimited category racer N332 Stiletto *as it appeared at the 1985 races at Reno, Nevada as the reigning champion and flown by Skip Holm; was originally P-51D-25NT 45-11471.*

Cavalier Turbo Mustang III N6167U as test flown in 1968.

First prototype Piper PA-48 Enforcer N481PE 1983.

F-82G Twin Mustang 46-0363 of the 68th F(AW)S USAF, Suwon, Korea 1951.

1941-42

30 November 1942: First flight of the XP-51B prototype (41-37352) with Packard V-1650-3 engine, the aircraft converted by North American Aviation from a standard P-51/Mustang IA airframe. Bob Chilton was the pilot. Extensive trails against other USAF fighters (P-38J, P-39N, P-40N, P-47D and P-51A) revealed the P-51B's superiority over all of them in almost every area of performance and dogfight capability and resulted in orders for some 2,200 aircraft being placed.

The report on the trials concludes that the P-51B has "good performance at all altitudes, but above 20,000ft the performance improves rapidly, and its best fighting altitude is between 25,000 and 35,000ft. The rate of climb is outstanding, with an average of about 3,000 feet per minute from sea level to 25,000ft. Above 25,000ft, the overall fighting qualities of this aircraft are superior to those of all the other types used in the trials."

Performance figures obtained from the XP-51B flight trials (conducted at a relatively light weight) included a maximum speed of 453mph (729km/h) at 28,800ft (this more than 60mph/96km/h faster than the Allison powered versions) and a maximum climb rate at war emergency power of 3,900ft (1,189m)/min. Time to 20,000ft at the same power setting was 5.5 minutes and service ceiling 44,200ft.

December 1942: By the end of 1942, 21 Mustangs intended for delivery to the RAF had been lost when the ships carrying them had been sunk during the Atlantic crossing. The ships were sunk by U-Boats or German aircraft, usually Focke-Wulf Fw 200 Condors. Combat and operational losses accounted for the destruction of 28 RAF Mustangs during 1942 while no fewer than 40 others were lost to 'other causes', usually training accidents.

A further 20 were lost on operations in the first six months of 1943 plus 39 due to non-operational causes. Therefore, by the end of June 1943 the RAF had written off 127 Mustangs to all causes, or 148 if the aircraft lost with their ships during delivery voyages are included.

North American Aviation also performed Merlin conversions, sharing information with Rolls-Royce while the engine manufacturer's own work was underway. As the XP-51B and fitted with a Packard V-1650-3 Merlin, the prototype conversion (41-37352) first flew on 30 November 1942.

RAF MUSTANG SQUADRONS

Note: The table summarises the Royal Air Force operational squadrons which operated Mustangs between 1942 and 1947. The table's headings list the squadron number, marks of Mustang operated, the dates between which it flew Mustangs, squadron codes and areas of operation.

Sqdn	Mark/s	Dates	Code/s	Operations/Notes
2	I/IA/II	04/42-01/45	XV	UK, France
4	I	04/42-01/44	FY	UK
16	I	04/42-11/43	KJ/KY	UK
19	III/IV	02/44-03/46	QV	UK, France
26	I	01/42-06/45*	RM	UK (* flew Spitfire Vs 03/44-12/44)
63	I/IA	06/42-05/44	–	UK
64	III/IV	11/44-05/46	SH	UK
65	III/IV	12/43-05/45	YT	UK, France
93	III/IV	01/46-12/46	HN	Italy
112	III/IV	06/44-12/46	GA	Italy
118	III/IV	01/45-03/46	NK	UK
122	III/IV	02/44-08/45	MT	UK, France
126	III/IV	12/44-03/46	5J	UK
129	III	04/44-05/45	DV	UK
154	IV	02/45-03/45	HT	UK
165	III	02/45-06/45	SK	UK
168	I/IA	11/42-10/44	QC	UK, France, Germany
169	I	06/42-09/43	VI	UK
170	I/IA	06/42-01/44	–	UK
171	IA	09/42-12/42	–	UK
213	III/IV	05/44-02/47	AK	Italy, Yugoslavia, Palestine, Cyprus
225	I/II	05/42-08/43	–	UK, North Africa
231	I	04/43-01/44	–	UK
234	III/IV	09/44-08/45	AZ	UK
239	I	05/42-09/43	HB	UK
241	I	03/42-11/42	–	UK, North Africa
249	III/IV	09/44-08/45	GN	Italy, Yugoslavia
250	III/IV	08/45-01/47	LD	Italy
260	III/IV	04/44-08/45	HS	Italy
268	I/IA/II	03/42-08/45	–	UK, France (also had Typhoons 07/44-12/44)
285	I	03/45-06/45	–	UK, target towing, gunlaying training etc
303	IV	04/45-12/46	PD	UK (Polish)
306	III	03/44-01/47	UZ	UK (Polish)
309	I/IA/III	07/42-01/47*	WC	UK (Polish) * flew Hurricanes 02/44-10/44
315	III	05/44-12/46	PK	UK (Czech)
316	III	04/44-11/46	SZ	UK (Polish)
516	I	04/43-02/44	–	UK
541	III	06/44-04/45	–	UK
611	IV	01/45-08/45	FY	UK
613	I	04/42-10/43	SY	UK

Mustangs were also operated by Nos 400, 414, 430 and 441 (Canadian) Squadrons.

1943

The final Allison powered Mustang, the P-51A, first flew in February 1943 and deliveries began the following month, initially to the 311th FBG in India. 43-6016 was the 14th P-51A off the line.

January: The beginning of 1943 saw a massive expansion of the Mustang programme with large numbers of the new Merlin powered models on order for both the USAAF and RAF. Production rates would increase by enormous amounts, resulting in North American's already large Inglewood plant being further expanded and a new facility built at Dallas. B-25 Mitchell bomber production was progressively transferred to the company's Kansas City site and that of the AT-6 Texan/Harvard models to Dallas. Like the Mustang, both of these aircraft were subject to very large orders and the Merlin-Mustang was built at both Inglewood (P-51B) and Dallas (P-51C). The P-51D was later also built at both plants and the P-51K at Dallas only.

20 January: A No 400 (RCAF) Squadron Mustang I is shot down in error by an RAF Hawker Typhoon near the Isle of Wight when returning from a cross-Channel reconnaissance mission. This is one of several such incidents due to the early model 'razorback' Mustang's resemblance to the Messerschmitt Bf 109.

A Mustang I (AG528) of No 400 (RCAF) Squadron based in Britain. In one of several incidents where early model Mustangs were mistaken for Messerschmitt Bf 109s, one of the squadron's aircraft was shot down by a Hawker Typhoon on 20 January 1943. (via Neil Mackenzie)

1943

A-36A 42-83685 was delivered to Britain in March 1943 for evaluation and allocated the RAF serial number EW998. In this shot the aircraft is shown with underwing bombs and air brakes deployed.

22 January: Mustang Is of No 268 Squadron RAF escort RAF Mitchell bombers from Britain to targets in Holland. The raiders are intercepted by Focke-Wulf Fw 190s and one of these is shot down, although the squadron loses two Mustangs, one in aerial combat and one by flak. Four other RAF Mustangs (from other squadrons) are lost while performing bomber escort duties on this and the following day.

February: The first Mustang X (AL975) is fitted with a 1,655hp (1,234kW) Rolls-Royce Merlin 70 engine optimised for high altitude operations. A fin of increased chord was also fitted. This aircraft and the other Mustang X conversions were used to test several Merlin variants during their flying lives.

3 February: First flight of the P-51A Mustang (43-6003), the last production variant powered by the Allison V-1710 engine.

The A-36A began combat operations in the North Africa/Mediterranean area from early June 1943, aircraft of the 27th Fighter Bomber Group initially participating in the invasion of Sicily. This example was photographed in Tunisia.

12 February: Mustang Is of No 268 Squadron RAF fly out over the North Sea to attack the SS barracks at Amersfoort in Holland. A Dornier Do 217 is shot down during the raid, caught on approach to Soesterberg.

13 February: First flight of the Mustang II for the RAF (FR890), equivalent to the USAAF's P-51A.

March: First deliveries of the P-51A to the USAAF, initially to the USAAF's 311th Fighter Bomber Group in India. In the same month, production of the 500 A-36As ended ahead of the dive bomber variant entering operational service in June.

March: The 26th A-36A (42-83685) is delivered to the RAF for evaluation as EW998.

March: No 39 Army Co-operation Wing RAF at Dunsfold in Surrey and its three Mustang squadrons (Nos 400, 414 and 430 RCAF) take part in Exercise *Spartan*, designed to assess operational efficiency during mobile operations. Air and ground crews lived in tents in the English countryside during the exercise which also involved other squadrons including Nos 26 and 239 with Mustangs. The exercise was one of the many rehearsals and trials undertaken in preparation for the invasion of Europe.

5 March: Establishment of the USAAF's Fourteenth Air Force in China with Brig-Gen Claire Chennault as its Commander-in-Chief. The Fourteenth AF replaced the existing China Air Task Force, also commanded by Chennault.

9 April: The P-51/F-6A enters USAAF operational service when the Twelfth Air Force's 68th Observation Group in North Africa and begins flying armed reconnaissance sorties over the Mediterranean from Tunisia. The aircraft involved in this first Mustang operational mission by the USAAF was the 154th Observation Squadron's P-51/F-6A 41-37328 flown by Lt Alfred Schwab.

23 April: The first US Mustang is lost in operational

1943

The A-36A played an important role in the Italian campaigns of 1943 and later in the same year was deployed against the Japanese in Burma and India.

service when a 154th OS P-51/F-6A is shot down in error by 'friendly' ground fire. Misidentification of Mustangs as Messerschmitt Bf 109s was a common problem until the P-51D with its cut down rear fuselage and bubble canopy entered service. In Europe especially, Mustangs were fired on by Allied fighters and anti aircraft guns on several occasions.

April-May: Eight P-51s are 'borrowed' from the USAAF by the RAF for use on tactical reconnaissance and bomber escort duties by Nos 14 and 225 Squadrons in North Africa. No 225 Squadron was already a Mustang operator but No 14 was a bomber unit flying Martin Marauders at the time.

5 May: First flight of the first production Packard Merlin powered P-51B Mustang (42-106429) from North American's Inglewood, California factory.

17 May: Avro Lancasters of No 617 Squadron RAF attack the Ruhr dams in Germany – the famous 'Dambusters' raid.

1 June: RAF Army Co-operation Command (with its 17 Mustang squadrons) disbands in favour of a new Tactical Air Force (the 2nd TAF from November 1943) created to support ground forces in the planned cross-Channel invasion of Europe. The Air Officer Commanding (AOC) was Air Marshal Trafford Leigh-Mallory, the controversial former commander of Fighter Command's No 12 Group during the Battle of Britain.

The Tactical Air Force Mustangs were used extensively on *Ranger* operations in the second half of 1943, these flown by a pair of aircraft at low altitude, the pilots searching for targets of opportunity. These were often very successful with the Mustangs regularly taking enemy aircraft by surprise. Several pairs of pilots returned from missions with multiple 'kills' to their credit.

6 June: After having first arrived in the North Africa area in April, the USAAF Twelfth Air Force's 27th Fighter Bomber Group begins combat operations over Sicily with the A-36A and its three squadrons, the 522nd, 523rd and 524th. The 86th FBG and its three squadrons (the 525th, 526th and 527th FBSs) joined them the following month. Both Groups were extensively used during the invasion of Sicily landings in July and August. The 111th Tactical Reconnaissance Squadron equipped with P-51/F-6As was also operational in the area at the time.

17 June: Yet another case of 'Mustang misidentification' when Mk.I AP206 of 414 (RCAF) Squadron is shot down by Spitfires off the Scilly Isles.

June: The Joint Chiefs of Staff issue a directive for the start of Operation *Pointblank*, the round-the-clock bombing of German industrial targets – especially aircraft factories – by the USAAF and RAF.

June: After spending the first half of 1943 in the USA and Britain studying various types of aircraft for licence production in Australia for the Royal Australian Air Force, the general manager of the Commonwealth Aircraft Corporation, Lawrence Wackett, issues a detailed technical report on the Merlin engined Mustang. This report led to the P-51D being selected for manufacture by CAC as the only source of Mustang production outside the USA. The report is reproduced almost in full in the 'Mustang Described' chapter of this book and provides much information on the aircraft's physical and industrial characteristics.

June: Deliveries of the Merlin powered P-51B Mustang to the USAAF begin, these replacing the Allison engined models on North American's production line.

July: In the North Africa/Mediterranean area, the RAF establishes No 1437 Strategic Reconnaissance Flight with Mustang IIs, this unit forming part of No 285 Wing Desert Air Force along with two South African Air Force squadrons.

9-10 July: The opening phases of the Allied invasion of Sicily. The A-36As of the 27th and 86th Fighter Bomber

1943

ROLLS-ROYCE'S MUSTANGS

Rolls-Royce's test centre at Hucknall had a large number of aircraft powered by its engines on strength during World War II, these used for various tests, trials, evaluation and trouble-shooting purposes. Among them were 21 Mustangs of various models including those Mk.Is which were converted to the Merlin powered Mk.X prototypes. These are listed below:

Mk.I AG518: Delivered 29 May 1942 and used for general performance calibration and as the pattern aircraft for the Merlin installation conversions.

Mk.I AL960: Delivered 7 June 1943 and dismantled to provide parts for cancelled rear engined flying testbed project.

Mk.I AL963: Delivered 26 June 1942 and converted to Mustang X with Merlin 65 installation. First flight after conversion 21 January 1943. AL963 was then evaluated several times by the Air Fighting Development Unit (AFDU) at Duxford with various modifications incorporated. It was later fitted with a low altitude Merlin 66 and disposed of for spares in November 1944.

Mk.I AL975: Delivered 27 June 1942 and converted to Mustang X with Merlin 65 installation. It was the prototype conversion, first flown on 13 October 1942. AL975 was later fitted with a high altitude Merlin 70 for testing as well as investigations into the engine cutting out, oil loss and coolant system problems noted elsewhere. After being fitted with a Merlin 71, AL975 force landed after an engine failure on 14 March 1945 and was disposed of for spares.

Mk.I AM121: Delivered 7 June 1942 and converted to Mustang X with Merlin 65. First flight after conversion 7 February 1943. AM121 was subsequently evaluated by the USAAF Eighth Air Force's VIII Fighter Command.

Mk.I AM148: Delivered 9 June 1943 and dismantled to provide parts for a cancelled rear engined flying test bed project.

Mk.I AM203: Delivered 9 August 1942 and converted to Mustang X with Merlin 65. First flight after conversion 12 December 1942. AM203 was subsequently evaluated by the Aircraft & Armament Experimental Establishment (A&AEE) at Boscombe Down and the Air Fighting Development Unit (AFDU) at Duxford plus the USAAF's VIII Fighter Command. It flew for the last time on 27 October 1943 before being sent to a Maintenance Unit.

Mk.I AM208: Delivered 3 August 1942 and converted to Mustang X with Merlin 65. First flight after conversion 13 November 1942; subsequently tested by A&AEE.

Mk.I AM245: Delivered 6 June 1953 and dismantled to provide parts for cancelled rear engined flying test bed project.

Mk.III FB356: Delivered 23 June 1944 and used for performance investigation of +25lb boost.

Mk.III FX852: Delivered 11 November 1943 and used for investigations into engine breather oil losses. Force landed 19 July 1944 and disposed of.

Mk.III FX858: Delivered 19 October 1943 and used for fuel consumption tests and investigations into engine breather oil losses. Converted to Merlin 100 engine early 1944 and evaluated by A&AEE and AFDU.

Mk.III FX901: Delivered 13 October 1943 and used for investigations into engine breather oil losses and the effects of high internal temperatures on spark plug performance. Later fitted with a Merlin 113 running at +25lb boost.

Mk.III FX935: Delivered 10 July 1944 and used for +25lb boost clearance trails.

Mk.III FX945: Same history as FX935, above.

Mk.III FX984: Delivered January 1944 and fitted with new exhaust manifolds; no other information known.

Mk.III FZ185: Delivered 21 January 1944 and used for check flight re engine breather oil losses.

Mk.III HB890: Delivered 17 August 1944 and used for evaluation of the Rolls-Royce governor controlled fuel injection pump which operated at high (+25lb) boost.

P-51B 43-6557: Delivered 12 June 1944 from USAAF and fitted with a Spitfire type header tank and flame damping exhaust manifolds.

P-51B 43-12425: Delivered 7 October 1943 from USAAF and used for engine breather oil loss investigations; returned to USAAF 21 October 1943.

P-51D 44-14244: Delivered 31 August 1944 from USAAF and fitted with interconnected throttle and propeller controls; returned to USAAF 17 January 1945.

Mustang I AM121 was delivered to Rolls-Royce in June 1942 and converted to the fifth and last Mk.X with a Merlin 65 engine in February 1943. It was subsequently handed over to the USAAF's Eighth Air Force VIII Fighter Command, retaining its British serial number but also carrying the 'VQ' codes of the Air Technical Section. This mishap occurred while flying with that unit.

Sovereign 2 – Mustang

1943

The first production Merlin powered P-51B (42-106429) flew in May 1943 and deliveries began the following June. 43-12201 is a P-51B-1NA from the first production batch.

Groups were used to attack *Luftwaffe* airfields in the Gerbini area during the week leading up to the invasion and then defensive positions and lines of communications. Casualties were heavy, the two Groups between them losing 20 A-36As over a two-and-a-half week period.

16 July: The two USAAF Twelfth Air Force Fighter Bomber Groups involved in the invasion of Sicily (the 27th and 86th) are relocated to a newly built advanced landing strip at Licata on the island. From there, they flew intensive operations supporting the US Seventh Army until resistance on Sicily collapsed in mid August.

July-October: Even though a single A-36A dive bomber was supplied to Britain for evaluation in March 1943, the type was not adopted by the RAF. However, six were 'bor-

With Mustang production greatly increasing following introduction of the P-51B, production space was stretched. This virtually complete aircraft is having its finishing touches applied under camouflaged netting at Inglewood. (NAA)

1943

Mustangs on the production line at Inglewood. (NAA)

rowed' from the USAAF between July and October 1943 for use by the RAF's No 1437 Strategic Reconnaissance Flight operating from Tunisia, Malta and subsequently the Italian mainland. The A-36As had their nose guns removed and cameras fitted in the fuselage.

5 August: The first P-51C Mustang flies from North American's Dallas, Texas facility.

17 August: USAAF daylight raids on the ball bearings works at Schweinfurt and Messerschmitt factory at Regensburg with very heavy losses – in the case of Schweinfurt 60 bombers out of 376 or 16 per cent. These raids emphasised more than any others to that point (and those before had also seen heavy losses) that the USAAF's dream of high altitude daylight precision bombing was unattainable without fighter escort all the way to and from the targets in Germany. The P-47 Thunderbolt and P-38 Lightning were incapable of doing that if combat was involved, so the arrival of the first P-51B Mustangs in England two months later was extremely fortuitous.

August: RAF Tactical Air Force Mustangs fly extensive operations in support of Operation *Starkey*, beginning in late August and continuing into the first week of September. The operation was designed to test the strength of *Luftwaffe* forces in the Channel area by drawing them into the air, an amphibious force putting to sea and basically sailing around in circles in the middle of the English Channel.

Some of the Mustangs joined other aircraft in strafing attacks on airfields and other targets in France, while photo-reconnaissance missions were also undertaken. Unfortunately, the *Luftwaffe* failed to take the bait and the exercise was regarded as unsuccessful.

8 September: Italy surrenders and five weeks later declares war on Germany. Italy still has to be invaded by the Allies, however, as German forces remain in control of the country.

9 September: The start of Operation *Avalanche*, the Allied landings at Salerno on the Italian mainland. The A-36As of the Twelfth Air Force's 27th and 86th Fighter Bomber Groups are involved shortly after completing

A new P-51B-1NA Mustang (43-12342) undergoing engine runs on the flight line at Mines Field after emerging from the Inglewood factory in July 1943. (NAA)

Sovereign 2 – Mustang 85

1943

P-51B TEETHING TROUBLES

As with any new aircraft, the Merlin powered P-51B encountered a few teething troubles after it entered squadron service in Europe late 1943. Operational problems included jamming of the guns under manoeuvring 'g' loads due to a belt feed feed problem and the discovery that the cabin heating system was inadequate to prevent the canopy from misting up during long endurance, high altitude bomber escort missions.

Other problems revolved around the new Merlin installation itself, Rolls-Royce and Packard charged with the job of sorting them out. These included oil loss from the engine breather system (which apart from making a dirty aircraft resulted in reduced oil capacity, a potential problem on long range missions); discovery that the engine would not run in auto rich when the supercharger was in fully supercharged (FS) gear (this resulting in the engine cutting out in a cloud of black smoke, indicative of an overly rich mixture); and overheating of the coolant temperature due to the radiator matrix tubes silting up.

The oil loss problem was difficult to trace and was eventually found to be mainly the result of piston blow-by, in which combustion gases were being forced past the piston rings and into the engine crankcase, creating excessive pressure. The problem was found to be worse at high revs, boost pressures and altitudes.

Packard Merlins were found to suffer much more badly from this than Rolls-Royce engines. In addition, the air capacity of the oil tank was found to be too small, this in conjunction with a lack of anti-frothing devices causing the oil to become highly aerated. A new and larger capacity oil tank was designed, while coupling the rocker cover and crankcase breathers to a common pipe which vented below the radiator reduced oil deposits on the aircraft's windscreen. Rolls-Royce used six Mustangs in trials aimed at solving this problem.

The auto rich problem was caused by the engine having a boost control unit which was too small for the 2-speed/2-stage Packard V-1650-3 as it was from a single-stage V-1650-1. A temporary fix was achieved by fitting stronger springs in the unit's boost aneroid and relay piston.

As for the overheating coolant, it was found to be caused by a combination of using radiator matrix tubes in the Packard which were considerably narrower than standard British practice and also the use of an American specification glycol coolant which had a high phosphoric acid content in its inhibitor, this very quickly corroding the copper tubes.

These were just a small proportion of the often detailed problems that had to be sorted out to ensure the Mustang's operational effectiveness and safety.

---

their contribution to the invasion of Sicily in July and August (see above). The two units subsequently moved to bases in southern Italy and retained their A-36As until April 1944 when they were replaced by P-47 Thunderbolts.

October: Some P-51A Mustangs arrived in China during the month to fly with the 76th Fighter Squadron, one of the units which had its origins in the American Volunteer Group – Chennault's Flying Tigers. The 76th FS was part of the Fourteenth Air Force's 23rd Fighter Group and was joined by the P-51As of the 51st Fighter Group's 26th FS shortly afterwards.

At around the same time, the Tenth Air Force began receiving P-51As and A-36As for its operations against the Japanese in Burma and India. The Mustangs were assigned to the 311th Fighter Bomber Group.

1 October: Establishment of the 8th Photo Reconnaissance Group within the USAAF Tenth Air Force in Burma-India, the unit equipped with F-6 Mustangs plus F-5 Lightnings and F-7 Liberators, a reconnaissance version of the heavy bomber. These aircraft performed extensive armed photographic and visual reconnaissance sorties over China, French Indo-China, Burma and Thailand along with strafing missions and in the case of the fighters, escorting bombers.

8-14 October: A disastrous week for USAAF bomber forces when 148 aircraft and nearly 1,500 crew are lost during daylight raids on Bremen, Marienburg, Danzig, Münster and Schweinfurt once again. The second Schweinfurt raid was conducted on 14 October (which became known as 'Black Tuesday') and resulted in an unacceptable loss rate of more than 20 per cent among the 280 bombers which took part.

16 October: After operating in North Africa and the Mediterranean since November 1942, the Ninth Air Force is established in England to become the USAAF's tactical air force for the planned invasion of Europe.

23 October: Arrival in England of the personnel of the first USAAF P-51B unit, the 354th Fighter Group comprising the 353rd, 355th and 356th Fighter Squadrons. The Group was initially based at Greenham Common in Berkshire and then Boxted in Essex. It was officially part of the Ninth Air Force but at first operated with the Eighth Air Force pending the arrival of its own Mustangs. The 354th FG's P-51Bs arrived in Britain on 11 November.

November: Establishment of the RAF 2nd Tactical Air Force, part of the organisational structure being put into place for the planned invasion of Europe. All of the RAF's Mustang squadrons came under the control of the 2nd TAF.

November: The first operational use of underwing drop tanks on Mustangs when two 75 USgal (284 l) units are fitted to P-51As of the 311th Fighter Bomber Groups' 530th Fighter Bomber Squadron which was sent to Bengal to escort B-24s and B-25s on raids in the Rangoon area. The use of the tanks pre-empted that of the Eighth Air Force in Europe by a couple of weeks. The 530th was part of the Tenth Air Force's 311th FBG and had previously operated with its fellow squadrons (the 528th and 529th) from Assam in support of American and Chinese

1943

Two views of 43-12102, the second of two XP-51D prototypes. The first aircraft (43-12101) flew for the first time on 17 November 1943 and both were converted from P-51B airframes. This latest Mustang with its bubble canopy was immediately put into mass production. (via Neil Mackenzie)

1943

P-51As 43-6003 (the first of the model) and 43-6005 were tested on retractable skis at Ladd Field, Alaska to see if the idea was operationally feasible. It was, but no need for it developed. (via Neil Mackenzie)

ground troops. The squadron lost eight aircraft to Japanese fighters during its stint in Bengal.

15 November: Inexplicably, unpopularly (and temporarily), RAF Fighter Command is renamed Air Defence Great Britain (ADGB), leaving it and the 2nd Tactical Air Force as the two commands controlling most of the RAF's fighters. It only lasted for 11 months.

17 November: Maiden flight of the first of two XP-51D prototypes with cut down rear fuselage and bubble canopy (43-12101), both converted from P-51Bs.

25 November: Fourteenth Air Force P-51A Mustangs and P-38 Lightnings plus B-25 Mitchells of both the Fourteenth and the Chinese-American Composite Wing perform a successful attack on Shinchiku airfield on Formosa. Flying across the Formosa Strait at low level, the raiders achieved surprise and destroyed 42 Japanese aircraft on the ground for no losses.

1 December: The first P-51B mission in Europe, a sweep over the Belgian coast by 23 aircraft of the 354th FG, led Lt Col Donald Blakeslee, an experienced fighter leader on loan from the 4th FG which was equipped with P-47 Thunderbolts at the time. The 354th's CO, Lt Col Kenneth Martin, flew as Blakeslee's wing man.

5 December: The 354th FG's P-51Bs conduct the type's first bomber escort mission, providing cover for B-17s during a raid on Amiens, France.

13 December: The 354th FG's first long range escort mission, a flight to Kiel which involved a round trip of just under 1,000 miles (1,610km) and was operated in conjunction with P-38 Lightnings of the 55th FG. This was the longest fighter mission to have been flown by anyone up to that point.

16 December: The 354th FG's and P-51B's first 'kill'

Many Mustangs carried dual British/US markings either permanently or temporarily. P-51B/Mustang III FX883 was one of them, diverted from an RAF order to the USAAF in December 1943.

1943

THE MALCOLM HOOD

Until the P-51D and its bubble canopy came along, visibility from the Mustang's sideways hinging canopy was marginal, especially to the rear. This was a problem with all 'razorback' canopy/upper rear fuselage configurations of mid-late 1930s vintage such as the Hurricane, P-40 Warhawk and even the initial P-47 Thunderbolts of the early 1940s.

By the mid war period a higher level of pilot visibility was regarded as necessary, resulting in bubble canopies being developed for the Mustang, Thunderbolt and Spitfire. As an interim measure, British company R Malcolm Ltd developed a new canopy design as a retrofit to the Mustang III. It replaced the original canopy with a bulged sliding unit which improved visibility to the rear and downwards and had the secondary benefit of providing increased headroom for taller pilots.

Universally known as the 'Malcolm Hood', the new canopy was successfully tested and subsequently fitted to many RAF Mustang IIIs as they were delivered from the USA. Several USAAF Eighth and Ninth Air Force units based in Britain also obtained Malcolm Hoods for their P-51Bs and Cs.

Interestingly, many Mustang pilots preferred the Malcolm Hood to the P-51D's bubble canopy, especially in relation to the excellent downwards view it provided to the front and sides of the aircraft.

Mustang III FX893 displays the improved visibility Malcolm Hood sliding cockpit canopy fitted to many RAF (and some USAAF) Mustangs after delivery to Britain.

when Lt Charles Gumm of the 355th FS brings down a Messerschmitt Bf 110 during an escort mission to Bremen. Gumm went on to become an ace but was killed on 1 March 1944 when his Mustang crash landed after experiencing engine troubles on takeoff.

December: F-6B reconnaissance aircraft in service with the Ninth Air Force's 67th Tactical Reconnaissance Group (the 107th TRS) begin a series of photo-reconnaissance missions along the Channel coast as part of the D-Day landings preparations.

December: The Mustang III enters RAF service with No 65 Squadron at Gravesend, replacing the Spitfire IX in that unit. This squadron – along with Nos 19 and 122 Squadrons – making up No 122 Wing. A further 17 squadrons were equipped with the Mk.III over the next few months, in many cases replacing Mk.I/IA/IIs. The other RAF squadrons to fly the Mustang III were Nos 64, 93, 112, 118, 126, 129, 165, 213, 234, 249, 260, 306 (Polish), 309 (Polish), 315 (Czech), 316 (Polish) and 541.

31 December: The 354th FG flew its tenth mission on this day, its nearly four weeks of operational service resulting in an even balance sheet with eight German aircraft shot down for the loss of a similar number of Mustangs. Most of these had been to technical problems.

One potentially dangerous and constantly recurring problem was jamming of the guns when manoeuvring 'g' forces were being applied. This was obviously a major impediment to combat effectiveness and was exacerbated by the fact that early P-51Bs had only four guns. Modifications to the ammunition belts helped solve the problem.

Other technical problems which showed up during early P-51B operations included frosting up windscreens as the heating system was inadequate (remembering that escort missions were being flown at higher altitudes than before), coolant leaks and the fouling of spark plugs because of long periods with low throttle settings on these long range missions.

It wasn't only the aircraft that were being tested by these new high altitude, long range and long endurance missions. Fighter pilots were experiencing 4-5 hour sorties for the first time, causing numerous discomforts and physiological factors which had never arisen before.

THE AMERICAN MERLIN

Rolls-Royce and Packard concluded their agreement for the manufacture of Merlins in the USA in July 1940. The British company had originally wanted Ford to build the engine at its French subsidiary and after the fall of France in June 1940, in the USA. Henry Ford was pessimistic about Britain's chances – thinking she would also be defeated by Germany – and decided not to participate in the Merlin programme.

The initial contract with Packard covered 1,500 engines with options on a further 10,000. Packard ended up building 55,523 Merlins or just under one-third of the 168,040 total. Average unit price for the Packard engines was $US12,000.

The first Packard Merlin V-1650-1 was bench tested in August 1941. Production began shortly afterwards and the rate increased steadily to 600 per month by July 1942, 1,300 per month by July 1943 and peaked at 2,700 per month in July 1944. Total production for that year reached 23,169 engines at an average of 1,930 per month. The rate declined after that, reducing to 1,500 per month in July 1945.

Packard introduced several important innovations to the Merlin including the Bendix-Stromberg injection carburettor, automatic supercharger gear shifting, water-alcohol injection, a ball bearing main water pump (replacing Rolls-Royce's plain bearing unit), a centrifugal air/oil separator to prevent foaming, and a new high altitude magneto.

Reliability was improved by the introduction of silver-indium-lead main bearings instead of copper, and nickel-chrome plating of both intake and exhaust valves for improved heat resistance qualities. Improved cam followers, magneto gears lubrication and a redesigned drive shaft spline were other engineering developments introduced by Packard, many of these incorporated into Rolls-Royce's own Merlins. It wasn't a one-way street, however, with information on development, reliability and engineering issues flowing freely between the two companies.

Packard Merlins were used in the P-51B/C, P-51D/K, P-51H and CAC Mustangs, Australian and Canadian built de Havilland Mosquitos, Canadian Hawker Hurricanes, Curtiss P-40F and P-40L Warhawk, Avro Lancaster III, Supermarine Spitfire XVI and Avro Lincoln B.2. The first production standard V-1650-3 with 2-speed/2-stage supercharger – as used in the P-51B/C Mustang – was delivered in April 1943.

The Merlin was a liquid cooled 60deg vee-12. All variants had the same basic specification with a capacity of 27.0 litres (1,647cu in), cylinder bore 5.4in (137.16mm), piston stroke 6.0in (152.40mm), compression ratio 6.0:1 and max engine speed 3,000rpm.

Power variations resulted from the type of supercharger installed (1-speed/1-stage, 2-speed/1-stage or 2-speed/2-stage), the maximum supercharger boost and fuel octane rating (ranging from +6$\frac{1}{4}$lb/42$\frac{1}{2}$in Hg) with 87 octane in the early engines up to +18lb (66in Hg) in later models with 100 octane fuel.

The Merlin III as installed in the Supermarine Spitfire I produced 1,030hp (768kW) at optimum altitude, while up to 1,720hp (1,282kW) was available in the later engines, including the Packard V-1650-7 as fitted to the P-51D/K Mustang. Some special engines ran at up to +25lb (80in Hg) boost using 150 octane fuel and were capable of turning out over 2,000hp (1,491kW). The most powerful Packard Merlin was the V-1650-9 fitted to the P-51H Mustang with 2,218hp (1,654kW) available at war emergency power with water/methanol injection.

The basic characteristics of the various Packard Merlin versions are as follows:

V-1650-1: 2-speed/1-stage supercharger; maximum boost 60in Hg (+15lb); equivalent to Rolls-Royce Merlin 28/29; maximum power 1,300hp (969kW) for takeoff, 1,240hp (925kW) at 11,500ft, 1,120hp (835kW) at 18,500ft. Applications: Lancaster III, P-40F/L Warhawk/Kittyhawk, Canadian Hurricane, Canadian Mosquito, Australian Mosquito.

V-1650-3: 2-speed/2-stage supercharger; maximum boost 60in Hg (+15lb); automatic supercharger drive shift; Bendix-Stromberg injection carburettor; equivalent of Rolls-Royce Merlin 61; maximum power 1,380hp (1,029kW) for takeoff, 1,595hp (1,189kW) at 17,000ft, 1,295hp (966kW) at 28,750ft. Applications: P-51B/C Mustang.

V-1650-7: 2-speed/2-stage supercharger; maximum boost 66in Hg (+18lb); equivalent of Rolls-Royce Merlin 69; maximum power 1,490hp (1,111kW) for takeoff, 1,720hp (1,282kW) at 6,200ft, 1,565hp (1,167kW) at 17,250ft. Applications: P-51B/C/D/K Mustang, CAC Mustang, Australian Mosquito Mk.41.

V-1650-9: 2-speed/2-stage supercharger; maximum boost 70in Hg (+20lb) standard or 80in Hg (+25lb) war emergency; water/methanol injection; equivalent to Rolls-Royce Merlin 102; maximum power 1,830hp (1,365kW) for takeoff (wet), 2,218hp (1,654kW) at 10,200ft (wet, war emergency), 1,930hp (1,439kW) at 10,100ft (wet), 1,630hp (1,215kW) at 23,500ft (dry). Application: P-51H Mustang.

Packard Merlin 266: 2-speed/2-stage supercharger optimised for lower altitudes; maximum boost 66in Hg (+18lb); Bendix-Stromberg injection carburettor; interconnected throttle/propeller controls; equivalent to Rolls-Royce Merlin 66; maximum power 1,372hp (1,023kW) for takeoff, 1,702hp (1,269kW) at 5,500ft, 1,630hp (1,215kW) at 16,300ft. Application: Spitfire XVI.

V-1650-11: Proposed version with direct fuel injection for cancelled P-51L Mustang.

1944

The Merlin powered P-51B Mustang entered USAAF Eighth Air Force service in Britain during January 1943, initially with the 357th Fighter Group. 43-7116 (a P-51B-10NA) is pictured before delivery.

January: P-51D production initiated at Inglewood.

January: The P-51B enters operational service with the USAAF Eighth Air Force's VIII Fighter Command in Britain via the 357th Fighter Group and its three squadrons.

January: The USAAF Chief of Staff, General H H ('Hap') Arnold, issues a New Year directive that sets the scene for air operations over Europe – the quick destruction of the *Luftwaffe* as a prelude to the planned invasion. The directive was clear: "Destroy the enemy air force wherever you find them, in the air, on the ground and in the factories of Europe." By the end of March and following a period in which a very large number of German aircraft had been claimed destroyed, a slight weakening of Germany's aerial defences started to become apparent with some raids encountering reduced opposition.

4 January: The 354th FG and its P-51Bs starts to improve its kill-loss ratio during an escort mission over Kiel when 18 Bf 110s and Fw 190s are shot down for no losses.

6 January: Major-General James Doolittle takes over command of the Eighth Air Force from Maj-Gen Frederick Anderson. Doolittle introduced a major change to fighter escort tactics by giving pilots the freedom to sweep ahead of the bombers instead of staying rigidly close to them. This gave the fighters the ability to not only gain a tactical advantage but also to engage enemy aircraft before they were able to get into a favourable attacking position.

7 January: The USAAF orders four XP-82 Twin Mustang prototypes, North American's solution to the perceived need for a two seat, long range escort fighter for use in the Pacific. The basic design of the XP-82 involved joining two modified P-51H fuselages and outer wing panels by a new wing centre section and tailplane.

11 January: Major James Howard, commanding officer of the 354th FG's 356th FS (and a former 'Flying Tiger') becomes the first three kill Mustang 'ace', the first European Theatre of Operations 'ace in a day' and Congressional medal of Honour winner. Flying P-51B 43-6315 *Ding Hao*, Howard found himself the only US fighter near a B 17 formation which came under attack from between six and eight *Luftwaffe* twin engined fighters with about two dozen Bf 109s and Fw 190s in close proximity.

Howard immediately attacked the enemy aircraft in order to protect the bombers, shooting down a twin (probably a Bf 110), Bf 109 and Fw 190 during the 30 minute engagement and damaging several others. Although only three kills could be confirmed, US bomber crews claimed Howard got at least six. By the end of the battle, Howard's P-51B had only one gun working due to icing and jamming, the result of constant high 'g' manoeuvring.

Howard's Medal of Honour was awarded for displaying "conspicuous gallantry and intrepidity above and beyond the call of duty in action with the enemy near Oscheresleben, Germany". His single handed actions undoubtedly saved the B-17 formation.

February: Thirty P-51As previously used by advanced training outfits in Florida arrive in Burma to serve with the USAAF's 5318th Provisional Unit. This group operated a

1944

The RAF began receiving Mustang IIIs in February 1944, the type eventually equipping 16 squadrons. This aircraft is of No 260 Squadron, operating in Italy. (via Neil Mackenzie)

varied collection of aircraft to support operations behind Japanese lines, the Mustangs used mainly for ground attack duties with underwing 500lb (227kg) bombs or rocket tubes. The 5318th was subsequently renamed the 1st Air Commando Group and remained in Burma until May 1944 when it was transferred to India.

February: The P-51B/C Mustang III enters service with the RAF, initially with No 19 Squadron at Ford, Sussex and No 65 Squadron at Gravesend. Most RAF Mustang IIIs were retrofitted with the bulged 'Malcolm Hood' sliding canopy for improved visibility and pilot headroom, replacing the original sideways hinging canopy.

The Mustang III went on to equip 16 RAF Squadrons (Nos 19, 65, 66, 94, 112, 118, 122, 126, 129, 165, 249, 260, 306, 309, 315 and 316). Nos 306, 309 and 316 were Polish squadrons and No 315 Czech. Most were used initially for bomber escort duties and as fighter-bombers with the 2nd Tactical Air Force operating from bases in France after D-Day.

10-11 February: On escort missions to Brunswick and Frankfurt, the 354th FG claims 22 German aircraft destroyed for the loss of only two Mustangs. By now, four of the Group's pilots were aces – Lts Beerbower, Bradley, Gumm and Turner.

11 February: The Eighth Air Force's first official P-51B unit, the 357th FG, takes its aircraft on operations for the first time, flying a sweep over Rouen. Although the 354th FG had been operating with the Eighth AF since the previous December it was officially part of the Ninth Air Force.

14 February: First flight of the prototype lightweight XP-51F Mustang (43-43332). Two others were built (43-43333-43334), one of which was sent to Britain for testing as the Mustang V with serial number FR409.

14 February: The 4th Fighter Group begins converting from P-47 Thunderbolts to P-51B Mustangs. P-51B/C deliveries to the Eighth Air Force gradually increase as the production rate grows with more Fighter Groups swapping their P-47s and P-38 Lightnings for the Mustang. Nine Eighth Air Force Groups eventually flew P-51Bs and Cs: the 4th, 20th, 339th, 352nd, 355th, 357th, 359th, 361st and 479th. All were re-equipped by the middle of the year.

MUSTANG *SANS* PROPELLER

Like most military aircraft, the Mustang was used for various tests and trials. One of the more unusual was a series of flights conducted in 1944, using a towed P-51B with its propeller removed.

The National Advisory Committee for Aeronautics (NACA) was seeking to correlate wind tunnel model and full scale aircraft test results and modified the P-51B so it matched the one-third scale model as closely as possible. This involved removing external racks, sealing intakes, applying a hard waxed finish and removing the propeller. An electric motor provided power to run the hydraulic system so the pilot (James Nissen) could operate the undercarriage and other systems before and during his free flight tests in what was a Mustang glider. A tow rope was attached through the spinner.

The Mustang was towed into the air by a Northrop P-61 Black Widow, the two aircraft operating from a dry lake bed near Los Angeles. Three successful flights were carried out, the P-51B reaching up to Mach 0.75 in dives after the tow rope was released, with on board cameras recording the necessary data.

On the fourth flight the tow rope broke soon after takeoff and the Mustang was damaged beyond repair in the forced landing that followed. The trials ended there, NACA having in the meantime gathered sufficient data to confirm the accuracy of the wind tunnel tests.

1944

The Eighth Air Force's 361st Fighter Group began receiving P-51Bs in May 1944, operating from Botisham.

20-25 February: The 'Big Week' in Eighth Air Force parlance when its bombers flew 3,300 sorties in a concentrated series of attacks on German aircraft production facilities by day, while the RAF contributed five massive night attacks to the campaign. By then, the 357th was still the only Eighth AF Fighter Group equipped with P-51B/Cs and was heavily involved, scoring its first aerial victories in the process.

One of these raids – against aircraft factories in Leipzig on 20 February – set a new benchmark for the longest penetration by fighters to date, a 1,100 mile (1,770km) round trip involving the 354th FG's P-51Bs. The Group claimed 16 enemy aircraft destroyed for no losses on this trip which was also the biggest strategic air attack in history to that time, involving 941 bombers and 700 fighters. Factories in the Brunswick area were also attacked during the same raid.

22 February: By this date the 354th FG in Europe had recorded 115 kills after 84 days of operations, 12 of them on this day. This score was significant to the Group because there had been considerable competition between it and the 56th FG (equipped with P-47 Thunderbolts) which had claimed 100 *Luftwaffe* kills in 86 days during 1943. Rivalry of this kind between the P-51 and P-47 Fighter Groups was typical and sometimes intense.

February-March: F-6 Mustangs of the USAAF's 67th Photographic Reconnaissance Group based at Middle Wallop in England carry out extensive photography of a 160 mile (257km) stretch of the French coast, their low level oblique pictures giving those planning the invasion of Europe the opportunity to study Germany's Atlantic Wall defences in detail, along with considerable amounts of other information which would be useful to troop commanders.

The 67th PRG was assigned to the Ninth Air Force in October 1943 and its 12th and 107th Squadrons became operational in January 1944. The task was taken over by the 15th and 109th Squadrons in April 1944.

Mustang dambusters. On 5 May 1944, RAF Desert Air Force Mustangs and Kittyhawks operating from bases in southern Italy attacked the Pescara dam with bombs and breached it. Some of the pilots involved were photographed after the mission. (via Neil Mackenzie)

1944

Airmen fixing rockets to a Desert Air Force Mustang, this particular aircraft belonging to No 260 Squadron RAF. (via Neil Mackenzie)

March: The USAAF Fourteenth Air Force in Burma begins receiving P-51B Mustangs; operations start the following month (see below).

3 March: The first raid by the Eighth Air Force on the 'Big City' – Berlin – when P-38 Lightnings escorted a small force of 29 B-17 Fortresses to the German capital. Interestingly, this was an 'accidental' raid on Berlin, the aircraft which got through not having heard a recall order which had been issued due to poor weather.

4 March: Mustangs fly over Berlin for the first time when 770 fighters including P-47s, P-38s and P-51Bs of the 4th and 354th FGs (the latter still on assignment from the Ninth AF) escort 500 B-17s and B-24s on another raid. The 4th FG's Don Blakeslee led the fighters. The P-51Bs and P-38s claimed eight *Luftwaffe* fighters destroyed but losses were heavy with 23 US fighters failing to return from the mission which was reduced in effectiveness because of poor weather with only a small number of bombers reaching the target.

Reichsmarschall Herman Goering was stunned by the appearance of the Mustangs and Lightnings over Germany's capital, later commenting, "The day I saw American fighters over Berlin was the day I realised Germany would lose the war."

6 March: The first successful large raid on Berlin by the Eighth AF when 702 B-17s and B-24s escorted by 800 fighters attacked the city. Bomber losses were heavy (69 destroyed and 105 damaged, some written off as a result) while the fighters claimed 81 *Luftwaffe* aircraft for the loss of 11 of their own. The 357th FG's Mustangs were credited with 20 destroyed for no losses while the other two Mustang groups involved between them claimed 25 victories.

Even though these early operations in Europe had revealed some mechanical reliability problems with the Merlin-Mustang and the 'turnback' rate was high, the value of the aircraft due to its combination of range and dogfighting abilities had already been amply demonstrated.

March: The P-51D Mustang enters USAAF service.

26 March: P-51Bs of the 354th FG fly the first officially sanctioned tactical support mission with a dive bombing attack on the Creil marshalling yards in France. The aircraft carried a 500lb (227kg) bomb under each wing for the mission. From now, this type of operation became increasingly common for the Mustang units operating in Europe, especially those of the

Mustang III FB353/PK-H of No 315 (Polish) Squadron RAF. The squadron converted from Spitfires to Mustangs in March 1944 and was subsequently involved in D-Day operations and interceptions of V-1 flying bombs. (via Neil Mackenzie)

1944

Ninth Air Force. The Eighth AF's fighters also flew tactical missions but bomber escort remained their primary duty.

April: RAF Mustang IIIs begin operating with the Desert Air Force in Italy, initially with No 260 Squadron at Cutella, replacing Curtiss P-40 Kittyhawks. Other RAF squadrons to convert to Mustang IIIs over the next couple of months included No 213 in Egypt before moving to Italy for operations with the Balkan Air Force; and No 112 which relocated from Tunisia to Malta in July 1944 and then Italy to support the Allied armies there.

April: The USAAF Tenth Air Force's 311th Fighter Group begins operating P-51Bs from bases in India near the Burmese border, flying sorties in support of airborne troops attacking Japanese lines of communication in northern Burma, some 200 miles (320km) behind enemy lines.

A bombed up Mustang III of 122 Squadron RAF is waved off by its ground crew before another mission. The squadron operated from airfields in France after D-Day. (via Neil Mackenzie)

April: The USAAF Fourteenth Air Force based in China starts operations with P-51Bs in some units, these being used for escort missions over the southern Himalayas ('The Hump') and ground attack. Field modifications were devised to provide even more fuel capacity and external stores ordnance capacity via additional underwing pylons. Up to 569 USgal (2,154 l) could be carried including the rear fuselage tank and four 75 USgal (284 l) underwing drop tanks, this providing a maximum range of 2,700 miles (4,345km).

April: The USAAF Fifteenth Air Force's 31st and 52nd Fighter Groups based in Italy replace their Spitfire Vs with P-51Ds. Both had previously flown the British fighter in the North African campaign. Two more Fighter Groups in Italy – the 325th and 332nd – also re-equipped with Mustangs over the next two months. The 52nd FG was used in a tactical role with the Twelfth Air Force while the other three groups were attached to the Fifteenth Air Force with bomber escort as their primary duty, although the other three also occasionally engaged in this activity. P-51Ds were introduced when they became available.

The 332nd FG was something of a curiosity for its time because it entirely comprised black American pilots who were not permitted to fly with units manned by white people. It has been written that pilots of the 332nd had to "battle discrimination and the Third Reich at the same time". As an example, the unit's top scoring pilot, Lt Lee ('Buddy') Archer, had his score 'reassessed' when he got his fifth kill so he would not be recognised as an ace (his first was changed to 'shared'); and others were sent home early so they would not reach the magic 'five'. By one measure the 332nd was the most successful of all the USAAF Fighter Groups involved in bomber escort duties – not a single bomber under its protection was lost on operations.

5 April: As 1944 progressed, Mustangs operating over Europe were used more often in strafing attacks on enemy airfields. An early example occurred on this date when Mustangs of the 4th and 355th Fighter Groups attacked airfields near Berlin and Munich, respectively, claiming the destruction of 43 aircraft on the ground and 10 in aerial battles.

10 April: The 354th FG in Europe flies two missions on a single day for the first time. The first was a dive bombing attack in the morning and the second an escort mission with Martin B-26 Marauders in the afternoon.

18 April: The USAAF Ninth Air Force based in England reorganises, creating within it the IX and XIX Tactical Air Commands (TACs), each intended to provide support for separate US Armies after the Allies were established on the Continent. The Ninth provided most of the transports and troop carrying gliders involved in the Operation *Overlord* invasion of Europe as well as medium and attack bombers and fighter-bombers.

A Mustang III of No 250 Squadron RAF with long rocket rails installed. (via Neil Mackenzie)

Sovereign 2 – Mustang 95

1944

A captured P-51B is examined by German pilots and technicians at the facility at Oranienburg near Berlin.

21 April: The first USAAF raid on the Ploesti oil refineries in Romania carried out by B-24 Liberators. The 31st Fighter Group's P-51Ds were tasked with escorting the bombers home from the target area. Near Bucharest, a formation of B-24s was attacked by about 60 enemy fighters. The Mustangs took the attacking fighters by surprise, 'bouncing' them out of the sun and claiming 17 destroyed, seven probably destroyed and ten damaged in the ensuing battle. Two Mustangs were lost and the 31st FG was awarded a Distinguished Unit Citation for its success.

May: No 2 Squadron becomes the first RAF operational unit to fly the Mustang II, keeping them until the end of 1944 when they were passed on to 268 Squadron. The squadron had first equipped with Mustang Is in April 1942 and the Mk.IIs were operated as part of the 2nd Tactical Air Force in Europe.

May: The P-51D begins arriving in England to supplement the P-51B/C in the Eighth Air Force, eventually equipping the nine Fighter Groups already flying the earlier models plus five new Groups – the 55th, 78th, 353rd, 356th and 364th for a total of 42 squadrons. All were equipped with the P-51D between June and the end of 1944 with the P-51K also coming on line later in the year. By the end of June, four VIII Fighter Command Groups were equipped with the P-51D. All but one of the Eighth AF's P-47 Thunderbolt Fighter Groups were ultimately re-equipped with the Mustang.

5 May: Mustang Dambusters – Desert Air Force aircraft in company with P-40 Kittyhawks operating from southern Italy attack and breach the Pescara dam by using bombs. The resulting floods provided considerable protection to part of the 8th Army and allowed it to move troops to reinforce the Fifth Army without impediment. This in turn had a positive effect on the offensive intended to destroy German forces south of Rome.

15 May: The 354th FG moves to Lashendon in Kent in preparation for the D-Day landings. It also receives a Distinguished Unit Citation for introducing the Merlin-Mustang to service and for providing a high standard of bomber escort over the previous five months.

21 May: The number of attacks on enemy airfields in France and the Low Countries by the Eighth and Ninth Air Forces' fighters intensifies as D-Day draws closer. On this day, no fewer than 617 Eighth AF Mustangs, P-47 Thunderbolts and P-38 Lightnings attacked such targets

MUSTANG TARGET MARKER

One little known aspect of Mustang operations in World War II was its use by Group Captain Leonard Cheshire – commanding officer of No 617 ('Dambusters') Squadron RAF – as a target marker. Cheshire had at first used one of his squadron's Lancasters to accurately mark targets and then a de Havilland Mosquito. He reasoned that if the fast and relatively small Mosquito could be used for this task, why not an even smaller and faster aircraft?

Unable to obtain a Mustang from the RAF, Cheshire asked the USAAF if he could borrow one of theirs. His request was granted and a P-51D was duly delivered to 617 Squadron's base at Woodhall. Strangely, Cheshire – who was a bomber specialist – had never before flown a single engined fighter or indeed any kind of single engined aircraft since his basic training days. A side issue was the fact that he hadn't needed to do his own navigating for some time. In addition, the Mustang's standard underwing racks couldn't carry the smoke markers used on the targets, so the squadron's armourers had to quickly rig up a makeshift system.

Due to its late arrival and the need to modify the racks, Cheshire first climbed into the Mustang only half an hour before the bombers departed on their early July 1944 raid against the V-2 rocket site at Siracourt in order to at least get a bit of a feel for it. He was asking a lot of himself – flying a completely unfamiliar aircraft, performing his own navigation which by definition had to be absolutely precise (as did his timing despite the Mustang cruising considerably faster than the Lancasters), and not even having the benefit of a practice landing in the aircraft. And in this case, his first landing would be at night!

Needless to say, this 'Master Bomber' overcame all that and from 500 feet put his smoke markers within a few feet of the concrete slab which protected the underground V-2 storage site. The Lancasters and their 12,000lb (5,443kg) Tallboy bombs did the rest. It was a magnificent piece of flying by a man who would subsequently be awarded the Victoria Cross.

Cheshire used the Mustang twice more during July 1944, again marking German V-weapon sites for 617 Squadron. He was then temporarily taken off operations having completed his 100th mission, but his successor (Wing Commander J B Tait) also used the Mustang for target marking on several occasions.

1944

Production of the P-51K with Aeroproducts rather than Hamilton Standard propeller began at NAA's Dallas plant in July 1944.

claiming 83 enemy aircraft destroyed on the ground (plus 67 probably destroyed or damaged) along with 91 locomotives destroyed. More than 130 other targets were attacked including river shipping and railway stations.

2 June: The first of the deep penetration 'shuttle' raids in which the aircraft involved – including the escorting Mustangs – landed in Russia or North Africa after taking off from British or Italian bases. After refuelling and re-arming, targets would be attacked on the way home. These missions were conducted under the title Project *Frantic* and were intended to allow the bombing of targets which otherwise would have been out of range.

The first raid involved 30 B-17s and 70 Mustangs from the Fifteenth Air Force, the aircraft departing their Italian bases and bombing the marshalling yards at Debrecon in Hungary before flying on to Russia. Another early raid was against Romanian railway targets and the USAAF aircraft were escorted into Russia by Yakovlev Yak-9s.

Negotiation with Soviet authorities to allow the use of Russian bases by American aircraft were protracted and difficult, starting in December 1943 and not concluded until April 1944. Sometimes the Soviets created the impression they were reluctant allies, unless they wanted something! The Americans requested the use of six bases but only three were approved in a devastated area near Kiev and only one of these was entirely suitable for handling heavy bombers. Between April and May 1944, American engineers extended runways and built new base facilities in order to bring the run down airfields up to a usable standard.

4 June: Two days before D-Day and all aircraft involved with the Allied Expeditionary Air Force and the invasion of Europe are painted with conspicuous black and white stripes on their fuselages and wings.

6 June: D-Day and the invasion of Europe – Operation *Overlord* – begins. By then, five RAF squadrons still operated Mustang Is and IAs while nine USAAF Eighth Air Force Fighter Groups were equipped with P-51B/Cs. Extraordinarily, one RAF squadron – No 168 – still had the first Mustang I received by the RAF (AG346 in October 1942) on strength in June 1944 but it was shot down by flak on 20 August.

A P-51B fitted with 3-inch HVAR (high velocity aircraft rocket) tubes in triple mountings, these becoming the standard ordnance for ground attack sorties.

1944

Five RAF squadrons still flew early model Mustang I/IAs in the tactical reconnaissance role by the time of the D-Day landings in June 1944. (via Neil Mackenzie)

June: After D-Day, USAAF Mustang units in Europe were increasingly used for ground attack missions, usually carrying two 500lb (227kg) bombs under the wings but also rockets. Some were fitted with a cluster of three 'bazooka' tubes under each wing to carry 4.5in M-8 high explosive rockets. Up to ten zero length rails could also be fitted under the wings for 5in high velocity aircraft rockets (HVARs), this number reducing to six if drop tanks were carried.

15 June: USAAF Boeing B-29 Superfortress bombers of the newly activated XX Bomber Command under General Curtiss LeMay begin attacking the Japanese mainland from bases in China. These operations were generally unsuccessful and it wasn't until technical problems with the B-29 were sorted out and they were able to operate from captured islands in the south-west Pacific that effective bombing of Japan (with Mustangs escorting) became feasible.

21 June: A combined force of 61 Mustangs from the Eighth Air Force's 4th and 352nd Fighter Groups provides a telling demonstration of the fighter's range capabilities when it escorts 163 B-17s from Britain to oil installation

1944

Multiple ace Captain Don Gentile of the Eighth Air Force's 4th Fighter Group in his P-51B 43-6913/VF-T Shangri-La. This photograph was taken on 8 April 1944, five days before Gentile completed his final operational mission and hit the runway during a low level pass at the end of it, breaking the Mustang's back. He then returned to the USA. Gentile scored 21.83 aerial 'kills', of which 15.5 were in the Mustang, 2 in Spitfires and 4.33 in Thunderbolts.

targets near Berlin and then fly on to bases in Russia. The distance involved was 1,470 statute miles (2,722km) and the flying time just under 7½ hours. The Mustangs then flew to Italy where they were temporarily attached to the Fifteenth AF to fly escort missions. The Mustangs were led by Lt Col Don Blakeslee.

For the B-17s, this mission made a major contribution to the Eighth Air Force suffering its highest number of losses in a 24 hour period. Even though all the bombers made it safely to their Russian base at Poltava – despite the formation being attacked by 25 Bf 109s en route – the base was heavily bombed by the *Luftwaffe* on the night the bombers were sitting on the ground. Forty-seven were destroyed and the remainder damaged. That in combination with other losses sustained on the same day in other operations brought the Eighth's loss tally up to no fewer than 91 aircraft.

25 June: The first RAF 2nd Tactical Air Force Mustang squadrons to move across the Channel to an advanced landing ground in Normandy are Nos 19, 65 and 122 at B.7 Martagny. No 168 followed four days later but the plan to move all of the 2 TAF Mustang squadrons to France was delayed due to the appearance of V-1 'flying bombs' over Britain two weeks earlier. The Mustang units allocated to dealing with the V-1 threat between them accounted for 254 in the two months period from mid June.

June: One of the 354th FG's P-51Bs (43-6877) was modified late in the month to incorporate a second seat behind the pilot in the space where radio equipment was normally located. The modification was performed at the request of the Supreme Allied Commander, General Dwight Eisenhower, who wanted to view the Normandy battlefields from the air. Eisenhower flew in the aircraft for the first time in early July.

June: Between D-Day and the end of the month the RAF Mustang squadrons operating over Normandy lost 63 aircraft in the face of a resurgence in German fighter opposition.

PAPER FUEL TANKS

One largely unsung but significant piece of kit developed for the Mustang was designed and built in Britain – the paper drop tank. The need for a larger drop tank than the standard 75 USgal (284 l) unit led to the USAAF Eighth Air Force asking one of its base depots to design such a tank. The task was taken on by British engineers Thomas O'Reilly and André Rousseau with the assistance of the chief engineer of British tank manufacturing firm Pytram Ltd.

The design for a 108 USgal (409 l) tank was quickly penned, but it was immediately realised that there was insufficient spare aluminium in Britain to meet the demand and shipping from the USA would be impractical. The decision was therefore taken to make the tanks out plastic impregnated compressed paper held together by glue. Experiments on using paper as a potential fuel tank material had been carried out in both Britain and the USA during the 1930s.

The concept was enormously successful and mass production was undertaken by two British firms assisted by 45 small sub-contractors at a peak rate of 24,000 per month. Fuel could not be stored in the tanks for more than a couple of days before the paper and glue began to come apart, but this did not matter as they were filled only shortly before takeoff and jettisoned during the mission after use.

Even if jettisoned over occupied territory the tanks contributed nothing to the enemy's war effort (unlike aluminium), and they could also be used as an incendiary weapon, pilots quickly learning to drop full tanks onto a target during a skip bombing run and then ignite the fuel with machine guns.

As is often the case with good, simple and practical ideas such as this, officialdom was somewhat tardy in recognising its merits. Even after 50,000 of the tanks had been successfully used in combat, the US War Department sent the Eighth Air Force a memo stating the idea was unworkable and that the tanks should not be acquired!

1944

P-51B-15NA 42-106923 of the Eighth Air Force's 357th FG, 364th FS undergoes some maintenance. The 357th was the first USAAF Group to fly the P-51B in Britain.

June: The RAF establishes the Balkan Air Force, the Mustangs of Nos 112 and 260 Squadrons moving to Crete the following month to join it. The new force's main intention was to operate in support of Marshal Tito's Yugoslav partisan forces. It carried out numerous attacks against rail traffic in Yugoslavia and northern Greece. In its first month of operations the Balkan Air Force's Mustangs and Spitfires destroyed or damaged a claimed 262 locomotives, of which many were pulling troop trains at the time of the attacks.

July: Production of the P-51K starts at Dallas, this variant similar to the P-51D but with an Aeroproducts rather than Hamilton Standard propeller. P-51Ds were also built at Dallas.

22 July: The 31st Fighter Group's P-51Ds are used on another escort mission to the Ploesti oil refineries in Romania (see 21 April, above), this time escorting bomb carrying P-38 Lightnings of the 82nd FG. The Mustangs flew on to Piryatin in Russia after completing the mission.

24 July: One of the war's largest air battles involving RAF Mustangs when No 65 Squadron Mk.IIIs encountered about 40 Focke-Wulf Fw 190s and Messerschmitt Bf 109s over France. Nine German fighters were shot down at a cost of four Mustangs.

25 July: Flying from Russia, the 31st Fighter Group and its P-51Ds earn a second Distinguished Unit Citation in the space of three months following the destruction of almost an entire *Luftwaffe* dive bomber wing. The action occurred when 35 Mustangs were escorting P-38s on a ground attack mission against the German held airfield at Mielec in Poland. On the return flight the American aircraft came across 36 Ju 87 Stukas on their way to bomb the Russian lines. Stukas were highly vulnerable to fighters even when unladen – bombed up it was a case of 'shooting fish in a barrel' and 27 of them were shot down in the space of a few minutes. The 31st FG returned to its normal base in Italy the following day.

28 July: Mustang pilots of the Eighth Air Force's 359th Fighter Group encounter the Messerschmitt Me 163 Komet rocket powered interceptor for the first time during an escort mission over Germany.

9 August: Mustangs of the 359th Fighter Group once again encounter Messerschmitt Me 163 Komet rocket fighters while escorting B-17s over Germany. One of the Komets is shot down by Lt Col John Murphy. Six others were subsequently destroyed by USAAF pilots and one by an Australian, Flg Off John Haslope, flying a Mustang III of 165 Squadron RAF in April 1945 (see separate breakout story).

10 August: First flight of the first of two prototype lightweight XP-51G Mustangs (43-43335), similar to the XP-51F but with a highly boosted Rolls-Royce (rather than Packard) Merlin. Some historians now doubt this date (with Ed Virgin as the pilot) is correct, with 9 August (Joe Barton at the controls) and 12 August (Bob Chilton) also quoted.

The second XP-51G (43-43336) was sent to Britain for testing by the Aircraft and Armament Experimental Establishment (A&AEE) at Boscombe Down and allocated the RAF serial FR410. For some reason the aircraft was dubbed 'Mustang IV' by the RAF, the same designation as the P-51D/K in British service, although there were few similarities between the two versions. Testing at Boscombe Down was completed in February 1945.

18 August: Mustang IIIs of No 315 (Polish) Squadron RAF attack about 60 *Luftwaffe* fighters taking off and landing at Beauvais airfield during a sweep over occupied France. During the 15 minute fight the Mustangs shot down 16 Fw 190s including three by the squadron's commander, Sqn Ldr Eugeniusz Horbaczewski. He went into the battle with 13 kills to his credit including 2½ on Mustangs, but was himself shot down and killed during the action.

100 Sovereign 2 – Mustang

1944

25 August: Now based in France and still flying P-51Bs, the 354th FG was engaged mainly in ground attack and fighter sweep operations. On this day it carried out six sweeps and destroyed 51 German aircraft, earning its second Distinguished Unit Citation as a result. Very much against its wishes, the pioneer Merlin-Mustang operator in Europe was re-equipped with P-47 Thunderbolts in November but following a series of protests to the powers-that-be, got its Mustangs back (P-51Ds this time) in February 1945.

31 August: Mustangs of the 52nd Fighter Group attack the *Luftwaffe* airfield at Reghin in Romania, destroying over 150 aircraft on the ground during multiple passes.

September: No 5 Squadron South African Air Force begins operating its Mustang IIIs from bases in Italy, these aircraft replacing P-40 Kittyhawks.

5 September: By this date, RAF Mustangs had been credited with the destruction of 232 V-1 'flying bombs' over Britain.

October: Air Defence Great Britain (ADGB) – established by renaming Fighter Command in November 1943 – reverts to its previous evocative title after a period of enormous unpopularity with RAF members and the public. The original decision to revive the ADGB name (which had been used prior to 1936) was seen as a major mistake by the British Air Ministry and one which had a detrimental effect on morale.

9 October: The Eighth Air Force scores its first Messerschmitt Me 262 kill when Lt Urban Drew of the 376th Fighter Squadron shoots down one of the new jet fighters.

10-17 October: With the threat to US bomber formations from the Messerschmitt Me 262 jet fighter growing, Eighth Air Force B-24s, B-17s and Mustangs performed a series of major 'jet fighter affiliation' exercise with four Gloster Meteors from No 616 Squadron RAF. Flying in normal formations, the 120 bombers involved were subject to simulated attacks by the Meteors, giving the

P-51D-15NA 44-14985 The Millie G of the 55th FG/343rd FS, flown by Ed Giller.

A trio of 356th FG/360th FS Mustangs with P-51D-10NA 44-14300 nearest the camera.

P-51D-5NA 44-13763 of the 361st FG/376th FS. Note the invasion stripes and the lack of dorsal fin fillet on this aircraft. Squadron code is E9-O.

(right) P-51D-5NA Mustangs of the 357th FG/362nd FS, all three aircraft in the background (44-1334, 44-13719 and 44-13596) lacking fin fillets.

Sovereign 2 – Mustang

1944

The first of two XP-51G lightweight Mustang prototypes flew in August 1944.

Mustang crews and the bombers' gunners a chance to work out tactics. The not surprising discovery was that having a height advantage gave the Mustangs a chance to negate their level flight speed deficit by being able to dive on the attackers. They needed to be 5,000ft higher than the jets to achieve this. By the end of the week's trials the Mustang pilots were regularly achieving successful interceptions of the Meteors and the tactics devised were applied to operations.

20 October: US landings in the Philippines begin.

November: No 3 Squadron Royal Australian Air Force based at Fano in north-eastern Italy replaces its P-40 Kittyhawks with Mustang IIIs and IVs. No 3 Squadron was part of the RAF's 239 Wing which was commanded by Australian Group Captain Brian Eaton. Eaton had recorded a notable achievement in September 1943 when he became the first Allied pilot to land on Italian soil.

November: The first Mustangs to serve in the South-West Pacific Area (SWPA) arrive at their base on the island of Morotai. They were F-6D reconnaissance aircraft operated by the 82nd Tactical Reconnaissance Squadron, replacing Curtiss P-40s. The 110th TRS also replaced its P-40s with F-6Ds, but not until February 1945.

6 November: Captain Charles ('Chuck') Yeager of the 357th Fighter Group shoots down a Messerschmitt Me 262 jet while leading a flight of Mustangs near Osnabrück. It took several attempts to score the kill. A group of three 262s was bounced by the Mustangs from a greater height, Yeager scoring hits on one of them before all three used their superior speed to pull away. The

P-51D production was initiated at Inglewood in January 1944 and at Dallas the following July, the same time as the P-51K. The rate quickly built up to a level considerably higher than had been achieved with the earlier Mustang models, the P-51D/K accounting for nearly two-thirds of all production. P-51D production ended immediately following Japan's defeat in August 1945. (NAA)

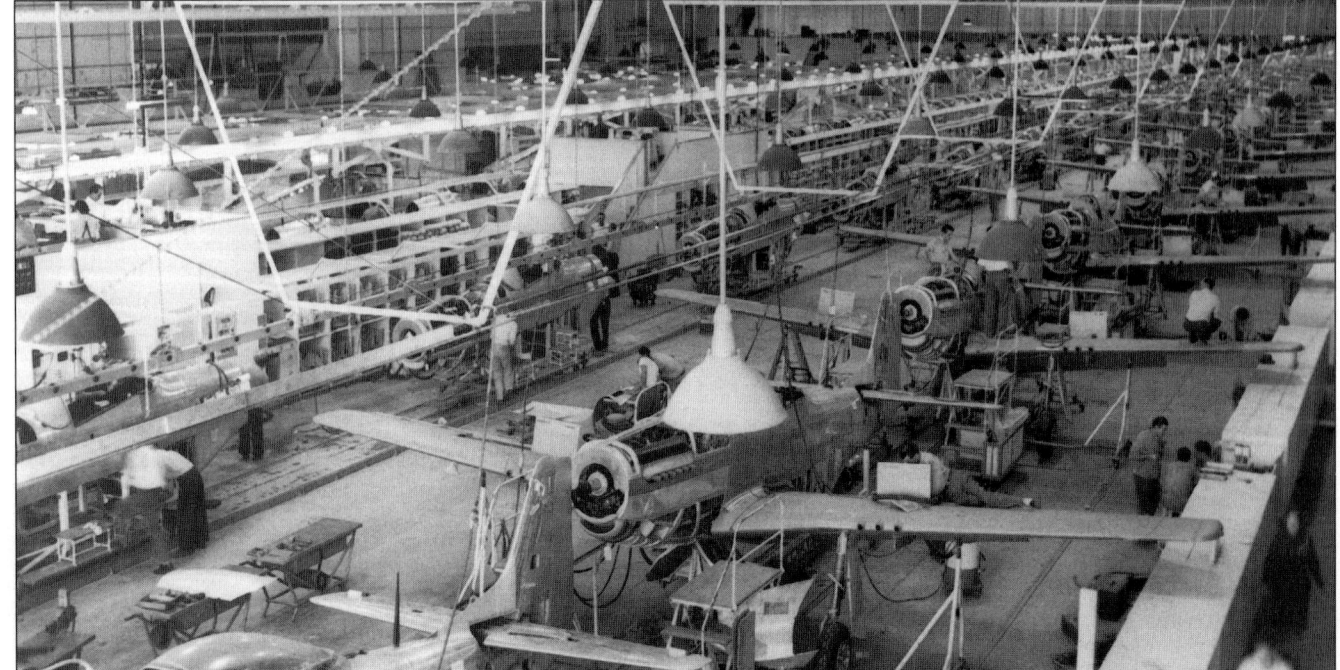

1944

same thing happened with the trio of 262s a few minutes later, Yeager this time hitting the leader before the jets escaped.

Finally, and ignoring intense anti aircraft fire, Yeager attacked another 262 which was approaching to land. Diving at 500mph (805km/h), he fired a burst into the jet fighter which came down short of the runway. Yeager ended the war with 11½ kills to his credit (including five in a single sortie later in November) and in October 1947 became the first man to officially exceed the speed of sound, flying the rocket powered Bell X-1.

15 November: The start of trials to assess the suitability of the Mustang for carrier operations when Lt R M Elder, USN makes the first of a series of unassisted takeoffs and arrested landings aboard USS *Shangri-La*. The P-51D (44-14017) was fitted with an arrester hook under the rear fuselage. Although the trials were successful, the Mustang was not adopted for use as a naval fighter. The test aircraft was subsequently fitted with a P-51H style tall fin and rudder and converted to a two seater as an ETF-51D.

21 November: One of the biggest air battles of the bombing campaign when the Eighth Air Force sends 1,291 B-17s on raids over Germany, mainly on Merseburg. The bombers are escorted by 954 fighters (most of them Mustangs) and are met by 300 *Luftwaffe* fighters. These sorts of numbers were common during November and the first part of December – very large raids met by stern opposition from the *Luftwaffe*. The Germans suffered heavy losses, a 26 November raid on oil installations near Hanover resulting in a claimed 114 enemy aircraft destroyed. After the first week of December the *Luftwaffe* suddenly disappeared from the skies as Germany gathered its forces together for a last ditch offensive a week or so later – the Battle of the Bulge.

December: RAF Mustang squadrons are taken out of the 2nd Tactical Air Force in Europe and transferred back to Fighter Command in Britain. From now, their duties include flying escort for Bomber Command's increasing number of daylight missions over Germany, Coastal Command's anti shipping strikes off the coast of Norway and accompanying Mosquito squadrons on their precision raids on targets in occupied Europe.

December: The Fifth Air Force's 3rd Air Commando Air Group begins P-51D operations, flying from the Philippines.

16 December: Germany launches its last major offensive of the war, the Battle of the Bulge in the Ardennes. The Allied air response was delayed for a week due to persistent very poor weather.

22 December: The USAAF Fifteenth Air Force based in Italy records its first jet 'kill' when Mustangs flown by the

A sequence of four photographs from a Mustang's gun-camera as it pursues and destroys a Focke-Wulf Fw 190 at low level. Claiming air superiority over the Luftwaffe was a major task for Allied fighters in 1944-45.

MATTERS OF BOOST

The use of the word 'boost' when talking about engine superchargers such as those installed in the Rolls-Royce and Packard Merlin results from the supercharger impeller which was driven off the rear of the engine's crankshaft through a series of gears. The impeller established a positive pressure in the engine's induction system.

This positive pressure was referred to as 'boost' and measured in pounds per square inch (psi) by the British and inches of mercury (in Hg) by the Americans.

The standard atmospheric pressure of around 15psi was taken as the datum point and called zero by the British, variations up and down measured as plus or minus so many pounds of boost. When an engine is noted as producing 1,546hp (1,167kW) at +15lb boost, for example, it is really operating at +30lb taking the standard atmospheric pressure into account.

Similarly, cruise power settings may see a negative boost figure. The minimum fuel consumption setting for the Spitfire V with Merlin 45 engine is listed as -4lb boost at 1,800rpm, the figure implying an impossible negative boost figure but in reality meaning +11lb.

The Americans take 30 inches of mercury as the datum point or zero (standard atmospheric pressure again) with each pound of boost equal to about 2 inches of mercury. Therefore a Rolls-Royce Merlin 66 produced its maximum power at +18lb boost while the US built Packard Merlin 266 equivalent produced the same power at 66 inches of mercury, remembering that 30in is the starting point, 18 x 2 = 36, and 36 + 30 = 66. All perfectly simple....!

Sovereign 2 – Mustang

1944

Allied air power in Europe was substantial from 1943 as the Americans began to arrive in ever larger numbers. This 1944 shot shows P-51Bs of the Eighth Air Force's 361st FG/376th FS. (via Neil Mackenzie)

P-51A Mustangs of the USAAF's 1st Air Commando Group over Burma in 1944.

No 3 Squadron Royal Australian Air Force based at Fano in Italy began replacing its P-40N Kittyhawks with Mustangs in November 1944 as the first RAAF unit to operate the type. This bombed up Mustang III is KH624. (via Neil Mackenzie)

1944

Christmas Day 1944 saw the death of Eighth Air Force ace Major George Preddy in P-51D 44-14906 Cripes A'Mighty. *Preddy scored 26.83 confirmed aerial victories with the 352nd FG/328th FS, all but the first three in a quartet of Mustangs named* Cripes A'Mighty. *In August 1944 Preddy shot down six Messerschmitt Bf 109s in a single sortie. This photograph was taken after that action. The aircraft is P-51D 44-13321* Cripes A'Mighty 3rd.

31st Fighter Group's Lts Eugene McGlauflin and Roy Scales shoot down a Messerschmitt Me 262.

23 December: Lt Col Edward McComas of the Fourteenth Air Force's 118th Tactical Reconnaissance Squadron claims six Japanese Nakajima Ki-43 Hayabusa (Oscar) fighters within an hour. McComas was leading a flight of 16 Mustangs back from an attack on the Wuchang-Hankow ferry terminals and strafed the Japanese airfield at Wuchang, destroying two aircraft on the ground and an Oscar in the air as he was departing the area. He also decided to strafe the airfield at Ehur Tao Kow and found more Oscars, shooting down five, two of them just as they became airborne in an attempt to intercept him.

24 December: The Battle of the Bulge produces the largest air strike of World War II when the USAAF's Eighth and Ninth Air Forces plus the RAF's 2nd Tactical Air Force attack enemy targets. The Eighth AF alone put up 2,046 heavy bombers escorted by 853 fighters. Allied fighters claimed 74 German kills for 10 losses.

25 December: Christmas Day 1944 was not a good one for the Eighth Air Force with the loss of Major George E Preddy, the seventh ranking USAAF ace of the war with 26.83 confirmed kills (25 plus four shared). The 352ndFG/328th FS pilot joined combat with a pair of Messerschmitt Bf 109s while patrolling near Koblenz in his P-51D. Preddy downed both of them to record his last two kills and then set out after a Focke-Wulf Fw 190 at low level. Both aircraft ran into heavy American machine gun ground fire. Preddy and his aircraft were hit, mortally wounding the pilot, the Mustang crashing into the ground at high speed. Preddy scored his first three victories in P-47 Thunderbolts but the remainder were in several blue nosed Mustangs all named *Cripes A' Mighty*. He had received the Distinguished Service Cross in August 1944 following an escort mission during which he shot down six Bf 109s.

Mustangs and Thunderbolts undergoing work at the Fifth Air Force's repair depot at Lingayen. The stripes on the wings are for identification purposes.

1944

THE US ARMY AIR FORCES

Eighth Air Force Mustang – P-51D-5NA 44-13926/E2-S of the 361st FG/375th FS.

With the establishment of the autonomous US Army Air Forces in June 1941 came not only a new name but a new philosophy for US air power based on preparing for a 'global mission'. Its basis was centralised planning and decentralised execution of directives through a number of regional Air Forces within the overall USAAF structure. In other words, the new system was preparing for what President Franklin Roosevelt considered to be an inevitable involvement in a global conflict. Its activities involved not just operational units but also the very necessary training, maintenance, supply, airfield construction, planning and support organisations.

A brief summary of the various US Air Forces is presented below.

First Air Force

Established at Mitchell Field, New York as the Northeast Air District in October 1940 and renamed First Air Force in 1941. It provided air defence for the eastern USA, trained new organisations and later on trained replacements for combat units. Apart from providing air defence for the eastern USA, the First's two Antisubmarine Wings also conducted patrols from bases in the USA, Newfoundland, Caribbean, north-west Africa and England until late 1943.

Second Air Force

Established at McChord Field, Washington State as the Northwest Air District in October 1940 and renamed Second Air Force in 1941. It provided air defence and also served as a training organisation, from 1942 mainly engaged in training replacements for heavy bomber and then very heavy bomber (B-29) units.

Third Air Force

Established at MacDill Field, Florida as the Southeast Air District in October 1940 and renamed Third Air Force in 1941. It had air defence responsibilities in 1940-41 and carried out anti submarine operations for a year from 1941. After that, the Third's major responsibility was training units, and air crews for bomber, fighter and reconnaissance operations.

Fourth Air Force

Established at March Field, California as the Southwest Air District in October 1941 and renamed Fourth Air Force in 1941. Like the US based First, Second and Third Air Forces, the Fourth provided air defence in its region (until 1943) as well as training, later the replacements for combat units.

Fifth Air Force

Established at Nichols Field, Luzon in the Philippines as the Philippine Department Air Force in August 1941, then renamed Far East Air Force in October 1941 and finally Fifth Air Force in February 1942.

Following Japan's defeat of US forces in the Philippines in late 1941, the Air Force lost most of its men and equipment and moved headquarters to Darwin, Australia. It relocated to Java in January 1942 in an attempt to help slow the Japanese advance in the Netherlands East Indies. Following Japan's successful invasion of the NEI, the Fifth temporarily ceased to function before re-establishing itself at Brisbane, Australia in September 1942 under the command of Lt-Gen George Kenney.

From Brisbane, the Fifth took control of USAAF organisations in Australia and New Guinea, participating in operations in that area and to the north before re-establishing itself in the Philippines from November 1944, firstly at Leyte then Mindoro and finally Clark Field. The Fifth moved to Okinawa in July 1945 and then Irumagawa, Japan in September following the surrender.

During 1944-45, the Fifth Air Force's V Bomber and V Fighter Commands controlled five Fighter Groups (the 8th, 35th, 49th, 348th and 475th); three Night Fighter Groups (418th, 421st and 547th); ten Bombardment Groups; two Recconnaissance and Photographic Groups; and four Transport Groups.

Sixth Air Force

Established at Albrook Field in the Canal Zone as the Panama Canal Air Force in October 1940, renamed Caribbean Air Force in August 1941 and Sixth Air Force in February 1942. The Sixth's main role was to provide air defence for the Panama Canal but it also undertook some anti submarine operations.

Seventh Air Force

Established at Fort Shafter, Hawaii, as the Hawaiian Air Force in October 1940 and renamed Seventh Air Force in February 1942. By then, the Seventh was headquartered at Hickam Field, Hawaii and remained there until December 1944 when it moved to Saipan and finally to Okinawa in July 1945. The Seventh provided air defence for the Hawaiian Islands but also had detachments operating in the central and western Pacific areas.

In 1945 the Seventh's VII Bomber and VII Fighter Commands had eight Fighter Groups (the 15th, 21st, 318th, 508th, 423th, 424th, 506th and 507th, of which the last four were attached from elsewhere); two Night Fighter Squadrons (548th and 549th); five Bombardment Groups; two Photographic Reconnaissance Squadrons (28th and 41st); one transport squadron and one liaison squadron.

Eighth Air Force

The Eighth is probably the best known of the US Air Forces in World War II due to its leading role in the bombing campaign against Germany. A huge organisation operating from no fewer than 129 airfields in England, the Eighth subsequently also flew from France and Germany after D-Day.

Mustang naval fighter. P-51D 44-14017 was used for aircraft carrier suitability trials aboard the USS Shangri-La *in November 1944. The flights were undertaken by Lt R M Elder USN, and although successful the Mustang remained a land based fighter.*

Established at Savannah, Georgia in January 1942 as VIII Bomber Command, an advanced detachment arrived in England the following month and bombing operations began in August 1942. The Eighth's first commander was Maj-Gen Ira C Eaker, those who followed including Brig-Gen Newton Longfellow (December 1942), Maj-Gen Frederick Anderson (July 1943), and Lt-Gen James Doolittle (January 1944-May 1945 and July-September 1945). Commands within the Eighth Air Force were VIII Bomber Command, VIII Fighter Command and VIII Air Support Command.

VIII Bomber Command conducted operations until February 1944 when it came under the control of the newly established US Strategic Air Forces in Europe, this also incorporating the Fifteenth Air Force's heavy bomber groups. The Eighth was transferred to Okinawa, Japan in July 1945 but without personnel, equipment or combat units. Although some of these were assigned to Okinawa

The aircraft of a legend. P-51D-10NA 44-14450 was the second Mustang to carry the Old Crow *name, flown by triple ace Clarence 'Bud' Anderson of the Eighth Air Force's 357th Fighter Group/ 362nd Fighter Squadron. The first* Old Crow *was a P-51B. Anderson ended the war with 16.25 aerial victories. He remained in the post war USAF as a test pilot and then flew combat operations in Vietnam in F-105 Thunderchiefs.*

1944

Tenth Air Force Mustangs – P-51D-5NT 44-11306 and others of the 311th FG/529th FS in China.

before the end of the war against Japan, none saw action. In England, the Eighth's headquarters were at Daws Hill from February 1942 and High Wycombe between May 1942 and July 1945.

In total, the Eighth Air Force controlled 47 operational Bombardment Groups, 24 Fighter Groups, three Reconnaissance Groups, four Troop Carrier Groups, eight specialist units (special operations, radio countermeasures, air-sea rescue etc) and seven miscellaneous units (target towing etc).

Eighth Air Force Fighter Groups and squadrons which operated the Mustang were:
4th FG (334th, 335th and 336th FS) from February 1944.
20th FG (55th, 77th and 79th FS) from July 1944.
55th FG (38th, 338th and 343rd FS) from July 1944.
78th FG (82nd, 83rd and 84th FS) from December 1944.
339th FG (503rd, 504th and 505th FS) from April 1944.
352nd FG (328th, 486th and 487th FS) from April 1944.
353rd FG (350th, 351st and 352nd FG) from October 1944.
355th FG (354th, 357th and 358th FS) from March 1944.
356th FG (359th, 360th and 361st FS) from November 1944.
357th FG (362nd, 363rd and 364th FS) from February 1944.
359th FG (368th, 369th and 370th FS) from May 1944.
361st FG (374th, 375th and 376th FS) from May 1944.
364th FG (383rd, 384th and 385th FS) from July 1944.
479th FG (434th, 435th and 436th FS) from September 1944.

Ninth Air Force

Established as V Air Support Command at Bowman Field, Kentucky in August 1941 and renamed Ninth Air Force in April 1942. The Ninth moved to Egypt in November 1942, playing a major role in the Egyptian, Libyan,

Twelfth Air Force Mustang – A-36A of the 27th FBG with 150 mission markings on its nose.

1944

Fourteenth Air Force P-51A Mustang at Kurmitola, India.

Tunisian and Sicilian campaigns and then the invasion of Italy.

The Ninth moved to England in October 1943 to act as the tactical air force for the planned invasion of Europe. It engaged in these activities before, during and after the invasion in June 1944 and was a major participant in the drive across Europe between then and Germany's surrender in May 1945.

The Ninth Air Force contributed a significant 'first' to the Mustang's history in November 1943 with the arrival in England of the first USAAF P-51B unit, the 354th Fighter Group comprising the 353rd, 355th and 356th Fighter Squadrons. The Group was officially part of the Ninth Air Force but at first operated with the Eighth Air Force pending the arrival of the latter's own Mustangs.

Commands within the Ninth Air Force were IX Bomber Command (later the 9th Air Division), IX Air Defense Command, IX Fighter Command, IX Tactical Air Command, IX Troop Carrier Command, XIX Tactical Air Command and XXIX Tactical Air Command.

Tenth Air Force

Established in February 1942 at Patterson Field, Ohio, the Tenth Air Force moved to India in May 1942, operating from there and Burma in the China-Burma-India theatre of operations until the end of the war against Japan. It was based in China from August 1945 before returning to the USA in January 1946.

The Tenth Air Force's groups were the 33rd, 80th and 311th Fighter Groups; 7th, 12th and 341st Bombardment Groups; 3rd Combat Cargo Group and 443rd Troop Carrier Group.

Eleventh Air Force

Established as the Alaskan Air Force at Elmendorf Field, Alaska in December 1941 and renamed Eleventh Air Force in February 1942. The Eleventh was involved in the actions which removed the Japanese from the Aleutian Islands and later participated in the bombing offensive against Japan. It remained based in Alaska and was again renamed in December 1945 as the Alaskan Air Command.

Twelfth Air Force

Established at Bolling Field, Washington DC in August 1942, the Twelfth moved to England the following month and then to Algeria in November, remaining in the Mediterranean area until the end of the war. From August 1943 it was based in Tunisia and from December 1943 in Italy. Commands were the XII Bomber, XII Tactical Air and XXII Tactical Air, Fighter Groups within these including the 7th, 27th, 57th, 63rd, 64th, 70th, 71st, 86th, 87th, 324th and 350th at various times.

The Twelfth Air Force's 68th Observation Group introduced the P-51/F-6A to USAAF operational service in April 1943 with the start of armed reconnaissance sorties over the Mediterranean.

1944

Fifteenth Air Force P-51B Mustang of the 332nd Fighter Group, a unit manned by black Americans.

Thirteenth Air Force

Established at New Caledonia in January 1943, the Thirteenth served in the south and south-west Pacific, taking part in the Allied drive north towards Japan. Bases were on Guadalcanal, Los Negros, Hollandia, Noemfoor, Morotai and finally Leyte in the Philippines from March 1945.

Fourteenth Air Force

Established at Kunming, China in March 1943 and commanded by Maj-Gen Claire Chennault of American Volunteer Group (Flying Tigers) fame, the Fourteenth replaced the China Air Task Force which was also commanded by Chennault. It operated against the Japanese for the remainder of the war, flying from Kunming until August 1945 and then Peishiyi for four months after hostilities had ended.

By the second half of 1945 the Fourteenth had two Bombardment Groups (the 308th and 341st) along with four Fighter Groups, the 23rd, 51st, 81st and 311th. Of these, three were equipped with Mustangs: 23rd FG (74th FS, 75th BS, 76th BS and 118th TRS); 51st FG (16th, 25th, 26th and 449th FS, the latter with P-38 Lightnings); and 311th FG (528th, 529th and 530th FS).

Fifteenth Air Force

Established at Tunis, Tunisia in November 1943 initially under the command of Maj-Gen James Doolittle, the Fifteenth Air Force was mainly used for the strategic bombing of targets in Italy, France, Germany, Poland, Czechoslovakia, Hungary, Austria and the Balkans, often operating in co-operation with the Eighth Air Force based in England. It was headquartered in Tunisia for only a few weeks, moving to Bari, Italy in December 1943 and remaining there until September 1945. From February 1944 the Fifteenth's heavy bomber groups operated under the control of the US Strategic Air Forces in Europe (USSTAFE), along with those of the Eighth Air Force's VIII Bomber Command.

By early 1945 the Fifteenth comprised 21 Bombardment Groups, seven Fighter Groups, one Special Group and one Weather Reconnaissance Squadron. The Fighter Groups which operated Mustangs were the 31st, 52nd, 325th and 332nd, while the 1st, 14th and 82nd flew the P-38 Lightning.

Twentieth Air Force

Established in Washington DC in April 1944 under the command of General of the Army Henry ('Hap') Arnold, the Twentieth was responsible for most Boeing B-29 operations, starting with the detachment of some combat elements to India in April-May 1944. Flying from satellite bases in China, the B-29s were used to bomb Japan, Thailand, Burma and Formosa but with only moderate success due to technical and logistical problems.

With the capture of islands in the Pacific, the B-29s moved to the Mariana Islands from which they could reach Japan escorted by P-51D Mustangs based on Iwo Jima. The Twentieth's strategic bombing campaign against Japan destroyed its industries and the dropping of atomic bombs on Hiroshima and Nagasaki in August 1945 delivered the *coup de grace*.

The Twentieth's main combat elements were XX Bomber Command, XXI Bomber Command and VII Fighter Command. Maj-Gen Curtiss LeMay took over command of the Air Force in July 1945.

US Strategic Air Forces in Europe

The heavy bomber units of the Eighth and Fifteenth Air Forces were combined into the newly established US Strategic Air Forces in Europe (USSTAFE) in February 1944, this co-ordinating USAAF activities in Europe and exercising some operational control over the Eighth and Fifteenth Air Forces. USSTAFE was commanded by Gen Carl Spaatz.

Far East Air Forces

Established in August 1944 to control the operations of the Fifth and Thirteenth Air Forces in the Pacific. Commanded by Lt-Gen George Kenney, the FEAF was headquartered initially at Brisbane, Australia and then Hollandia, New Guinea and finally Fort McKinlay in the Philippines.

Continental Air Forces

Established at Washington DC in December 1944, the CAF controlled the activities of the Air Forces which remained in the USA during the war – the First, Second, Third and Fourth.

1945

The winter of 1944-45 was an extremely cold one in Britain and Europe. Here, ground crews work on 343rd Fighter Squadron Mustang at its Wormingford base in very difficult conditions during January 1945.

January: The Mustang IV enters RAF service with No 611 Squadron at Hawkinge followed by Nos 112 and 213 in Italy during February and Nos 65 and 234 in March. Others re-equipped over the next few months – Nos 19, 64, 93, 118, 122, 126, 154, 249, 250, 260 and 303 (Polish). The RAF received its Mustang IVs relatively late due to the USAAF having first priority over deliveries of the P-51D/K models.

11 January: Major William Shomo of the 71st Tactical Reconnaissance Group's 82nd Tactical Reconnaissance Squadron becomes the second Mustang Congressional Medal of Honour recipient following a mission over northern Luzon in the Philippines. Attacked by a large number of Japanese fighters, Shomo pulled off the extraordinary feat of shooting down seven of them in this single action. Shomo was flying an F-6D Mustang on this occasion rather than his usual P-51D 44-72505 *The Flying Undertaker*, so named because of his pre-war occupation.

14 January: By now, Germany's air defences were desperately trying to thwart Allied bombers as the end came closer. On this date, intelligence reports had suggested that the German fighters were going to try a new tactic, using heavily armoured Focke-Wulf Fw 190s to attack the bombers in line abreast formation. This proved to be correct, the 66 Mustangs deployed by the 357th Fighter Group to escort B-17s and B-24s attacking oil installations in the Magdeburg-Brunswick area taking on the Fw 190s. The result was 56 German fighters shot down, the superiority of the American pilots proving to be the difference in this and subsequent air battles.

Germany was by now scraping the bottom of the barrel to find fighter pilots and was putting up an increasing number of inexperienced and inadequately trained pilots as more and more veterans became casualties. The opposite was true for the Americans, who had large numbers of highly experienced and skilled pilots available. This action earned the 357th FG a Distinguished Unit Citation.

17 January: Warsaw 'liberated' by the Russians.

February: *Luftwaffe* Me 262 jets were very active during this month as Germany slid towards inevitable defeat. Eighth Air Force Mustang pilots reported 118 encounters with 262s during the month and bomber crews 163. Mustang pilots claimed 15 of them during this period including seven on 25 February by the 55th Fighter Group during a sweep near Giebelstadt airfield. The Group also shot down an Arado Ar 234 jet bomber on the same day.

February: The Fourteenth Air Force in China starts concentrating largely on the interdiction role, its Mustangs assigned the job of attacking bridges and locomotives. The aircraft had claimed 142 locomotives destroyed and 37 bridges made temporarily unserviceable within a month.

February: Units of the USAAF Seventh (based in Hawaii) and Twentieth Air Forces begin receiving P-51Ds, starting with the Seventh AF's 15th and 21st Fighter Groups, both initially part of the Hawaiian air defence system with detachments sent out for operations in the central

1945

The Mustang IV (P-51D/K) entered RAF service in January 1945, later than the USAAF due to the Americans having priority. KM232 is a P-51K of 239 Wing carrying the personalised markings of Wng Cdr Joe Stottard. (via Neil Mackenzie)

and south Pacific areas. The Twentieth Air Force was still officially headquartered in the USA at the time but some of its combat units had moved to India in mid 1944 and the Mariana Islands in the Pacific later in the year. The Twentieth formally transferred to Guam in July 1945.

February: France's *Armée de l'Air* receives a batch of P-51Ds for operation initially by 2/33 'Savoie' *Escadre*.

3 February: Maiden flight of the first P-51H Mustang (44-64160), the only one of the 'lightweight' models to achieve production.

19 February: Start of the US Marine Corps assault on the volcanic island of Iwo Jima, this successful operation a significant event in the conduct of the last six months of the Pacific war as it provided a secure base from which USAAF Mustangs could join XXI Bomber Command's B-29 Superfortresses and strike the Japanese mainland. The island was not wholly occupied by the Americans until 16 March, but US air operations began while the fighting was still underway (see 6 March, below).

March: Fifth Air Force combat units based in the Philippines begin converting to P-51D Mustangs, starting with the 35th and 348th Fighter Groups and in both cases replacing P-47 Thunderbolts. The 3rd Air Commando Group also moved to the Philippines, this unit operating a mixed fleet including P-51Ds and using them initially to support ground forces on Luzon and then to provide bomber escorts for raids on Formosa and China.

The Fifth's Mustangs were also involved in the important campaign against Japanese shipping in the South China Sea in an attempt to disrupt this vital lifeline to the mainland. By April 1945 they had succeeded in effectively removing Japanese air cover for the ships and sinkings increased accordingly.

6 March: P-51Ds of the Seventh Air Force's 15th and 21st Fighter Groups arrive at Iwo Jima's South Field, which

P-82B Twin Mustang mockup showing the new wing centre section joining the two fuselages and the gun ports within it. The pod under the centre section was intended to carry additional guns. (NAA)

112 Sovereign 2 – Mustang

1945

P-51K Mustang IV KH716 of No 3 Squadron RAAF in the rubble and slush of Fano, Italy during early 1945. (via Neil Mackenzie)

remained under the threat of Japanese artillery attack for a time. They flew their first mission two days later, the first of many in support of the troops on the ground on other parts of the island where the fighting was continuing. The Mustangs were also used to attack Japanese forces on the neighbouring islands of Chichi Jima and Haha Jima.

Operations from Iwo Jima were difficult as the island was covered in volcanic dust which was kicked up every time an aircraft (or even a person) moved. The dust had a considerable effect on aircraft maintenance and especially on engine life, which reduced considerably. The island was also used as a staging base and emergency airfield for the B-29s of XXI Bomber Command, based in the Mariana Islands about 650 miles (1,040km) to the south.

14 March: After two-and-a-half years of test flying, the first Merlin powered Mustang X conversion (AL975) is written off following a wheels up forced landing at Fradswell in Staffordshire. This resulted from the failure of the Merlin 71 engine installed at the time.

P-51D Mustang of the 361st Fighter Group's 375th Fighter Squadron. The Mustangs and other Allied aircraft continued intensive operations throughout the first few months of 1945 until Germany surrendered.

1945

The first P-51H Mustang flew on 3 February 1945. This is 44-64164, the fifth aircraft off the line. (NAA)

21 March: The precision raid by de Havilland Mosquitos drawn from Nos 21, 464 (RAAF) and 487 (RNZAF) Squadrons against the Gestapo headquarters inside Shell House in the middle of Copenhagen. Twenty-eight Mustang IIIs and IVs from Nos 64, 125 and 234 Squadrons RAF flew as escorts, these providing fighter cover for the Mosquitos and also acting as flak suppressors. The prime aim of the raid was to destroy Gestapo records of Danish Resistance members, these stored within the building

Even though the raid was a success, it had its problems. The attack had to be made at very low level (100 feet) to ensure accurate placement of the bombs to avoid damaging the surrounding civilian dwellings and other buildings. One of the first wave of Mosquitos hit a 130ft (40m) tall floodlight pylon on the way in and crashed into a school. Following aircraft saw the smoke and flames, assumed they were coming from the target and bombed the school by mistake with the deaths of 103 civilians, 86 of them school children.

Some of the Mosquitos did attack the correct building and it was destroyed, killing more than 100 Germans and Danish collaborators and destroying most of the records. In the confusion, Danish Resistance workers somehow managed to remove the five safes and two filing cabinets which had survived the bombing. In them was found a complete list of Danes who were on the Germans' payroll. A number of prisoners in the building were able to escape, although some were killed. Two Mustang IIIs were lost.

24 March: P-51D pilots of the USAAF's 31st Fighter Group shoot down five Messerschmitt Me 262 jet fighters during a bomber escort mission to Berlin.

March-April: *Luftwaffe* jet fighter activity reaches a peak and is sustained throughout these two months. During this period, USAAF fighter pilots reported 438 encounters with Me 262s, the 280 combats which resulted ending in claims for 43 Me 262s destroyed in the air, three probables and 45 damaged. Another 21 were destroyed on the ground.

April: The Royal Australian Air Force takes delivery of the first of 214 P-51Ds and 84 P-51Ks from US production. The last is delivered in September 1945.

April: Sweden orders and immediately takes delivery of 50 surplus USAAF P-51Ds, these given the local designation J 26. A further 107 P-51Ds were subsequently delivered, the last of them in March 1948.

7 April: P-51Ds of the 15th and 21st Fighter Groups fly their first B-29 escort mission to Japan and back from Iwo Jima, the more than 1,500 miles (2,415km) journey requiring the fitting of two 165 USgal (625 l) underwing tanks. The target on this first raid was the Nakajima-Musashi factory and involved 108 Mustangs. It was also the first occasion that US land based fighters had flown over the Japanese mainland and was symbolic of the beginning of the end for Japan. The 15th and 21st FGs were joined by the 506th FG in mid May. With the maximum possible external and internal fuel on board, the P-51D had an absolute range 2,080 miles (3,347km) and an endurance of 8½ hours.

7 April-30 June: The three P-51D equipped Fighter Groups based on Iwo Jima and escorting B-29s to Japan saw little air-to-air action but added extensive ground strafing activities to their repertoires while over Japan. During this period they claimed 666 Japanese aircraft destroyed, the vast majority on the ground in Japan.

8 April: It wasn't all one way traffic in favour of the Allies in the closing stages of the air war over Europe. On

1945

These photographs of Eighth Air Force P-51Ds were taken in April 1945 when the war with Germany was nearly over. The 356th FG/360th FS aircraft (top) was photographed during that month at Martlesham Heath, while 44-14169 of the 355th FG/358th FS was snapped at Steeple Morden.

this day, Me 262 jets directed their attacks against fighters escorting USAAF bombers on a raid into Germany and shot down 28 Mustangs, P-38 Lightnings and P-47 Thunderbolts in a wide ranging air battle. On the other side of the ledger the USAAF fighters claimed the very substantial tally of 133 Messerschmitt Bf 109s and Focke-Wulf Fw 190s during the same encounter.

10 April: The effective end of the Messerschmitt Me 262 threat to Allied bombers when more than 1,000 B-17s and B-24s attacked the jet fighter bases at Parchim, Rechlin, Brandenburg-Briest and Oranienburg. Even though the Me 262s shot down 10 of the bombers, their bases were devastated and their units forced to scatter and withdraw. By then, Me 262 operations had already started to suffer from a lack of fuel, supplies of this essential commodity drying up completely shortly afterwards.

10 April: In China, the Fourteenth Air Force's efforts to block Japanese supply lines had been successful, resulting in the enemy launching attacks against the American airfields at Chihchiang using an army of 60,000 men supported by fighter squadrons. The offensive lasted nearly two months, Chinese troops working closely with the

Sovereign 2 – Mustang 115

1945

The first of two XP-82 Twin Mustang prototypes (44-83886) flew on 15 April 1945. This is F-82B 44-65162, the third production aircraft photographed well after the war when flying as a warbird.

Fourteenth AF in repelling the Japanese, the Air Force's medium bombers and fighters attacking with guns, bombs and napalm in a situation of air superiority. The result was a major defeat for the Japanese, who were forced to retreat from eastern China and the Yangtze area and never return.

12 April: US President Franklin D Roosevelt dies. Vice-President Harry Truman takes over from him.

15 April: First flight of the prototype XP-82 Twin Mustang (44-83886).

16 April: Mustang IVs from No 611 Squadron are the first RAF aircraft to 'greet' Russian aircraft over Berlin.

17 April-11 May: USAAF B-29s and Iwo Jima based Mustangs carry out attacks on Japanese Kamikaze bases on the southern Japanese islands of Shikoku and Kyushu. For these raids, the Mustangs carried six high velocity

The first Australian built CAC Mustang Mk.20 flew at the end of April 1945. A68-63 was delivered to the RAAF in March 1946. (via Neil Mackenzie)

1945

P-51K Mustang IV TK589 wearing RAF markings but still carrying traces of its USAAF serial 44-1332. The aircraft was delivered to the RAF in 1945 for tests and trials.

aircraft rockets (HVARs), this in combination with long range fuel tanks increasing their takeoff weights to a figure well above the normal maximum of 12,100lb (5,488kg).

23 April: First flight of the prototype XP-51J Mustang (44-76027), the last of the trio of experimental lightweight models developed in 1944-45. The XP-51J reverted to the Allison V-1710 engine, albeit in its more powerful -119 form with two speed/two stage supercharger and water injection.

30 April: Adolf Hitler commits suicide in Berlin.

30 April: The 354th Fighter Group – the pioneer USAAF Mustang unit in Europe – flies its last operational sorties of the war from airfield R.45 at Ansbach in Germany. Since starting operations on 1 December 1943, the 354th had flown 1,384 missions, 18,334 individual aircraft sorties, claimed 956 enemy aircraft destroyed (including 701 in air-to-air combat, the highest of any USAAF Group in WWII), 32 probably destroyed and 428 damaged. Against that, the Group had lost 178 pilots on operations. The 354th then became part of the Army of Occupation before being sent back to the USA in February 1946. It was disbanded the following month.

30 April: First flight of the Australian built Commonwealth Aircraft Corporation (CAC) CA-17 Mustang Mk.20, the first of 200 to come from the only source of Mustang production outside the USA.

May: No 268 Squadron relinquishes its Mustang I/IA/IIs as the last RAF operational unit to fly the Allison powered variants. The squadron was operating in France as part of the 2nd TAF at the time and had previously also flown Hawker Typhoons. Spitfires XIVs replaced the

Mustangs everywhere, a graphic illustration of US air power in Europe during World War II. The occasion is a 'Victory Open Day' at Duxford near Cambridge in June 1945 and the aircraft are from the Eighth Air Force's 78th Fighter Group. Those with visible serial numbers are P-51Ks.

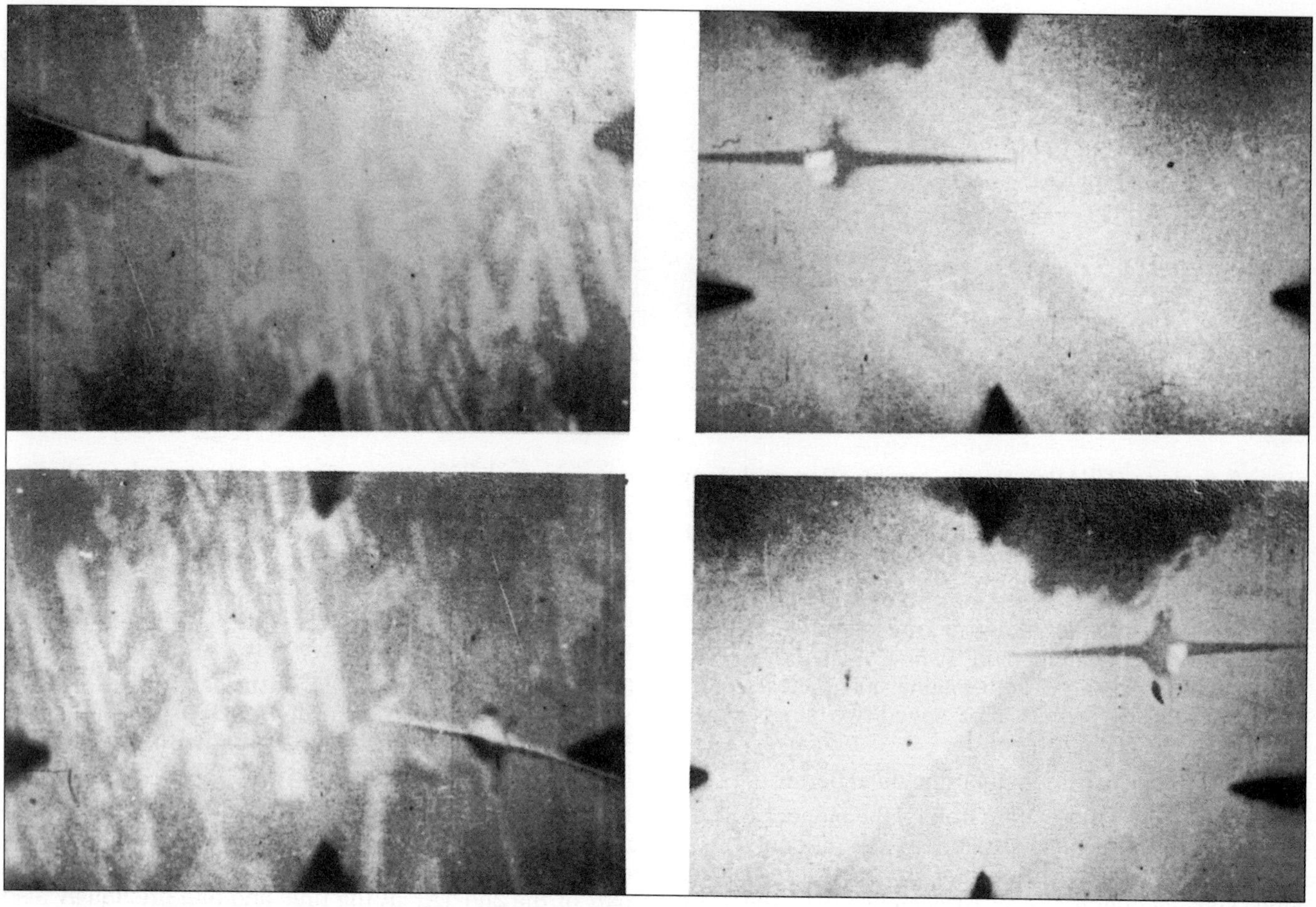

1945

The view from the gun-camera of John Haslope's Mustang as he chases and fires on the Messerschmitt Me 163 during his successful action of 10 April 1945.

The Mustang III of No 165 Squadron RAF in which John Haslope shot down the Me 163 rocket powered fighter. Haslope dived after the Messerschmitt firing as he went, but badly bent his aircraft in the resulting high 'g' pullout.

1945

Mustangs, although the last example was not removed from the squadron's strength until August 1945.

5 May: No 3 Squadron RAAF's Mustangs (based in Italy) fly their last mission of the war, a reconnaissance over Fiume in Yugoslavia and Udine in Italy.

8 May: The war against Germany officially ends at one minute past midnight. Victory in Europe (VE) Day proclaimed. Some fighting continued, however. Two F-6 Mustangs of the 12th Tactical Reconnaissance Squadron were patrolling near the Danube when they were bounced by five Focke-Wulf Fw 190s. Flight leader Robert C Little in one of the Mustangs shot down an Fw 190 during the fight, thus claiming the last German aircraft destroyed in combat over Europe in World War II.

Interestingly, it may not have been the last kill as a Soviet pilot is recorded as having shot down a Messerschmitt Bf 109 near Prague on the following day. Despite the ceasefire, German forces were still offering resistance in this area, not so much to continue the fight for their country but to avoid being captured by the Soviets. The vast majority of defeated German soldiers were horrified at the prospect of having to surrender to the Russians and much preferred doing so to the Americans or British.

14 May: The daylight B-29 raids on Japan produced a variety in the level of resistance offered by Japanese fighters, but on this date they were out in full force. The raid was an incendiary attack on Nagoya and involved 472 B-29s plus escorting Mustangs. More than 2,500 tonnes of incendiaries were dropped on Nagoya, destroying a substantial part of the city. A large number of Japanese fighters rose to meet the raiders, shooting down 10 B-29s and damaging 64 more. The Mustangs claimed 18 kills.

June: The first RAF squadron to be equipped with the Mustang I – No 26 – is transferred to Germany and loses its North American fighters. The squadron had swapped them for Spitfire Vs in March 1944 but in October 1944 it returned to the Mustang I to fly reconnaissance sorties over V-2 bases from Britain. It then moved to France in April 1945 where the Mustangs were used as spotters for the naval guns attacking German garrisons near Bordeaux.

1 June: Between the start of operations in early April 1945 and the beginning of June, the three USAAF Mustang equipped Fighter Groups in the Pacific area had between them claimed the destruction of 666 Japanese aircraft.

5 June: The first RAAF 'home' squadron (No 84) to receive Mustangs takes delivery of its first aircraft, P-51K A68-506.

15 June: The last of the USAAF's series of B-29 incendiary raids on Japanese urban areas, this one on Osaka leaving the city destroyed.

17 June: The start of a new phase in the USAAF's bombing of Japan. With the end of incendiary raids on urban areas, the emphasis switches to day and night attacks on Japan's industrial centres, especially those involved with aircraft, aero-engine and oil production.

6 August: Atomic bomb dropped on Hiroshima.

9 August: Atomic bomb dropped on Nagasaki.

MUSTANG VERSUS Me 163

The records indicate that eight Messerschmitt Me 163 Komet rocket powered interceptors were shot down by Mustang pilots between August 1944 and April 1945, the first seven by USAAF flyers escorting bomber formations into Germany. The eighth was credited to an Australian, Flying Officer John 'Slops' Haslope DFC on 10 April 1945.

Haslope was flying a Mustang III of No 165 Squadron RAF on a daylight mission escorting Lancasters and Halifaxes on a raid to Leipzig. During the mission, Haslope found himself in a position to attack an Me 163 which had penetrated the formation and appeared in front of and below his Mustang. The Komet dived and Haslope followed, ignoring his airspeed indicator's red line and concentrating solely on claiming the German fighter, firing as he went.

The Komet suddenly pulled up sharply out of the dive and Haslope attempted to follow, pulling enormous positive 'g' and blacking himself out in the process. When he came to, Haslope noticed two things: firstly that he was several thousand feet lower than he'd been when the action started; and secondly that his Mustang was handling badly, as if it was damaged.

And indeed it was. After the long and tense flight back to 165's base at Bentwaters in Suffolk, the full implications of Haslope's multi-g pullout from the dive were revealed and they included several degrees of extra dihedral on the Mustang's wings plus severe wrinkling of the wing skins. On the positive side, Haslope also became the only Commonwealth pilot to claim victory over a Komet in aerial combat.

What transpired was that Haslope had successfully hit the Komet with his gunfire during the dive, the enemy fighter then going out of control when the Mustang pilot was blacked out. The Messerschmitt looped and dived before finally plunging to the ground and exploding, this probably indicating that its pilot was immobilised. The incident was witnessed by several other pilots and Haslope was awarded the Distinguished Flying Cross for his successful engagement.

After the war, John Haslope became an airline pilot, but sadly he was killed in August 1951 when the Trans-Australia Airlines Douglas DC-3 he was flying crashed at Barilla Bay near Cambridge, Tasmania.

---

14 August: Japan agrees to unconditional surrender – the fighting stops and World War II is over.

14 August: The final Mustang operational mission of WWII flown by USAAF P-51Ds of the 15th, 21st and 506th Fighter Groups based on Iwo Jima. This last mission was typical of many performed by these units in the last few months of the Pacific War, escorting B-29 bombers to Japan in what were the longest missions regularly flown by single seat, single engined fighters during the war. They typically lasted up to eight hours. On this day, the aircraft flew a 1,500 miles (2,415km) round trip to Osaka and back, the mission taking 7¼ hours to complete.

1945

A P-51C of the 311th Fighter Group's 530th Fighter Squadron photographed over China in July 1945.

August: With the cessation of hostilities with Japan, the Chinese Nationalist Government purchases almost the entire surplus stock of USAAF Mustangs (about 1,000 aircraft) based in the Far East, including those previously used by the Fourteenth Air Force.

August: The Royal New Zealand Air Force had negotiated to acquire 370 Mustangs earlier in 1945 but most were cancelled with the end of WWII. An initial batch of 30 P-51Ds was already on its way, however, and these were delivered, albeit directly to storage. They remained in that state for six years until finally being activated in late 1951 to briefly equip four RNZAF Territorial Air Force (reserve) squadrons.

2 September: Victory over Japan (VJ) Day – surrender documents are signed aboard the battleship USS *Missouri* in Tokyo Bay.

September: A survey of USAAF aircraft types built and delivered between January 1940 and August 1945 reveals their comparative cost. A P-51 Mustang cost the US taxpayer $US50,985 per aircraft compared with $US97,147 for a Lockheed P-38 Lightning, $US50,666 for a Bell P-39 Airacobra, $US44,892 for a Curtiss P-40 Warhawk and $US83,001 for a Republic P-47 Thunderbolt.

Of other types, a Boeing B-17 Flying Fortress cost $US187,742, a Douglas C-47 Skytrain $US85,035 and a North American B-25 Mitchell $US116,752. The least expensive aircraft in the US arsenal was the Piper L-4 Grasshopper at $2,701 per aircraft, while the most expensive was the Boeing B-29 Superfortress, its $US509,465 price tag reflecting its size, complexity and highly advanced technology for the time.

At the end of World War II the USAAF had 5,500 Mustangs on strength, the vast majority P-51D/Ks and their F-6D/K tactical reconnaissance derivatives. The pre-war National Guard auxiliary service was reconstituted after the cessation of hostilities and replaced by the renamed Air National Guard in 1947. Some 700 P-51D/Ks were supplied to the NG/ANG as the initial equipment of about 44 squadrons, while 75 eventually flew the type. Of the 700, about 600 were removed from storage at Newark, New Jersey, all of them new aircraft with only delivery time in their logbooks.

November: Delivery of the final single engined Mustang from US production, a P-51H (44-64714) built at Inglewood. Manufacture of the P-51D had ended immediately after Japan's surrender.

12 December: The USAF orders 100 P-82E long range escort fighters, development of which had continued even though contracts for 480 P-82 Twin Mustangs had been cancelled with the end of the war against Japan.

US P-51 Mustang production ended in November 1945 with delivery of the 555th and last P-51H.

1946-84

Even though US production of the Mustang had ended by late 1945, it continued in Australia by the Commonwealth Aircraft Corporation at a low rate until 1951 when the last of 200 was handed over. This is a general view of the CAC Mustang production line at Fishermen's Bend, Victoria. (HDHV)

9 March 1946: The first Royal Australian Air Force Mustang arrives at Iwakuni in Japan as part of the British Commonwealth Occupation Force (BCOF). The RAAF's No 81 Wing, comprising Nos 76, 77 and 82 Squadrons, made up the contingent. Nos 76 and 82 Squadrons ended their Japanese tour of duty in October 1948 while No 77 stayed on as a single unit. It was just about to return to Australia in June 1950 when the Korean War broke out, delaying departure for another three years.

21 March 1946: The formation of Strategic Air Command within the USAAF, to which was assigned three P-51D Mustang Fighter Groups between then and later in 1946. They were the 33rd FG, which had previously served in India and comprised the 58th, 59th and 60th Fighter Squadrons (based at Roswell, New Mexico); the 27th FG (522nd, 523rd and 524th FS) which was not operational until July 1947 due to a lack of aircraft and based at Kearney, Nebraska; and the 82nd FG (95th, 96th and 97th FS) at Grenier, New Hampshire. The 33rd and 27th FGs subsequently became part of the newly established US Air Force and re-equipped with Republic F-84 Thunderjets.

30 June 1946: The 120th Fighter Squadron of the Colorado National Guard (Air National Guard from 1947) becomes the first of this service's units to take delivery of the P-51D Mustang. It was followed by the 110th FS, Missouri NG in September. Eventually, 73 NG/ANG squadrons were equipped with Mustangs, 44 as their initial equipment (with P-51Ds) and 29 converting from other types to F-51Ds and Hs. In addition, seven ANG squadrons flew RF-51Ds. The Mustang and P-47 Thunderbolt made up the bulk of the NG/ANG's initial fighter equipment.

August-September 1946: The start of a whole new chapter in the Mustang story – privately owned and modified aircraft for racing – with the revival of the US National Air Races at Cleveland. In the Bendix Trophy race – a 2,048 mile (3,296km) dash from California – Mustangs were dominant in a field which included a Bell P-63 Kingcobra, 14 Lockheed P-38 Lightnings, a P-39 Airacobra, a B-26 and a Corsair.

Three P-51Cs and a P-51D took the first four places, Paul Mantz's P-51C winning at an average speed of 435.5mph (700.8km/h) and an elapsed time of 4hr 42min 14sec. Jacqueline Cochrane's P-51C was second. Mantz's Mustang set the scene for the modified aircraft which would follow. It featured 'wet' wings with integral fuel tanks, and a smooth and wet sanded finish to reduce drag. In addition, the fuel was chilled by

RAF use of the Mustang continued until 1947. P-51K Mustang IV KH348 of No 213 Squadron is photographed at Nicosia, Cyprus in 1946.

1946-84

P-51D Mustangs began equipping the National Guard from June 1946, the aircraft eventually flying with 73 NG (later Air National Guard) units of which 44 had it as their initial equipment. P-51D-25NT 45-11676 from the final Dallas production batch is shown in Nevada NG markings.

wrapping the fuel filler in dry ice, thus decreasing its mass and allowing the tanks to hold more gallons than their actual capacity. This technique was and is used in motor racing.

The Thompson Trophy race – over 10 laps of a 30 mile (48km) course – was won by a P-39 followed by Tony LeVier's P-38 with Mustangs finishing in third, fourth, fifth and seventh places.

Ever more heavily modified Mustangs enjoyed more success at the National Air Races over the next three years but the 1949 event was the last. In that year's Thompson Trophy race, William Odom's radically modified P-51C (with the engine radiators mounted in pods at the wingtips) crashed into a residential area after stalling while negotiating a pylon. Odom and a mother and child on the ground lost their lives, the resultant negative publicity leading to the withdrawal of sponsorship and the end of the event.

With the benefit of hindsight it is apparent that the writing had been on the wall since the 1947 event as far as safety is concerned. In that year's Thompson Trophy event, four out of the field of 13 crashed and three others retired with various mechanical problems. In 1948 the fields were much smaller – the result of 1947's accidents and the ever increasing expense of running former military aircraft – but Paul Mantz made history when he took his P-51C to victory in its third successive Bendix Trophy event.

After the unfortunate events of 1949 it would be another 15 years before pylon racing of these former World War II fighters restarted, this time well out of harm's way in the desert at Reno, Nevada.

September-October 1946: The USAAF places orders for 150 P-82F and G radar equipped night fighters for operation by Air Defense Command.

The National Guard became the Air National Guard in 1947 and the P-51 became the F-51 in June 1948. 44-72777 is an Inglewood built P-51D-25NA operated by the Rhode Island ANG.

122 Sovereign 2 – Mustang

1946-84

GROUND CONTROL IN KOREA

The Mustangs of the Royal Australian Air Force's No 77 Squadron built up a good reputation in the ground attack role in the early stages of the Korean War, their operations typical of those also being undertaken by USAF and South African Mustang units in the conflict.

The squadron was based at Iwakuni in Japan for the first three months of the war before moving to Pohang in South Korea. During that initial period and because of the long distances between Iwakuni and the targets, a typical daily routine was to depart Japan early in the morning, stage through the Korean airstrip at Taegu to refuel and arm, attack the allocated targets, return to Taegu to rearm and refuel and if possible attack another target before returning to Iwakuni for the night.

The squadron's maintenance personnel would fly to Taegu every morning by Dakota in advance of the Mustangs in order to perform their duties at the airstrip and then return to Iwakuni in the evening. After that, their work was still not done as some of them then had work through the night repairing any damage and preparing the aircraft for the next day's operations. Next morning, they would be back on the Dakota to repeat the process.

Ground attack operations were intensive in the opening phases of the battle, the squadron's main role being to provide close support for UN ground forces. The Mustangs worked in close co-operation with ground controllers who would guide the aircraft to targets, often needing to respond quickly to calls from units which needed immediate assistance. The controller was normally positioned close to the enemy to help ensure an accurate strike, but sometimes an air controller – flying a light aircraft such as an Auster – would be needed to direct the Mustangs to their targets.

An example of this kind of operation took place on 1 August 1950 and is described in a 77 Squadron history: "Four Mustangs led by Flg Off T McCrohan were tasked with providing close air support to the UN forces in the Chingju area. After making contact with the ground controller, the Mustangs were directed to attack three anti-aircraft gun positions.

"The Mustangs carried out a strafing run and quickly silenced the enemy guns. The controller then directed the four aircraft to a building which housed a number of 50-calibre machine guns, this was attacked with rockets and then strafed with machine gun fire. The pilots then turned their attention to another enemy position 200 yards further west which they again rocketed and strafed but with no visible results.

"Before departing, the Mustangs strafed a number of enemy vehicles claiming five trucks and one tank destroyed and a further three trucks probably destroyed."

May 1946: The last home based RAF squadron equipped with the Mustang IV (No 64 at Horsham St Faith) replaces its aircraft with the de Havilland Hornet F.1.

February 1947: The last Mustang IVs withdrawn from RAF front line service, the final operator No 213 Squadron based at Nicosia in Cyprus. The squadron's Mustangs were replaced by Hawker Tempest F.VIs. A few aircraft remained on RAF strength until later in 1947.

28 February 1947: A demonstration of the Twin Mustang's range capability is given when P-82B 44-65168 *Betty Jo* flown by Lt Col Robert Thacker and Lt J M Ard flies non stop between Hickam Field in Hawaii to La Guardia Airport, New York, a distance of 4,968 statute miles (7,995km). The flight took 14hr 31min 50sec to complete at an average speed of 342mph (550km/h), this slower than anticipated due to an electrical problem which prevented the release of three out of four drop tanks as planned. No autopilot was fitted, so the two pilots had to fly the P-82B by hand, while extra fuel tanks were installed behind the pilots' seats to bring total capacity up to 2,215 USgal (5,851 litres).

July 1947: Establishment of the Philippine Air Force, initial equipment including sufficient F-51Ds to equip a single fighter-bomber squadron.

18 September 1947: The United States Air Force formally established as an independent military service, entirely separate from the Army. As a result, the United States Army Air Force (USAAF) ceases to exist, replaced by the USAF.

P-51 Mustangs remained in USAF service for some time after this date, equipping or partially equipping 15 Tactical Fighter Wings, one Fighter Wing, two Tactical Reconnaissance Wings, one Tactical Fighter Group, two Fighter Groups, and two Fighter Bomber Wings. Most had relinquished their Mustangs by 1950-51 but a few continued to use the type for a while after that. The 18th TFW operated from the Philippines, Korea and Okinawa and kept its Mustangs until 1953, the 452nd TRW at Long Beach, California used F-51s and TF-51s as reserve aircraft until 1953-54, and the 445th Fighter Bomber Wing (Composite) at Buffalo, New York kept some Mustangs until as late as 1956 to maintain fighter-bomber operational proficiency. Other small units had a few Mustangs on strength to maintain combat efficiency and for communications and miscellaneous duties.

11 June 1948: The USAF changes its fighter designation prefix from P for 'pursuit' to F for 'fighter'. The P-51 Mustang therefore became the F-51 and its F-6 reconnaissance variants the RF-51. The P-82 Twin Mustang was redesignated F-82.

23 June 1950: The Mustangs of No 77 Squadron RAAF perform what was supposed to be their last sortie from their base at Iwakuni in Japan before returning to Australia after four years' service as part of the British Commonwealth Occupation Force. Two days later, North Korean troops crossed the border into South Korea and 77 Squadron quickly found itself in action again.

25 June 1950: North Korean troops advance into South Korea, signalling the start of the Korean War. The first US troops landed in South Korea on 2 July. At the time, about

Sovereign 2 – Mustang   123

1946-84

Pennsylvania ANG P-51H 44-64622 in formation with two of its replacements – a North American F-86A Sabre and a Republic F-84F Thunderstreak.

30 USAF F-51Ds were in storage in Japan, of which ten were quickly issued to the Republic of Korea Air Force.

26 June 1950: Two F-82G Twin Mustang squadrons of the 347th Fighter (All-Weather) Group based in Japan (with a third on Okinawa) are quickly moved to Itazuke in southern Japan (the closest Japanese base to Korea) and begin operating patrols over the Inchon area within a day of the North Korean advance into South Korea. As such, these are the first members of the Mustang family to see operational service in the conflict. The Group's three squadrons are the 4th, 68th and 339th, and the F-82s are the only fighters in Far East Air Force service with sufficient range to fly sorties over Korea from Japan.

27 June 1950: F-82G Twin Mustangs of the 68th Fighter Squadron record the first USAF kills of the Korean War, destroying a Yak-9 fighter and a Yak-11 trainer. The first kill – one of the Yaks – is officially credited to Lt William Hudson although some think it may have actually been Lt 'Chalky' Moran who achieved it. Moran was credited with the other Yak and Major J Little (leading the 339th FS in the same engagement) with a Lavochkin La-7 fighter.

In February 1947 P-82B Twin Mustang 44-65168 Betty Jo flew non stop from Hawaii to New York, a distance of 4,968 miles (7,995km). The aircraft was fitted with substantially extra fuel capacity including four 300 USgal (1,135 l) underwing drop tanks, two of which can be seen here.

28 June 1950: F-80 Shooting Stars and a flight of Mustangs orbit over Suwon airfield to cover the arrival in Korea of General Douglas MacArthur in a Douglas C-54 transport. Shortly after MacArthur's arrival, four Yak-9s tried to attack the airfield and all were shot down by the Mustangs, giving the General a grandstand view of the action.

30 June 1950: General George Stratemeyer, Commander-in-Chief of the Far East Air Forces, sends an urgent request for an additional 164 F-80 Shooting Stars, 25 F-82 Twin Mustangs and 64 F-51 Mustangs for service in Korea. Additional requests were made the next day, covering two F-51 wings (including RF-51s) and two F-82 squadrons.

A shortage of F-82s made the second request impossible but with 764 F-51s in service with Air National Guard units in the USA and another 794 in storage, it was possible to quickly move some of these to Korea (see 15 July, below). Getting additional aircraft to Korea was only part of the problem faced by the air commanders. Extensive work had to be performed on existing airfields to bring them up to scratch, Air Force engineers performing this duty in quick time.

2 July 1950: Only one week after North Korean troops moved into the South, Mustangs of No 77 Squadron Royal Australian Air Force conduct their first operational sortie, escorting Douglas C-47 transports carrying wounded soldiers to Japan. 77 Squadron at first operated from its base at Iwakuni in Japan.

3 July 1950: The Mustangs of 77 Squadron RAAF fly their first combat mission in Korea, eight aircraft attacking targets on the ground and claiming the destruction of two locomotives, a truck and six other vehicles plus a bridge damaged.

15 July 1950: The carrier USS *Boxer* departs California for Korea with 145

1946-84

Mustangs in post war USAF service with P-51D-25NA 44-73227 in the foreground.

Mustangs on board drawn from Air National Guard squadrons. On the same day, the 51st (Provisional) Fighter Squadron starts operations from Taegu in South Korea using the about 20 F-51Ds which had been stored in Japan and not issued to the ROKAF. Shortly afterwards, the 40th FS swapped its F-80 Shooting Star jets for Mustangs and started operations from Pohang as part of the 35th Fighter Bomber Group.

August 1950: By the end of the month, six USAF F-51D Mustang squadrons were operational in Korea and would be joined by two tactical reconnaissance units equipped with F-51Ds and RF-51Ds in November plus Australian and South African Mustang squadrons. The USAAF units bore the brunt of close support operations in the opening phases of the Korean War.

August 1950: The Republic of Indonesia formally constituted following the war of independence against the Dutch. As part of the settlement, P-51D Mustangs and other aircraft are handed over to the new Indonesian Air Force.

5 August 1950: Major Louis Sebille, commanding officer of the 18th FBW's 67th FBS, posthumously becomes the Korean War's first pilot Congressional Medal of Honour recipient when he flies his F-51D (44-74394) into a concentration of enemy troops in order to help protect allied soldiers. Major Sebille had been unable to release one of the two 500lb (227kg) bombs he was carrying and his aircraft had been hit during a strafing run. Ignoring advice to turn away, Major Sebille made another pass, during which the Mustang crashed into enemy troops, still with the bomb attached to the aircraft. Major Sebille was the third and last Mustang pilot to win his country's top bravery award.

31 August 1950: North Korean troops launch a major offensive against the southern city of Pusan, South Korea's major port. This was considered *the* vital battle because if Pusan was lost, so was the rest of the country. The Mustangs were especially effective against the waves of North Koreans which attacked the city, using guns, rockets and napalm and inflicting substantial casualties. Air strikes in combination with amphibious landings by the US Marines broke the North Korean push, which was over by the third week of September. Many thought that this would also mean the end of the conflict, but China's entry in November changed everything.

27 September 1950: The personnel of No 2 ('Cheetah') Squadron, South African Air Force, set sail from Durban en route to Korea where they will operate F-51D Mustangs. Combat operations began in November.

1 November 1950: A major milestone in the Korean War. Four 18th Group Mustangs were patrolling an area south of the Yalu River (the frontier between North Korea and China) when they were attacked by six swept wing jet fighters. The jets made one firing pass without hitting anything before flying back across the river. They were Chinese MiG-15s flown by Russians, although that wasn't known at the time. This and subsequent appearances by the MiG-15 caused a major rethink of US air power in Korea because the previously unknown jet quickly proved superior to any other fighter in the area. Its appearance led directly to the deployment of F-86 Sabres to Korea.

Bill Odom's P-51C N4845N Beguine was one of the first highly modified Mustang racers with its wingtip mounted radiators and special Hamilton Standard propeller with thin section blades. Unfortunately, this aircraft was involved in a fatal accident during the 1949 National Air Races at Cleveland (including two people on the ground), this effectively ending the sport in the USA for 15 years.

Sovereign 2 – Mustang

1946-84

The Korean War saw the Mustang in combat again, the old piston engined fighter proving to be especially effective in the ground attack and close support roles. This F-51D of the 18th Fighter Bomber Wing has four 5-inch high velocity aircraft rockets (HVARs) under its wings and still has space for napalm or conventional bombs.

The arrival of the MiGs and other Chinese aircraft at around this time marked a major change in the Korean War. Until now, it had seemed the conflict would be quickly over, but China decided to get involved in a substantial way with both its air and ground forces, causing the war to drag on for another two and half years.

8 November 1950: The first recorded and conclusive jet-versus-jet combat when a Lockheed F-80C Shooting Star of the USAF's 51st Fighter Interceptor Wing flown by Lt Russell Brown shoots down a Chinese MiG-15 over the Yalu River. Despite this early victory, the F-80 was no match for the MiG-15 in aerial combat.

19 November 1950: The F-51Ds of No 2 (Cheetah) Squadron South African Air Force become operational at Pusan for service in the Korean War after working up in Japan. The squadron was attached to the USAF's 18th Fighter Bomber Wing at Chinhae on the south coast of Korea.

19 January 1951: Mustangs of No 77 Squadron RAAF attack the Chinese Communist Forces headquarters at Pyongyang in North Korea using bombs, rockets and napalm. The target was destroyed but one Mustang was lost and its pilot taken prisoner.

February 1951: The USAF's 18th Fighter Bomber Wing and its Mustangs developed a fine reputation for expertise in the armed tactical reconnaissance role in the first half of 1951, especially its 'truckbuster' activities. In February alone the unit destroyed 728 enemy vehicles and damaged another 137.

6 April 1951: No 77 Squadron RAAF flies its last Mustang combat mission in Korea before re-equipping with Gloster Meteor F.8 jets. The mission involved attacking a large convoy of Chinese trucks of which 12 were destroyed and many others damaged. Of the 56 Mustangs flown by the squadron during its nine months of Korean operations, 18 were lost. The human cost was eight pilots killed.

No 77 Squadron Royal Australian Air Force was the first unit to deploy Mustangs in Korea, its aircraft performing their first mission only eight days after North Korean troops advanced into the South. This RAAF Mustang and personnel was photographed at Yonpo.

1946-84

Two Republic of Korea Air Force (ROKAF) fighter wings operated Mustangs during the war, the early aircraft coming from USAF stocks in Japan.

May 1951: The 35th Fighter Interceptor Wing's 40th Squadron becomes the first USAF Mustang unit in Korea to exchange its piston engined fighters for jets. The squadron moved to Japan and swapped its Mustangs for Lockheed F-94 Starfires. As 1951 progressed, the demand for Mustangs increased but the number available diminished due to attrition and wear and tear on the ageing airframes as a result of very high sortie rates. As an example of this, the 35th FIW's two Mustang squadrons between them flew 400 sorties over a four day period in June.

20 June 1951: An air battle involving Mustangs of the USAF's 18th Fighter Bomber Wing when a flight of them come across eight enemy Ilyushin Il-10 *Shturmoviks* heading to Sinmi-do to strafe Allied troops. The Mustangs shot down two Il-10s and damaged three more before other aircraft from both sides were called in. Another flight of Mustangs engaged six Yak-9 fighters, one of which was shot down but a Mustang was also lost.

8 July 1951: There had been a couple of instances in late June where US Mustangs had been attacked by MiG-15s,

Changing of the guard. After nine months of Mustang operations in Korea, No 77 Squadron RAAF changed its F-51s for Gloster Meteor F.8 jets. Here, the squadron's last Mustang taxies past some Meteors at Iwakuni, Japan in May 1951.

1946-84

Mustangs found numerous civil uses after they ended their military careers, many earning their keep before becoming warbirds. VH-BOZ was the second last Australian built Mustang and was used for target towing and radar calibration duties on behalf of the Royal Australian Navy and Army. Note the target winch apparatus below and behind the cockpit. This photograph was taken at Sydney's Bankstown Airport in 1966. (Vance Ingham)

but in both cases the piston engined fighters were able to outmanoeuvre the jets and escape at very low altitude. On 8 July a squadron of Mustangs was attacked by 20 MiG-15s, the F-51s lucky to escape this time and due entirely to the intervention of 35 F-86 Sabres, these shooting down three MiGs and forcing the others away.

August 1951: The 200th and last Mustang built in Australia by the Commonwealth Aircraft Corporation is delivered.

November 1952: Although Israel had acquired two P-51D Mustangs following establishment of the new state in May 1948, deliveries in quantity began in November 1952 with the purchase of 25 from Sweden. A further 15-20 were later acquired from Italy.

December 1952: No 2 Squadron South African Air Force ends Mustang operations in Korea, replacing its F-51Ds with F-86F Sabres.

February 1953: The USAF withdraws its last F-51D from service in Korea.

27 July 1953: Korean War Armistice signed.

October 1953: Six Australian built CAC Mustangs (including the first example, A68-1) had been flown to the Outback in the north-west of South Australia to be sub-

A pair of Cavalier remanufactured F-51 Mustangs, this pair wearing USAF markings but soon to be provided to Bolivia under the USA's Military Assistance Program. Note the taller than standard fins. Two seats are fitted to both but the aircraft in the background is a TF-51D with modified canopy and dual controls.

1946-84

The re-introduction of big time air racing at Reno, Nevada in 1964 sparked a rush to make Mustangs (and other types) faster around the pylons. Some Mustangs race in virtually standard configuration but there has been a number of modified aircraft prepared over the years, some of them radically. One example is this device, fitted with a modified Learjet wing, Rolls-Royce Griffon engine and contra-props. (Paul Merritt)

jected to the effects of a British atomic bomb test. They remained surprisingly intact after the explosion, most of the damage sustained being inflicted later by vandals and souvenir hunting military personnel. As the least damaged of the sextet, A68-1 was restored to a condition of basic airworthiness and flown out of the area in October 1967 with undercarriage locked down. It was eventually fully restored in the USA.

July 1954: Guatemala receives the first three of 30 P-51Ds it eventually operates, the last of them not withdrawn from service until 1972.

January 1955: Nicaragua acquires 28 ex Swedish P-51Ds, these remaining in service until 1965.

27 January 1957: The end of the Mustang's career with the USAF when F-51D 44-72948 is retired from service with the West Virginia Air National Guard's 167th Squadron and flown to the Air Force Museum at Wright Patterson AFB, Ohio.

February 1959: The US FAA grants Trans-Florida Aviation (later Cavalier Aircraft Corporation) Type Approval for its remanufactured Executive Mustang models.

The first of two Piper PA-48 Enforcer COIN aircraft takes to the air for the first time on 9 April 1983. This final expression of the Mustang line which had begun 43 years earlier failed to find any customers.

1946-84

Apart from Cavalier's effort with the Turbo Mustang III, another Dart-Mustang conversion was performed in Australia during 1971-72, again using a powerplant from a Viscount. This privately performed conversion of an ex RAAF CAC built aircraft was very similar to the Cavalier aircraft and was completed, although it never flew in the new configuration. It was subsequently restored to standard.

June 1960: The last of five RAAF Citizen Air Force squadrons (No 24 City of Adelaide) to operate the Mustang is relegated to non flying status, ending the type's career in Australian military service.

12-20 September 1964: Big time air racing returns to the USA with the first of the events at Reno, Nevada. Started by Bill Stead and properly organised with sponsorship and television coverage, 'Reno' has since developed into *the* air racing event around the pylons, featuring not only the Unlimited category with Mustangs, Bearcats, Furies and the like but also races for T-6 Texans, Formula One aircraft and others.

The 1964 event included an Unlimited trans-continental race plus pylon races, the inaugural US Aerobatics Championship and the US Hot Air Ballooning Championship. It attracted over 100,000 spectators and encouraged other promoters to stage air races at several venues the following year.

The 1964 trans-continental race was won by Wayne Adams' P-51D and the main pylon race by Bob Love's Mustang, but a Grumman Bearcat won the overall championship. A feature of the 1964 and subsequent events was the flying start using a Mustang flown by Bob Hoover as a pace aircraft, the combination continuing to perform that role for many years. Hoover would lead the field around the course line abreast and pull up to signal the race start with the now famous words: "Gentlemen, you have a race!"

The Reno races have inspired the creation of many highly modified aircraft in the quest for greater speed, not only Mustangs but also other types. One of the best known Mustangs was Charles Hall's P-51D N7715C *Miss R J* which set a new world closed record of 416.16mph (669.72km/h) at Reno in 1972. This aircraft featured a cut down canopy, souped up Merlin and clipped wings with Hoerner tips. After being sold to Ed Browning, it appeared in 1975 in much more radically modified form as the RB-51 *Red Baron* with a Rolls-Royce Griffon 57 engine from an Avro Shackleton driving six bladed counter-rotating propellers. It also featured a broader chord fin and rudder plus a new ventral fin.

In the hands of Darryl Greenamyer, *Red Baron* went on to win Reno's main event – the Unlimited Gold race – in 1977, and in August 1979 Steve Hinton flew the RB-51 to establish a new world speed record for piston engined aircraft of 499.047mph (803.116km/h), agonisingly close to the 'Holy Grail' target of 500mph. That was the *Red Baron's* last hurrah, the aircraft suffering a non fatal crash and destruction shortly afterwards at the 1979 Reno races.

December 1967: First flight of the Cavalier Mustang II, developed for the ground attack and counter insurgency (COIN) roles.

17 July 1969: The last Mustang to be lost in aerial combat is a Salvadorean F-51D flown by Captain Humberto Varela, shot down by a Honduran F4U-5 Corsair during the brief 'Football War' between the two nations.

29 April 1971: First flight of the first of two turboprop powered (Lycoming T55) and substantially redesigned Cavalier Enforcer (N202PE). A second aircraft (N201PE) quickly followed. The design rights were sold to Piper later in the same year.

12 July 1971: The first Cavalier Enforcer prototype crashes after flutter caused an elevator to separate from the tailplane. The pilot ejected safely.

7 February 1978: The last flight by a Mustang in the active inventory of the US military when F-51D 44-72990 is flown from Edwards AFB, California to the Army Aviation Museum at Fort Rucker, Alabama. The Mustang was one of two Cavalier upgrades used by the US Army as chase aircraft for the Lockheed AH-56A Cheyenne attack helicopter's test programme, equipped with cameras and flight test recorders.

4 September 1981: After pressure from the US Congress, Piper receives a $US12m contract to build two PA-48 Enforcers for flight testing and evaluation by the USAF. Some within the Congress had lobbied for the Enforcer since its days as a Cavalier project, envisaging a role for it as a low cost ground attack/counter insurgency (COIN) aircraft for supply to friendly smaller nations.

9 April 1983: First flight of the first of two Piper PA-48 Enforcers (N481PE) with further modifications over the original Cavalier versions.

1984: The Dominican Republic's *El Cuerpo de Aviación Militar* (Dominican Aviation Corps) retires its last 12 Mustangs as the final examples of the aircraft to remain in operational service. The Mustangs were sold to private buyers for use as warbirds.

A LAST HURRAH

The Dominican Republic was the final military operator of the Mustang, retiring its last F-51Ds in 1984. The year before, *Fuerza Aerea Dominicana* (FAD) Mustangs took part in the type's final military operation when they strafed a Cuban intelligence gathering ship which had refused to leave Dominican waters when requested to do so.

The incident invited retaliation from Cuba, which obliged by sending some MiG-21s to beat up the Mustangs' base. Perhaps wisely, the Dominican pilots declined the opportunity to give the Mustang one last chance at combat glory, preferring instead to stay on the ground until the MiGs had left the area and returned to their own bases.

One of the 30 P-51Ds flown by the Royal New Zealand Air Force's Territorial Air Force between 1951 and 1955.

MUSTANG OPERATORS

MUSTANG OPERATORS

The Royal Australian Air Force received a total of 499 Mustangs, 200 of them manufactured locally by the Commonwealth Aircraft Corporation. These are US built P-51Ks of No 84 Squadron photographed in 1945. (via Neil Mackenzie)

Note: The following summary of Mustang operators excludes the USA and United Kingdom as details of their use of the aircraft are contained within the other chapters of this book.

Australia

The Royal Australian Air Force operated 499 Mustangs, 200 of which were manufactured in Australia by the Commonwealth Aircraft Corporation (CAC). Australia was the only country outside the USA to build the Mustang (see 'Marks and Models' chapter).

Even before the first US built Mustangs began arriving in Australia in mid 1945, the type had already seen considerable combat in the hands of the Australian pilots of No 3 Squadron in the northern hemisphere. Operating under British control and flying RAF aircraft, 3 Squadron had spent its war playing a significant role in the North African, Sicilian and Italian campaigns flying Kittyhawks and from late 1944, Mustangs.

Many Australians also flew with RAF Mustang squadrons in Europe, one of them – Flying Officer John Haslope – recording a memorable victory against a Messerschmitt Me 163 Komet rocket powered interceptor near Leipzig in April 1945. Haslope was flying with 165 Squadron RAF at the time.

The RAAF's own procurement of Mustangs began in April 1945 when the first of 298 P-51Ds and Ks arrived, with deliveries spread over the next five months. Serialled A68-500 to 583 (P-51K) and A68-600 to 813 (P-51D), these Mustangs were purchased to make up for cancelled orders of the locally produced versions, deliveries of which began in June 1945.

The end of the war meant that many of the imported Mustangs had very limited flying careers, although they did serve with Nos 84 and 86 Squadrons briefly before hostilities ended, but saw no action.

The decision to manufacture the Mustang in Australia was made in April 1944 after an extensive evaluation of available types. Initial orders covered 690 aircraft but with the end of the war the need for them reduced, resulting in just 200 being built at a leisurely pace with production stretched out to keep CAC's factory employed.

Australian production was preceded by the arrival of a P-51D 'pattern' aircraft in 1944 (A68-1001) although this was used for extensive ground testing and didn't fly in Australia until April 1945, just before the first Australian built CAC CA-17 Mustang Mk.20 (A68-1) took to the air for the first time.

The 200 Australian built Mustangs comprised 80 CA-17 Mk.20s (A68-1 to 80) which were built up from 100 sets of imported components; 28 CA-18 Mk.22s (A68-81 to 94 and 187 to 200); 26 CA-18 Mk.21s (A68-95 to 120); and 66 CA-18 Mk.23s (A68-121 to 186). All were based on the P-51D but with some minor modifications. The Mk.22 was a tactical reconnaissance version with two cameras in the rear fuselage,

Bolivia was one of several Central and South American countries to fly Mustangs well into the 1960s and 1970s. This former Bolivian Cavalier F-51D was one of the last in service, remaining on strength until 1977.

and the Mk.23 featured a Rolls-Royce rather than Packard built version of the Merlin engine.

The first batch of 80 Mk.20s had been handed over to the RAAF by July 1946 but it would be another year before deliveries of the next group started. The last Mustang (Mk.22 A68-200) was delivered in August 1951.

The Mustang's main RAAF service was with Nos 76, 77 and 82 Squadrons which went to Japan for occupation duties early in 1946. 76 and 82 Squadrons returned to Australia in 1950, while 77 Squadron was due to follow them when the Korean War started and the Australian Mustangs found themselves in the thick of it.

Operating from Iwakuni in Japan, 77 Squadron flew its Mustangs in combat for ten months from June 1950 until they were replaced by Meteors. Most of the aircraft flown in Korea were American built P-51s, although a handful of CAC built Mustangs were also on the squadron's strength at the time.

Back in Australia, the Mustang was also operated by No 4 (later 3) Tactical Reconnaissance Squadron, and Nos 75, 76 and 78 Squadrons, all of which quickly changed to jets as they became available.

The last squadrons to fly Mustangs were the five Citizen Air Force squadrons, Nos 21 (City of Melbourne), 22 (City of Sydney), 23 (City of Brisbane), 24 (City of Adelaide) and 25 (City of Perth). With one exception, these units relinquished their Mustangs for Vampires in 1955-56, 24 Squadron keeping its Mustangs until June 1960 when the CAF squadrons were relegated to non flying status.

Bolivia

The *Fuerza Aérea Boliviano* (FAB) operated a total of 25 Mustangs from 1954, starting with the acquisition of three F-51Ds and a single TF-51D in 1954 and followed by other F-51Ds (including eight purchased from Uruguay for a token $US1 each in what was really an MAP redeployment) and finally, in 1967-68, eight Cavalier F-51Ds and a TF-51D supplied under the USA's Military Assistance Program (MAP). The Mustangs equipped a single squadron until 1977.

The Royal Canadian Air Force operated several squadrons equipped with Mustangs during World War II, these operating from Britain under RAF control. Post war, the RCAF received 130 ex USAAF P-51Ds.

Two P-51D Mustang IVs of 402 (City of Winnipeg) Squadron RCAF, photographed in 1948.

Canada

Like its fellow members of the British Commonwealth, Canada made a substantial contribution to the RAF's war effort in Europe including five squadrons which at some stage flew Mustangs.

Three of them (Nos 400, 414 and 430) were designated as army co-operation units and were among the first to fly the Mustang Mk.1, relinquishing their Curtiss Kittyhawks in favour of the new fighter in 1942. All three eventually re-equipped with Spitfires but in the meantime conducted extensive tactical reconnaissance duties over occupied Europe in 1943-44. In the case of 414 Squadron, it operated its Mustangs in support of the ill fated Dieppe landings in August 1942, while both it and 430 squadron were extensively involved in operations surrounding D-Day.

Other wartime RCAF squadrons were Nos 441 and 442, both of which swapped their Spitfires for Mustang IVs just as the European war was ending.

Post war, the RCAF received 130 P-51Ds from the USAF in 1947. Locally designated the Mustang Mk.IV Tactical Fighter, they were obtained specifically to equip the RCAF's new Auxiliary Fighter Squadrons – Nos 402 (City if Winnipeg), 403 (City of Calgary), 420 (City of London), 424 (City of Hamilton), 442 (City of Vancouver) and 443 (City of New Westminster). Two regular squadrons (Nos 416 and 417) also briefly flew Mustangs and the auxiliary units operated the aircraft until 1956.

China

The USAAF supplied 50 surplus P-51Ds to the Chinese Nationalist Air Force shortly before VJ Day along with large numbers of other types in the immediate post war years including a further batch of 53 P-51Ds.

When hostilities ended in August 1945, General Chiang Kai-shek's government purchased almost the entire surplus stock of USAAF aircraft (about 1,000) based in the Far East at the time, including P-51Ds and P-51Bs which had served with USAAF's 14th Air Force in China.

Many of these were used in the civil war against Mao Tse Tung's communists before the Nationalists were forced to flee the mainland and re-establish themselves on Formosa (Taiwan) in 1949. A few P-51Ds were

The Chinese Nationalist Air Force received its first Mustangs from USAAF stocks shortly before VJ Day but subsequently purchased large numbers of surplus P-51Ds from the same source.

The Dominican Republic was the final military operator of the Mustang, not retiring its last F-51Ds until 1984. Most were acquired second hand from Sweden.

captured by the communists and subsequently operated by the Peoples' Republic of China Air Force.

Cuba

It has always been assumed that the pre revolutionary Cuban Aviation Corps (*Cuerpo de Aviación*) received a number of F-51Ds from the USA from late 1947 as part of the Inter-American Treaty of Reciprocal Assistance (or Rio Pact), but this is now being challenged by some Mustang historians.

It is certain, however, that Fidel Castro's *Fuerza Aérea Revolucionaria* did acquire three civilian registered Mustangs in 1958, these apparently remaining on strength for a short time after the revolution. They saw no combat during the revolution, although it is thought that the pre revolution Batista regime had a small number of F-51s at its disposal during the fighting and did deploy them.

Dominican Republic

The Dominican Republic's *El Cuerpo de Aviación Militar* has the distinction of being the last air force to fly operational Mustangs, the final 12 examples not retired until the end of 1984. They were quickly snapped up by private owners.

The nation's association with the Mustang began in 1948 when six aircraft (a mixture of P-51Bs, Cs and Ds) were acquired, but the main force arrived in 1952 when 44 P-51Ds were purchased from Sweden to equip one fighter-bomber squadron. Another squadron operated a mix of de Havilland Vampire F.1s (also purchased from Sweden in 1952) and Republic P-47 Thunderbolts. It is thought that one or two additional Mustangs were also acquired from Haiti when it retired its aircraft in 1974-75.

About 30 of the Mustangs were overhauled and upgraded by Trans-Florida Aviation in 1965 (these seeing extensive service in the same year's civil war) and plans to replace them with F-86F Sabres never came to fruition due to budgetary constraints. By 1978 only 13 or 14 remained in service with what was now called the *Fuerza Aérea Dominicana* and these soldiered on for another six years before being retired.

France

The *Armée de l'Air* became a Mustang operator near the end of the European war when the 2/33 'Savoie' *Escadre* received P-51Ds in February 1945 for the tactical reconnaissance role operating out of Colmar. 1/33 'Belfort' also received Mustangs.

Both squadrons were units of the 33ème *Escadre de Reconnaissance* and moved to Freiburg-im-Breisgau in southern Germany in May 1945, remaining there until May 1950 when they relocated in Cognac. The Mustangs remained in service until replaced by Republic F-84G Thunderjets from August 1952.

Guatemala

The *Fuerza Aérea de Guatemala's* officially received a total of 30 F-51Ds delivered in several batches and obtained from different sources. The first three arrived in July 1954, delivered to the revolutionary Castillo forces who were trying to oust the existing government. It was regarded as communist by the USA which had previously refused to supply Mustangs because of that. The Castillo forces were supported by the US Central Intelligence Agency (CIA).

Two more Mustangs were clandestinely supplied by the USA via Honduras and after Castillo invaded 11 further aircraft were delivered to the FAG courtesy the US Government. The Castillo aircraft were absorbed into the force. Another 14 arrived in 1957, some of the former Canadian aircraft, while it has also been suggested that others were obtained from Israel.

The FAG's Mustangs were operated by its single fighter-bomber squadron until the last was retired in 1972.

Haiti

The *Corps d'Aviation d'Haiti* acquired six P-51Ds in 1951, these initially equipping a composite squadron with various training aircraft such as the T-6 Texan and then the force's sole fighter-bomber squadron. Based at Bowen Field, Port-au-Prince, the Mustangs were used mainly for internal policing and coastal patrol duties and were retired in 1975.

Honduras

It has always been thought that the Honduran Republic's small air force, the *Fuerza Aérea Hondoreña* operated a small number of F-51Ds. Latest evidence suggests this was not the case, although the FAH reportedly did investigate the purchase of 22 ex French aircraft in 1953. The confusion probably results from the fact that two F-51Ds were clandestinely supplied to Guatemala's revolutionary Castillo forces via Honduras.

Indonesia

Following its war of independence against the Dutch in 1946-49, the former Netherlands East Indies was formally reconstituted as the Republic of Indonesia in August 1950. Part of the settlement was that the Dutch handed over most of its aircraft in the area to the new Indonesian Air Force (*Angkatan Udara Republik Indonesia* – AURI). Among them were P-51D Mustangs, these forming the backbone of the AURI's initial fighter strength, equipping No 3 Squadron.

The Mustangs survived being 'replaced' by Soviet supplied MiGs as these were more often than not unserviceable due to a shortage of spares and support.

By 1973, Indonesia's Mustang force had been reduced to only a handful of aircraft, but the number was then increased by a dozen with the purchase of additional aircraft from foreign sources. Operated in the fighter-bomber and counter-insurgency (COIN) roles, some Mustangs remained on Indonesian strength into the late 1970s.

Israel

The proclamation of the State of Israel in May 1948 began an armed struggle to secure the new nation's independence and the establishment of an air force with a motley collection of aircraft obtained by clandestine means.

Among the fighters acquired and operated during the fighting of 1948-49 were Avia S 199s (Czech built Messerschmitt Bf 109s), Supermarine Spitfires and two P-51D Mustangs. The Mustangs were part of the Israeli Defence Force/Air Force's first fighter squadron – No 101 – and flew numerous combat missions. Kills were recorded against an RAF Mosquito and an Egyptian Fiat G.55.

A further 25 F-51Ds were purchased from Sweden and delivered between November 1952 and June 1953, equipping No 102 Squadron. About 15-20 more ex Italian aircraft were also obtained via scrap merchants.

IDF/AF Mustangs saw extensive action during the Suez Crisis which began with Israeli attacks on Egypt in late October 1956. One of the more interesting missions performed by two of the Mustangs was an attempt to cut Egyptian telephone lines by using hooks trailing from long cables. When this method failed, the pilots used their Mustangs' propellers to do the job, sustaining only minor damage in the process.

Israel's Mustangs were retired from front line use after the Suez Crisis but some remained in service as advanced trainers until 1958.

Israel acquired its first two P-51Ds by surreptitious means in 1948 and subsequently obtained about 45 more from Sweden and Italy.

Italy

The *Aeronautica Militare Italiano* operated 48 P-51Ds obtained from US stocks between 1948 and 1953, some of these subsequently passed on to the Somali Air Force, which had been established with Italian assistance. Some also eventually found their way into Israeli service, the airframes purchased from Italian scrap merchants.

Netherlands

The Netherlands began receiving 40 P-51Ds originally intended for the RAF shortly before VJ Day, these to equip the Netherlands East Indies Air Force's (NEIAF) Nos 121 and 122 Squadrons. They arrived in 1946 against a background of continuing unrest in the area as the push for independence and the establishment of the Republic of Indonesia grew.

As a result, the three fighter squadrons operated by the Netherlands Army Air Corps in the NEI saw considerable ground attack combat in 1948-49 as the fighting increased. A further 20 Mustangs were acquired during this period to replace the Curtiss P-40N Warhawks which had been operated by No 120 Squadron since 1943.

With the cessation of hostilities in late 1949 and the proclamation of the Republic of Indonesia in August 1950, the surviving Mustangs were handed over to the newly established *Angkatan Udara Republik Indonesia* – AURI.

New Zealand

The acquisition of 370 Mustangs for the Royal New Zealand Air Force had been negotiated during 1945, these intended to supplement the RNZAF's Vought F4U Corsairs in the fight against Japan. Deliveries were scheduled to comprise an initial batch of 30 P-51Ds followed by another 137 of the same model and a final batch of 203 P-51Ms.

The abrupt end of the war against Japan in August 1945 made the acquisition superfluous but as the first batch of 30 P-51Ds was already on its way, these aircraft were delivered but placed directly into storage.

They remained in that state for six years until 1951 when the RNZAF decided to reactivate its reserve component, the Territorial Air Force. The TAF's No 4 Squadron was the first to receive Mustangs in late 1951 and was subsequently joined by Nos 1, 2 and 3 Squadrons.

The Mustangs remained in service only until August 1955 when they were withdrawn following a series of undercarriage and coolant system corrosion problems, these probably resulting from the period of storage. Four aircraft carried on until 1957 as target tugs.

Nicaragua

The *Fuerza Aérea de Nicarauense* acquired 26 ex Swedish F-51Ds in January 1955 for operation by one fighter squadron alongside a fighter-

The Royal New Zealand Air Force ordered 370 Mustangs in early 1945 but these were cancelled when peace came. However, 30 P-51Ds were already on their way and delivered directly to storage. They remained in that state until briefly reactivated six years later.

bomber unit equipped with P-47 Thunderbolts.

Before the Mustangs were purchased, P-51s flown by Guatemalan rebel forces had operated from bases in Nicaragua. Nicaragua later obtained about nine more ex USAF and Air National Guard F-51Ds (including TF-51 trainers) and they remained in service until 1965.

Philippines

The Philippine Air Force was established in July 1947 – one year after the Philippine Republic had been proclaimed – with sufficient F-51Ds to equip one fighter-bomber squadron. The aircraft were subsequently involved in action against Hukbalahap rebels. The Mustangs were replaced by F-86F Sabres in 1957-58.

Salvador

The *Fuerza Aérea de Salvadorena's* small air arm has the distinction of being the last to use the Mustang in sustained action in the so-called 'Football War' with Honduras in July 1969 (see 'Mustang Chronology' section).

To supplement its only combat unit – a flight of Vought F4U-4 Corsairs – Salvador took delivery of five single seat Cavalier F-51Ds and a two seat TF-51D in 1969, the refurbished aircraft supplied by the USA. More Mustangs were sought by the Salvador Government and overall, 14 appeared on strength. By the end of the brief Football War conflict, 10 remained. The last examples were sold in 1974, replaced by Dassault Ouragan jets.

Somalia

The small *Cuerpo Aeronautica della Somalia* was established under the control of Italy, the AMI contributing a few Mustangs to its initial strength. When Italian trusteeship of Somalia ended in July 1960 with the foundation of the Somali Democratic Republic, the Air Corps was handed over to the new government but remained under Italian sponsorship with the Mustangs still in service as the sole combat type. Somalia then came under the influence of the Soviet Union and began receiving MiG-15s and -17s in exchange for basing facilities.

South Africa

The South African Air Force flew F-51Ds borrowed from the USAF in the Korean War. The SAAF's No 2 'Cheetah' Squadron was committed to the United Nations effort in Korea and although the Mustangs were owned by the USAF, they carried full SAAF livery and serial numbers.

Flying as part of the USAF's 18th Fighter-Bomber Wing, SAAF combat missions in Korea started in mid November 1950, the Mustangs operating from several bases (some of them near to the front line) mainly on hazardous close support missions using rockets, bombs and napalm. They completed 10,373 sorties up to the end of December 1952 when they were replaced by F-86F Sabres.

The squadron added another 2,032 sorties to the total with its Sabres and after the conflict received the rare distinction – especially for a foreign unit – of being awarded a US Presidential Citation for "extraordinary heroism in action against the enemy of the United Nations...."

Of the 95 Mustangs supplied to No 2 Squadron, no fewer than 73 were lost – 58 to ground fire, two were shot down by MiG-15s and 13 were lost in operational accidents. Twelve pilots were killed in action, 30 were missing or captured and others were wounded.

In WWII, No 5 Squadron SAAF operated Mustangs in Italy from October 1944, these replacing P-40 Kittyhawks.

South Korea

Until the outbreak of the Korean War in June 1950, the Republic of Korea Air Force (ROKAF) comprised mainly training and liaison types such as the North American T-6 Texan and Piper L-4 Cub. With the start of hostilities, F-51D Mustangs were transferred to the ROKAF and South Korean pilots were given conversion training in Japan.

The Philippine Air Force had a small number of F-51Ds to equip a fighter-bomber squadron when it was established in July 1947.

Sweden took delivery of its first batch of 50 surplus USAAF P-51Ds in April 1945 and received a further 107 post war. The Mustang was designated J 26 in Swedish service.

The ROKAF's first operational squadron was commanded by Colonel Kim Shin, a veteran of General Chennault's American Volunteer Group – the Flying Tigers – which had fought the Japanese in China.

Mustangs were operated by the ROKAF's 10th and 11th Fighter Wings during the Korean War, initially for defensive purposes but from the second half of 1952 on close support missions. They began to be replaced by F-86F and F-86D Sabres supplied under the Military Assistance Program from 1955.

Soviet Union

Ten RAF Mustang Is were supplied to the Soviet Union in 1942 but the type never entered service and it is believed that no more were delivered.

Sweden

Neutral Sweden's first contact with the Mustang occurred in 1944 when ten US and British aircraft made forced landings on Swedish soil and were interned. Four of these (two P-51Bs and two P-51Ds) were put into *Flygvapnet* service for evaluation under the local designation J 26.

As a result, Sweden ordered 50 surplus USAAF P-51Ds in April 1945, significantly shortly *before* the war in Europe had ended. Also designated J 26 in Swedish service, delivery of these P-51Ds began immediately. A further 107 P-51Ds were subsequently ordered with the last of them delivered in March 1948. Twelve were later converted to S 26 photo-reconnaissance aircraft.

Sweden's Mustangs flew with four *Flygflottilj* (Wings), initially F 16 then F 4, F 20 and F 21. Most were disposed of in 1952-54 as the de Havilland Vampire and Saab J 29 jets came on strength, buyers including Israel, Nicaragua and the Dominican Republic.

Switzerland

Switzerland's *Flugwaffe* purchased 100 surplus F-51Ds from US stocks in 1948 while awaiting delivery of new de Havilland Vampires from Britain and to replace the Messerschmitt Bf 109E. The last of these was retired in December 1949. The Mustangs remained in front line service until 1956 when re-equipment with the Vampires had been completed, although a few stayed on strength until 1958.

Uruguay

The *Fuerza Aérea Uruguaya* received 25 F-51Ds from the USA in 1950 after first refusing an offer to be supplied with P-47 Thunderbolts. The Mustangs equipped the FAU's sole fighter-bomber squadron (Grupo 2) until 1960 when they were replaced by Lockheed F-80 Shooting Star jets. Eight were sold to Bolivia for a token $1 each as part of a deal done under the MAP.

Switzerland purchased 100 surplus P-51Ds from the USAAF in 1948 while awaiting the delivery of de Havilland Vampire jets.

MUSTANG SERIAL NUMBERS

Notes: NA designation suffix denotes aircraft built at North American Aviation's Inglewood, California plant; NT designation suffix denotes the Dallas, Texas factory. Abbreviations: ff – first flight; del – delivered; cvtd – converted.

USAAF P-51/A-36 MUSTANGS

Serials	Model	NAA No	Qty	Notes
NX19998	NA-73X	NA-73X	1	prototype, ff 26 Oct 1940
41-038/41-039	XP-51	NA-73	2	ff 20 May 1941
41-37320/41-37351	P-51-NA	NA-91	32	ff 29 May 1942
41-37352	XP-51B	NA-101	1	ff 30 November 1942
41-37353/41-37420	P-51-NA	NA-91	68	
41-37421	XP-51B	NA-101	1	
41-37422/41-37469	P-51-NA	NA-91	48	
42-83663/42-84162	A-36A-NA	NA-97	500	ff 21 September 1942
42-102979/42-103328	P-51C-1NT	NA-103	350	ff 5 August 1943
42-103329/42-103378	P-51C-5NT	NA-103	50	
42-103379/42-103978	P-51C-10NT	NA-103	600	
42-106429/42-106538	P-51B-10NA	NA-104	110	ff 5 May 1943
42-106539/42-106540	P-51D-NA	NA-106	2	ff 17 November 1943
42-106541/42-106738	P-51B-10NA	NA-104	198	
42-106739/42-106978	P-51B-15NA	NA-104	240	
43-6003/43-6312	P-51A-NA	NA-99	310	ff 3 February 1943
43-6313/43-7112	P-51B-5NA	NA-104	800	
43-7113/43-7202	P-51B-10NA	NA-104	90	
43-12093/43-12492	P-51B-1NA	NA-102	400	
43-24752/43-24901	P-51B-15NA	NA-104	150	
43-24902/43-25251	P-51C-10NT	NA-103	350	
43-43332/44-43334	XP-51F-NA	NA-105	3	ff 14 February 1944
43-43335/43-43336	XP-51G-NA	NA-105	2	ff 10 August 1944
44-10753/44-11152	P-51C-10NT	NA-103	400	
44-11153/44-11352	P-51D-5NT	NA-111	200	
44-11353/44-11552	P-51K-1NT	NA-111	200	
44-11553/44-11952	P-51K-5NT	NA-111	400	
44-11953/44-12552	P-51K-10NT	NA-111	600	
44-12553/44-12852	P-51K-15NT	NA-111	300	
44-12853/44-13252	P-51D-20NT	NA-111	400	
44-13253/42-14052	P-51D-5NA	NA-109	800	
44-14053/44-14852	P-51D-10NA	NA-109	800	
44-14853/44-15752	P-51D-15NA	NA-109	900	
44-63160/44-64159	P-51D-20NA	NA-122	1000	
44-64160/44-64714	P-51H-NA	NA-126	555	ff 3 February 1945
44-72027/44-72626	P-51D-20NA	NA-122	600	
44-72627/44-74226	P-51D-25NA	NA-122	1600	
44-74227/44-75026	P-51D-30NA	NA-122	800	
44-76027/44-76028	XP-51J-NA	NA-105	2	ff 23 April 1945
44-84390/44-84609	P-51D-25NT	NA-124	220	
44-84610/44-84611	TP-51D-NT	NA-124	2	built 1944
44-84612/44-84989	P-51D-25NT	NA-124	378	
45-11343/45-11442	P-51D-25NT	NA-124	100	
45-11443/45-11450	TP-51D-NT	NA-124	8	built 1944
45-11451/45-11742	P-51D-25NT	NA-124	292	
45-11743	P-51M-1NT	NA-124	1	built 1945
67-14862/67-14865	F-51D		4	Cavalier, to Bolivia
67-14866	TF-51D		1	Cavalier, to Bolivia
67-22579/67-22582	F-51D		4	Cavalier, to Bolivia
68-15795/68-15796	F-51D		2	Cavalier, to USAF
72-1536/72-1541	F-51D		6	Cavalier, to El Salvador

F-6 conversions: 57 F-6A included in P-51 listing; 35 F-6B included in P-51A listing; 91 F-6C included in P-51B/C listing. 146 F-6D included in P-51D listing: 44-13020/44-13039; 44-13131/44-13140; 44-13181; 44-84509/44-84540; 44-84566; 44-84773/44-84778; and 44-84835/44-84855.
163 F-6K included in P-51K listing: 44-11554; 44-11897/44-11952; 44-11993/44-112008; 44-12216/44-12237; 44-12459/44-12471; 44-12523/44-12534; and 44-12810/44-12852.
TF-51D conversions: 44-84654/44-84658; 44-84660; 44-84662/44-84663; 44-84665/44-84670; and 44-84676; total 15 by Temco plus 10 new build as listed in table.

RAF MUSTANGS

Serials	Mark	NAA No	Qty	Notes
AG345-664	I	NA-73	320	ff 23 April 1941, del from Oct 1941, 20 lost in transit
AL958-999	I	NA-83	42	
AM100-257	I	NA-83	158	
AP164-263	I	NA-83	100	
EW998	A-36A	NA-97	1	del Mar 1943 for evaluation, ex USAAF 42-83685
FB100-124	III/P-51B	NA-104	25	entered service December 1943
FB125-399	III/P-51C	NA-103	275	
FD418-567IA/P-51	NA-91		150	FD418-437, FD450-464, FD466-469 and FD510-527 (57 aircraft) not delivered
FR409	IV/XP-51F	NA-105	1	for evaluation
FR410	V/XP-51G	NA-105	1	for evaluation
FR411	III/P-51B	NA-104	1	for tests
FR890-939	II/P-51A	NA-99	50	
FX848-999	III/P-51B/C	NA-103/104	152	
FZ100-197	III/P-51B/C	NA-103/104	98	
HB821-961	III/P-51C	NA-103	141	
HK944-947	III/P-51B/C		4	ex USAAF
HK955-956	III/P-51B/C		2	ex USAAF
KH421-640	III/P-51B/C	NA-103/104	220	
KH641-670	IV/P-51D		30	first delivery September 1944
KH671-870	IVA/P-51K		200	
KM100-492	IVA/P-51K		393	ex USAAF
KM493-743	IV/P-51D		251	ex USAAF, KM744-799 (56 aircraft) not delivered
KN987	IV/P-51H	NA-126	1	for evaluation
SR406-440	III/P-51B/C	NA-103/104	34	ex USAAF, SR439 not allocated
TK586	IV/P-51K	NA-111	1	ex USAAF for trials
TK589	IV/P-51K	NA-111	1	ex USAAF for trials

P-82 TWIN MUSTANG

Serials	Model	NAA No	Qty	Notes
44-83886/44-83887	XP-82-NA	NA-120	2	ff 15 April 1945
44-83888	XP-82A-NA	NA-120	1	
44-65160/44-65179	P-82B-NA	NA-123	20	44-65169 cvtd to P-82C, 44-65170 to P-82D
46-0255/46-0354	P-82E-NA	NA-144	100	
46-0355/46-0383	P-82G-NA	NA-150	29	
46-0384/46-0388	P-82H-NA	NA-150	5	cvtd from P-82Gs
46-0389/46-0404	P-82G-NA	NA-150	16	
46-0405/46-0495	P-82F-NA	NA-149	91	
46-0496/46-0504	P-82H-NA	NA-149	9	cvtd from P-82Fs

Note: The 14 P-82Hs were converted from P-82Fs (9) and P-82Gs (5) on the production line.

LIMITED EDITION AVIATION ART POSTERS

Limited edition, **quality colour collectable posters** with artwork by internationally renowned aviation artist **Juanita Franzi**. The colour posters are printed on quality 200 gsm art board and are ideal for framing or mounting. They are of a manageable size (B3, 500 mm x 353 mm) with each of the five images approximately 25-26 cm long. Five quality drawings for the price of one.

An ideal adornment for the study, office or club house. The perfect gift for the aviation enthusiast.

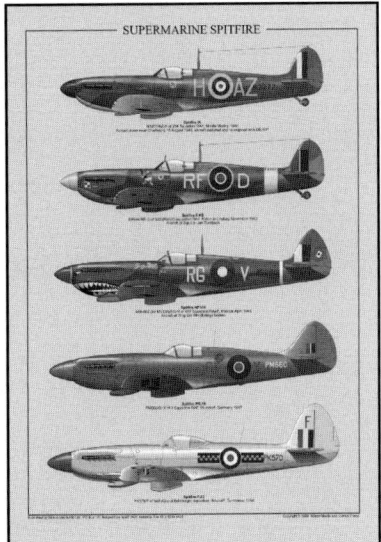 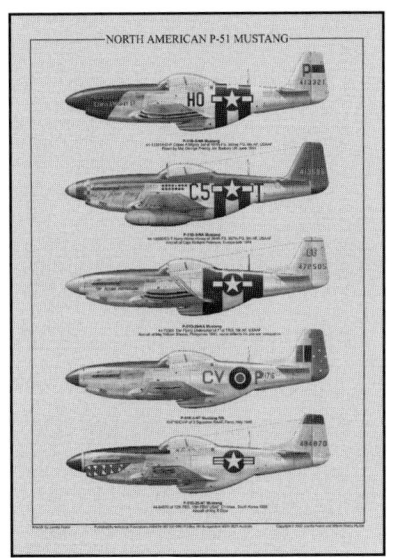 

Supermarine Spitfire: The five drawings represent the evolution and development of arguably the world's most famous and charismatic fighter. The five drawings depict the Mks. I, V, VIII, XIX and 22 ranging from a Battle of Britain aircraft to Wng Cdr Bobby Gibbes' RAAF Mk.VIII and a post war Mk.22.

North American P-51 Mustang: The USA's most famous fighter of WWII is celebrated by drawings of the P-51Ds of 8th Air Force aces Maj George Preddy and Capt Richard Peterson plus 5th Air Force ace Maj William Shomo, Korean War pilot Maj P Dow and a Royal Australian Air Force P-51K.

McDonnell Douglas F-4 Phantom: One of the most significant and effective combat aircraft of any era, Mr Mac's 'Phabulous Phantom' is represented by drawings of a USN F-4B, a Vietnam era USAF F-4D, the famous 'Playboy Bunny' F-4J, a Royal Navy FG.1 and a Royal Australian Air Force F-4E.

LIMITED EDITION AVIATION POSTERS ONLY $A20.00 each (GST included)
Postage and handling $A4.00 per order in Australia (overseas $A8.00)
Please allow two weeks for delivery in Australia.

VISIT OUR WEB SITE AND GET THE LATEST INFORMATION ON PRODUCTS AND EVENTS
WWW.NOTEBOOKPUB.COM

Or mail us at: **Notebook Publications** (ABN 94 082 531 066)
PO Box 181, Bungendore NSW 2621 Australia
Telephone: +61 2 6238 1620   Facsimile: +61 2 6238 1626

Also available:

Aviation Notebook Series: McDonnell Douglas F-4 Phantom by Stewart Wilson
Boeing 747 by Stewart Wilson
BAe/MDC Harrier by Stewart Wilson

LIMITED EDITION AVIATION ART POSTERS

Limited edition, quality colour collectable posters with artwork by internationally renowned aviation artist Juanita Franzi. The colour posters are printed on quality 200 gsm art board and are ideal for framing or mounting. They are of a manageable size (635, 500 mm x 355 mm) with each of the five images approximately 25-20 cm long.

Five quality drawings for the price of one.

An ideal adornment for the study, office or club house. The perfect gift for the aviation enthusiast.

Supermarine Spitfire: The five drawings represent the evolution and development of arguably the world's most famous and best loved fighter aircraft. The five drawings depict the Mk.I, Vb, IXe, XIV and 22 starting from the initial prototype aircraft to the very last production variant Mk.22.

North American P-51 Mustang: The USA's most famous fighter of WWII is celebrated by drawings of the P-51B, P-51D/K Air Force aces Maj George P. Preddy and Capt Don Gentile, P-51D racer Precious Metal, William Stroeb, Korean War pilot

McDonnell Douglas F-4 Phantom: One of the most significant and effective combat aircraft of any era, Mc Mac's Fabulous Phantom is represented by drawings of the USAF F-4B a Vietnam era USAF RAU, the famous 'Flavoy Bunny' F-4J, a Royal Navy F-4K and a Royal Australian Air

LIMITED EDITION AVIATION POSTERS ONLY $49.50 each (GST included)

Aviation Notebook Series: McDonnell Douglas F-4 Phantom by Stewart Wilson
Boeing 747 by Stewart Wilson
PZL / WDK Farmer by Stewart Wilson

SPITFIRE

SPITFIRE Stewart Wilson's 45th book, is one the author promised himself to write for many years, the intention being to provide a different approach to a history of Britain's most famous fighter.

The heart of the book is a chronological history of the aircraft, in diary form and tracing its progress from conception to phasing out of service and covering all versions of Spitfire and Seafire.

Included in the chronological section of the book are numerous "breakout boxes" highlighting various aspects of the aircraft, its operational history, personalities, industrial background, political influences and other points of interest.

Additional to the chronological section is a narrative introductory chapter tracing the Supermarine company's history and background to the Spitfire plus coverage of foreign operators, marks and models, the Merlin and Griffon engines, specifications and performance data, serial numbers, production variants and squadrons.

Spitfire is profusely illustrated by photographs, colour profiles and technical drawings, both of the latter commissioned especially for the book.

The result is a comprehensive reference work on the Spitfire which is intended to provide a self contained source of information for the reader and to complement existing books on the subject.

This very different look at the Spitfire is something every enthusiast or anyone interested in World War 2 aviation history cannot afford to be without!